Pauline
Boss

More Advance Acclaim for

Loss, Trauma, and Resilience
Therapeutic Work with Ambiguous Loss

"Pauline Boss has written a comprehensive guide to understanding and healing one of the most painful of human experiences. In clear, accessible prose, she links together a wide range of theories, practices, and vivid cultural references. Sure to become a classic that will be widely read by those who've suffered ambiguous loss as well as those attempting to provide a therapeutic pathway that transforms suffering into newfound strength."
> —*Peter Fraenkel, Ph.D. Associate Professor of Clinical Psychology, The City University of New York, and co-author of* The Relational Trauma of Incest: A Family-Based Approach to Treatment

"In a world with wars, migration, disastrous events like the 9/11 attacks, and personal tragedies such as Alzheimers, ambiguous loss is all around us. Many people experience separation, be it of mind or body, without closure, leaving them with the distinctive problems of managing grief, stress, and trauma. This poses major challenges for society in general, and for therapists in particular. Pauline Boss's book is illuminating, useful, and informative. It develops original theory through numerous examples drawn from the author's research. *Loss, Trauma, and Resilience* is an important contribution to the psychosocial literature on loss and trauma, essential for therapists, researchers, and anyone seeking to reflect on contemporary life."
> —*Celia J. Falicov, Ph.D., Clinical Professor of Psychiatry, University of California, San Diego, and past President, American Family Therapy Academy*

LOSS, TRAUMA, AND RESILIENCE

LOSS, TRAUMA, AND RESILIENCE

Therapeutic Work With
Ambiguous Loss

PAULINE BOSS

W. W. Norton & Company
New York • London

For information about permission to reproduce selections from this book, write to Permissions, W. W. Norton & Company, Inc., 500 Fifth Avenue, New York, NY 10110

Production Manager: Leeann Graham
Manufacturing by R.R. Donnelley, Harrisonburg

Library of Congress Cataloging-in-Publication Data

Boss, Pauline.
Loss, trauma, and resilience : therapeutic work with ambiguous loss / Pauline Boss.
  p.   ; cm. — (Norton professional book)
Includes bibliographical references and index.
ISBN 0-393-70449-1
1. Loss (Psychology). 2. Grief. 3. Resilience (Personality trait). I. Title. II. Series

BF575.D35B68 2005
155.9'3—dc22   2005054733

W. W. Norton and Company, Inc., 500 Fifth Avenue, New York, NY 10110
www.wwnorton.com
W. W. Norton & Company Ltd., Castle House, 75/76 Wells St., London W1T 3Qt

1   3   5   7   9   0   8   6   4   2

For Dudley

Contents

Foreword

Life is filled with joys and with pains, with gains and with losses—both circumstantial and normative. Gains will be slowly assimilated until they become somehow part of our selves. In turn, those chunks of our selves that are lost with any loss will become slowly decathectizied, and ultimately allowed to fade away, perhaps to remain only at the edge of our awareness. We may emerge a bit richer from any gain and a bit poorer from any loss, but, throughout that never ending process of metabolizing happiness and sorrow, our core identities not only remain recognizable to ourselves and others but maintain their resilient capacity to adapt, change, grow, and evolve. Unless . . . . This process occurs *unless* a gain or a loss lays in the grey zone of ambiguity. Under those circumstances, in those gray zones, time freezes and evolution stops.

Social ambiguity and personal ambivalence are omnipresent in the human condition. In situations of ambiguity we are, as the etymology of the word shows, "driven in both ways" and so cannot find a single course. In case of personal ambivalence (a term coined by Eugen Bleuler in the early 20th century) we simultaneously experience two conflicting and apparently unsynthesizable feelings. Do we welcome another year of life or do we regret the passage of time? Do we celebrate our kid's first day of school or mourn the loss of his or her family-centered, homebound life? Do we express joy for a graduation or convey our sympathy for the beginning of a life of work? Do we throw rice and confetti with our blessings to the newlyweds or do we shower them with pessimistic advice for a safe navigation of the uncharted and perhaps dangerous territory ahead? And so on–from the sublime to the ridiculous, each event that enlightens our lives has its dark shadow, and each negative event has a positive aspect. Well rehearsed and deeply rooted emotional processing, not to mention social rules and mores, provide us with normative ways of behaving and even instructions about what to feel and when to have these emotions. These cultural guidelines carry us through times of transition, even those that "drive us both ways." They help *unless,* again, ambiguities of circumstances are such that all prior norms and guidelines collapse or don't apply.

In turn, social rituals are containers of values and are ceremonies that help us through tough transitions. A birthday party, a Bar or Bat Mitzvah or a First Holy Communion, a wedding ceremony, a graduation, an award granting ceremony, a wake, a funeral—these all help to remind us and those around us that a transition (with its gains and losses) has taken place. At the same time, rituals create a social space for unrestrained (but culturally informed) expression of emotions and for active connection with our personal social network that enhances social support and resonates with joys, appeases pains, shares hopes, and mourns the truncation of dreams. Rituals help, unless. . . . Rituals help, *unless* they cannot be performed, as when ambiguity of circumstances makes a ritual socially inappropriate and a display of emotion questionable. Again, under those conditions, in those gray zones, time freezes, evolving stops.

This gray zone within the already gray territory of ambiguity has been the subject of the pioneering exploration of Pauline Boss. She started that adventure some thirty years ago, investigating the until-then uncharted field of *ambiguous loss* and enriching it progressively by describing its many nooks and crannies, its multiple presentations, its pervasiveness, the varied ways in which different cultures cope with this type of loss, and the labyrinth out of the quagmire associated with ambiguous loss. Equipped with an inquisitive mind and a scientific tradition of social psychology, cross-cultural psychology, and family dynamics, Boss has accumulated a depth of research data and a breadth of world-wide clinical experience that is unsurpassed in the field.

And now she is offering us *Loss, Trauma, and Resilience: Therapeutic Work with Ambiguous Loss.* It is her grand synthesis. Conceptual guidelines, research distillation, multicultural explorations, and rich clinical experience all coalesce in a work that goes way beyond the boundaries of her previous books and articles. This book discusses the conceptual lens for identifying ambiguous loss within the broader frames of loss and mourning, of resilience and health, and of therapy in a variety of contexts. Anchored firmly in theory and in practice, Boss's conceptual lens offers clear treatment orientations and key guidelines for clinical practice.

Loss, Trauma, and Resilience also orients researchers as to what is currently known as well as regarding new questions this knowledge raises (the mark of good research). Boss models for the reader stances and nuances for multicultural practices, and she thereby enriches the practices of therapists and counselors across the board, whether they are involved on the international scene working with victims of the political violence, in community-based practices focused on the plight of the poor, in practices centered on the elderly and their families, or they are generalists who day in and day out help people to deal with the many untenable ambiguous losses that accompany living in what is sometimes a dreadful world. Ultimately, Boss highlights the humanness of the ambiguous loss perspective. In doing so she also encourages us, with kind hand and wise words, to do the same with our own unavoidable ambiguous losses, helping us emerge from that journey with new clarities, new strengths, and new joys.

To Pauline Boss, good friend and admired colleague, I offer my deep appreciation for her wisdom and clarity. And to the reader, my wish is that you may experience the same sense of professional and personal enrichment that I had while reading this book.

Carlos E. Sluzki, M.D.
Research Professor, College of Health and Human Services and Institute
for Conflict Analysis and Resolution, George Mason University Clinical
Professor of Psychiatry, George Washington University

Preface

Five years ago, the idea of ambiguous loss—an unclear loss that defies closure—was introduced to the general public (Boss, 1999). I now write about its application.

My basic theoretical premise is that ambiguous loss is the most stressful kind of loss. It defies resolution and creates long-term confusion about who is in or out of a particular couple or family. With death, there is official certification of loss, and mourning rituals allow one to say goodbye. With ambiguous loss, none of these markers exists. The persisting ambiguity blocks cognition, coping, and meaning-making and freezes the grief process (Boss, 1999, 2004a).

The theory of ambiguous loss is based on decades of research and the work of professionals who treat families traumatized by war, terrorism, natural disasters, and chronic illnesses and disabilities. The ideas have also been honed by decades of clinical work with couples and families, as well as from my personal experiences with ambiguous loss. In the early 1970s, through the Center for Prisoner of War Studies at the Naval Health Research Institute in San Diego, I interviewed wives of pilots missing in action (MIA) in Vietnam and Southeast Asia. In 1989, I met with psychologists exhausted by their work in Armenia and Azerbaijan after the Armenia earthquake. In 1997, I met with therapists and community leaders in the aftermath of the flooded Red River Valley in the upper Midwest, and on numerous occasions I have met with military family personnel, rehabilitation counselors, clergy, and healthcare professionals to discuss ambiguous loss and trauma. After the terrorist attacks on 9/11/01, and at the invitation of labor union leaders,

I collaborated with New York therapists to shape interventions for families of the missing. I continue training therapists for that kind of work. At the invitation of the International Committee of the Red Cross (ICRC), I trained professionals and community leaders in Kosovo to work with the nearly 4,000 families with loved ones still missing since the late 1990s from ethnic cleansing. In private practice, I have worked since 1974 with individuals, couples, and families, most of whom had some kind of ambiguous loss—a depressed mate, a parent with Alzheimer's disease, a child with brain injury, a loved one with an addiction or other chronic mental illnesses. From all of this work, I have gained a profound respect for the many who manage to live well despite an ambiguous loss with no resolution. They have taught me what resilience is.

Overall, what has become clear to me is this: Ambiguous loss is a relational disorder, and not an individual pathology. It follows, then, that family- and community-based interventions—as opposed to individual therapy—will be less resisted and thus more effective. It should come as no surprise that when loved ones disappear, the remaining family members yearn to stay together. They resist therapy if it means more separation. Separating family members for individual therapy may only add to the trauma of ambiguous loss.

This book is meant to help professionals learn about the concept of ambiguous loss, its impact on resilience and health, and the guidelines for interventions. Rather than offering a concrete list, however, I provide theoretical ideas and treatment guidelines for each professional's particular need. This allows for tailor-made interventions that fit the culturally diverse people we serve today.

In this book, I merge family-based approaches begun by the pioneers of family therapy (Framo, 1972) with community-based approaches (Landau & Saul, 2004; Speck & Attneave, 1973) and theories from sociology, psychology, and family therapy. Social and systemic relational approaches are useful with catastrophic physical absence and chronic psychological absence—traumatic head injury, Alzheimer's disease, mental illnesses, and addictions. In addition, the family- and community-based interventions can support resiliency with couples and families experiencing the ambiguous losses of immigration, migration, and diasporas, as well as divorce, remarriage, adoption, and the placement of loved ones in institutionalized or foster care. When it comes to the trauma of ambiguous loss, individual therapy is insufficient. Although family therapy and community interventions are not new ideas, they appear to be so in the fields of trauma and resiliency.

Human relationships are often traumatized by ambiguous loss, but this unique kind of loss is just beginning to be discussed in professional texts and training courses. Even veteran therapists may miss it. What I learned from experience is that I could not recognize ambiguous loss in others until I had first recognized my own. For me it was immigration, addiction, divorce, and aging parents. Other family histories may contain more catastrophic ambiguous losses through genocide, slavery, holocaust, mysterious disappearances, Alzheimer's disease, and mental illnesses. Rife with ambiguity, losses that cannot be clarified or verified become traumatic, but they can be discussed in community with others to gain meaning and hope. As a colleague said after reflecting on his own experience, "It's not easy, but an untenable situation *can* be maintained indefinitely. I *can* stand not knowing."

HOW TO READ THIS BOOK

There are three sections to this book. The first discusses the developing theory of ambiguous loss. The second offers therapeutic goals and guidelines for treating the trauma of ambiguous loss. The epilogue provides information and support for therapists who are experiencing their own situations of ambiguous loss, personally or professionally. Recognizing one's own ambiguous losses is a necessary adjunct to reading this book.

Part I: The Developing Theory of Ambiguous Loss

In this section, I summarize the developing theory about ambiguous loss. Chapter 1 focuses on the psychological family; Chapter 2, on trauma and stress; and Chapter 3, on resilience and health. This first section lays the groundwork for a stress-based therapeutic model, emphasizing resilience and health more than pathology. What does this mean? Although stress is viewed as a natural part of family life due to maturational transitions, there are times when people experience stress and change that go far beyond normal human experience and expectation. Ambiguous loss is one such example, and it is inevitable in human experience. The ambiguity surrounding a loss of a friend, spouse, partner, coworker, teammate, or relative can traumatize and paralyze individual, dyadic, and family coping processes. It can harden people into a frozen grief drained of resilience (Boss, 1999).

Part II: Therapeutic Goals for Treating Ambiguous Loss

The second section of the book provides therapeutic goals and guidelines for treatment and prevention of trauma by centering on how to gain or maintain resiliency through finding meaning (Chapter 4), tempering mastery (Chapter 5), reconstructing identity (Chapter 6), normalizing ambivalence

(Chapter 7), revising attachment (Chapter 8), and discovering hope (Chapter 9). The first chapter in this part of the book (Chapter 4) launches the circular process of building resilience through finding meaning and sets all the others in motion. The resiliency process is systemic, circular, and sometimes—as with conflicting feelings and actions—a combination of both. Although this process is stressful for clients, it is less so than the trauma of doing nothing in response to ambiguous loss. In essence, this section is about finding resiliency despite an irresolvable loss and no solution to the problem.

Epilogue: The Self of the Therapist

This section of the book addresses the self of the therapist. The end is, paradoxically, the place to begin. That is, having read about how to shape therapies for ambiguous loss, you are now ready to *begin with yourself.* This means recognizing one's own ambiguous losses and finding some personal understanding before trying to help others. This self-work helps to increase your own tolerance for ambiguity and thus increases your professional resiliency.

Self-reflection is essential, and I have included examples of my own self-reflection throughout this book. I encourage you to use the process of self-reflection as you read the entire book, reflecting on your own experiences and feelings in the light of even the didactic information. Reflective and cognitive processes are, after all, intertwined.

COMING FULL CIRCLE

My work in New York, in Kosovo, and with people affected by the 2004 tsunami has solidified my views about including family- and resiliency-based approaches in treating loss and trauma. The common focus on individual treatment and pathology after loss and trauma must be broadened to include safeguarding natural family and community strengths and rebuilding resiliency. This is the underlying thesis of this book.

Working in New York after 9/11 brought me out of the ivory tower and into the community, and it pushed my thinking and my feelings to the brink. My experiences with the families of workers who vanished on that terrible day tested my assumptions—and me—more rigorously than any research test could have. The challenge was to apply the theory to this catastrophe and to help this immensely diverse group of families. The work was exceedingly difficult during the first few weeks and called for frequent time-outs to reflect. On one of those early days, I looked out of the window from the 21st floor of the union building where we were working with the families. The smoke was still rising from Ground Zero. I hungered for another view, but only later did I find a more comforting one. At a friend's high-rise home in lower Manhattan, in the late afternoon sun, I saw the Statue of Liberty—the same statue that welcomed my father and my maternal grandparents into the New York harbor so long ago. I realized then that I had come full circle, back to where my family had begun life in the United States. I felt a deep calm. Hope and loss had merged for them, and now for me, too. Out of this insight came renewed strength.

Many of the families we worked with had come to this shore, like my elders, hoping for a better life. By uprooting, they, too, had lost contact with parents and siblings. After 9/11, they faced an ambiguous loss even more horrendous. Could they regain their resiliency and strength while being cut off from loved ones in faraway islands or countries? Thankfully, with family- and community-based interventions, many have.

LOSS, TRAUMA, AND RESILIENCE

Introduction

Loss and Ambiguity

Absence and presence are not absolutes.[1] Even without death, the people we care about disappear physically or fade away psychologically. The Alzheimer's patient, the brain injured, and the stroke victim, as well as the kidnapped or imprisoned, are out of reach. This ambiguity between absence and presence creates a unique kind of loss that has both psychological and physical qualities.

The amalgamation of the ideas of loss and ambiguity has always been—and still is—the stuff of good literature. Bayley (1999) writes an elegy for his beloved but demented Iris, Albom (1997) writes about Tuesdays with his dying professor, Fadiman (1997) writes about the spirit catching you in a new country after forced immigration, and Styron (1990) writes about his own depression. Yet it is only within the past 30 years that the idea of ambiguous loss as traumatic has reached therapeutic circles, and that research has provided us with an initial theoretical base (Boss, 1972, 1975, 1977, 1980c, 1986, 1987, 1992, 1993b, 1993c, 1993d, 1999, 2002a, 2002b, 2002c, 2004a, 2004b; Boss, Beaulieu, Wieling, Turner, & LaCruz, 2003; Boss, Caron, & Horbal, 1988; Boss & Couden, 2002; Boss & Kaplan, 2004). The premise is that ambiguity coupled with *loss* creates a powerful barrier to coping and grieving and leads to symptoms such as depression and relational conflict that erode human relationships. For this book, I extend this work to link ideas about ambiguous loss with a resiliency model that allows for diverse interpretations and interventions.

Loss is not always simply death or physical absence. Human relationships are more complex. For many, the psychological family in our hearts

1

and minds is as important for assessing stress and maintaining resiliency as the physical family we live with. We do not necessarily disconnect from loved ones just because they are physically gone, nor do we always connect to people just because they are physically present at home or in our daily lives. Such ambiguity can be a benefit or a detriment. In times of trauma and stress, we often reach for loved ones kept present in our hearts and minds, not just the people we live with physically, in order to stay resilient and carry on. On the other hand, not knowing if a loved one is absent or present, dead or alive, can create so much ambiguity that the stress is traumatizing and immobilizing. This new view of loss, trauma, and resiliency centers on this psychological family and making sense of ambiguous absence and presence.

THE CONTEXTUAL VIEW

Many people never achieve the complete detachment described by Western psychotherapists as necessary for normal grieving. A lack of closure after loss, however, is not always an indication of weakness in the individual or family.

The force that causes loss to remain fresh decades later and thus be labeled as pathological often lies in the context *outside* of the person rather than in their ego, psyche, or family. When a person or family suffers loss within an external context of ambiguity, the situation understandably has high potential for causing symptoms of unresolved grief. From this more contextual perspective, pathology is attributed to a client's situational context and environment rather than to the psyche or family. Using this broader view, clients are more receptive to therapy and therapists are better able to treat people in the context of particular loss experiences that range from merely stressful to traumatic.

With a broader lens, we also become more multiculturally sensitive in assessments of *maladaptations* to the trauma of ambiguous loss, which require treatment and change, versus *healthy adaptations* which may be creative ways of coping and being resilient. We can assess perceptions, feelings, behaviors, relationships, and symptoms more broadly by asking questions such as: What losses have you had? Have you experienced any *ambiguous* losses? How do you see this situation? What did you lose? What do you still have? How do you feel about the ambiguity now? Rather than focusing only on problematic symptoms, we are more likely to see the unique ways individuals, couples, and families within diverse contexts manage to live well despite the stress of ambiguous loss.

When contextual factors are outside a client's control, our therapeutic task is to help individuals, couples, and families *differentiate* between what can and cannot be changed. Specifically, we need to take into account the external factors of culture, history, economics, development, and constitutional heredity (Boss, 2002c). Each of these factors influences how a particular individual, couple, family, or even community perceives and copes with loss and ambiguity. Being born into one culture or another, during times of war or peace, into affluence or poverty, being old or young, having heritable strengths or vulnerabilities, experiencing discrimination or privilege—all can influence human resiliency.

The research on resiliency and family stress within a more contextual view is relatively new. Among the pioneers are Reiss and Oliveri (1991), who broadened the contextual perspective by emphasizing the community context as the major source of meaning and thus a major influence on how families respond to stress, and Conger, Rueter, and Elder (1999) who studied couple resilience in the context of economic hard times. Resiliency and family functioning in African-American families despite the stress caused by discrimination was studied by Murry, Brown, Brody, Cutrona, and Simons (2001). Harriette McAdoo (1995) also studied African-American families but focused on the stress levels, family help patterns, and religiosity of single-parent mothers in middle- and working-class families. Cultural psychiatrists Kirmayer, Boothroyd, Tanner, Adelson, and Robinson (2000) followed that line as well in describing cultural protective factors for psychological stress among the Cree in northern Canada. In addition, diverse contexts are being studied and incorporated into support for the chronically ill. For example, Wood, Klebba, and Miller (2000) linked the hopelessness about chronically ill children with parental attachment issues. Focusing on spirituality in nursing work Lorraine Wright (1997) summarized her ideas in an essay on suffering and spirituality based on her research with colleagues on healing and family religious beliefs (Wright, Watson, & Bell, 1996). From a more secular perspective, Swedish researchers Strang and Strang (2001) provided support for the idea that more secular values such as optimism are also conducive to healing. This sampling of research supports the point that context can influence the complexity of family loss, trauma, and resilience. Knowing this broader perspective is necessary in helping diverse people after the trauma of loss confused by ambiguity (Boss, 2002c; Boss & Mulligan, 2003). What this means is that each couple or family must be viewed within their unique context so that interventions can be tailored to fit their particular needs.

With a broader contextual lens, this research based theory of ambiguous loss is useful in guiding interventions in diverse situations with diverse populations. Regardless of class, race, ethnicity, generation, gender, or sexual orientation, we have here a less pathology-based lens for viewing unresolved loss and its outcomes of anxiety, somatic symptoms, and relational conflict.

AMBIGUOUS LOSS AND TRAUMATIC STRESS

Ambiguous loss is inherently traumatic because the inability to resolve the situation causes pain, confusion, shock, distress, and often immobilization. Without closure, the trauma of this unique kind of loss becomes chronic. To understand the trauma of ambiguous loss, it is helpful to recognize the distress of more ordinary loss. In modern cultures, loss is difficult to talk about because it reminds family members as well as trained professionals that something could not be fixed or cured. Most people cannot tolerate for long the feeling of being in a situation that is outside of their control. A death in the family may be viewed as failure—a failure to find a cure or make things better. To many in cultures that value mastery, the goal is to win, not lose. Because of this strong value, there is in our culture a tendency to deny loss. Grieving is acceptable, but we should get over it and get back to work. Whereas finding closure is difficult with ordinary losses, it is impossible with ambiguous loss because there is no official recognition of there even being a real loss.

Freud (1917/1957) labeled long-term preoccupation with the lost person *complicated grief* or *melancholia*. Erich Lindemann (1944), who worked with the surviving family members of the people lost in the Coconut Grove nightclub fire, also saw lack of closure as individual pathology. He said that grief reactions depended on how well the bereaved perform their *grief work*. Indeed, in current diagnostic manuals, the inability to complete one's grief work is called *unresolved grief* and defined as pathological due to its lack of resolution or closure. Unresolved grief, they say, can involve a range of emotions, but in general, according to Freud (1917/1957), these emotions result from the patient's refusal to relinquish the "love object." The question for us here, however, is this: What happens when a person is faced with an ambiguous loss, which by its very nature is irresolvable? What happens when it is the external situation, not the person's psyche, that makes letting go of the lost object impossible?

Feigelson (1993), a psychoanalyst, writes explicitly of such a situation. Her husband, also a psychoanalyst, sustained massive brain injury after he fell down an elevator shaft in their apartment building. Feigelson called her experience, an "uncanny" loss due to a "personality death" (p. 331). Using what she learned from this personal experience of ambiguous loss, she firmed up Freud's indirect suggestions about "an 'uncanny' union of opposites" (p. 331). She wrote, "Something unknown amalgamates with something known to produce an uncanny sensation. The anxiety of the uncanny involves something on the border of what we both know and don't know, both cognitively murky and affectively alarming" (p. 331).

From a psychoanalytic perspective, ambiguous loss is indeed an uncanny situation of traumatic anxiety produced by a combination of the known and the unknown (physically present but psychologically absent, or vice versa). The intellectual and relational uncertainty of living with someone both here and not here produces a terrible anxiety of bizarre human experience. Terr wrote, "My intention is not to supplant repressed internal conflict as a possible causality for weird human experience, but to *add* externally precipitated psychic trauma to the very short list of underlying reasons for the 'uncanny.' When the ego is overwhelmed by external events, everything outside a person may begin to look spooky, eerie, and overdetermined" (1985, pp. 495–496). This may be why women with husbands missing in Vietnam, after 9/11, and in other settings tell of talking with their mates after they disappear (Boss, 1975, 1999; Boss et al., 2003). Other therapists report similar phenomena (Becvar, 2001; Falicov, 1998). In such cases, the psychological family is very real, and often helps to assimilate sudden loss.

But what of situations where a loved one's mind is missing instead of his body? Both types of ambiguous losses have in common the trauma-related anxiety that "is felt when there is a sudden change from the ordinary dependable way things are in everyday life to the extraordinary and bizarre distortions that occur when a known person is profoundly altered" (Feigelson, 1993, p. 332). The absent quality of a person who is still physically present distresses even healthy and resilient family members. This idea applies even more systemically to those who are psychologically attached to the patient because of the cessation of reciprocal relationships and clear identity. They feel as loss their mate's changes in memory and cognitions, but according to Feigelson, "Changes in temperament overshadow by far the most intractable intellectual losses. Profound dependence, egocentricity, eccentric habits of personal hygiene and rigidities of dressing set in. Interests and hobbies wither. Brashness and coarsening of speech, friction with others over trivia, aspontancity, restlessness, irritability, attacks of rage, panic, anxiety, depression, apathy, withdrawal, and loss of empathic fine tuning render many head-injured people complete social outcasts" (1993, pp. 333–334). In such cases, life is altered dramatically for the spouse, children, and the family as a whole. And no one sends a sympathy card or sits shivah for this. Instead, there is a lonely and oft misunderstood mourning with an indefinite beginning and indefinite end. Feigelson asks painful questions: "How is it possible to lose half a person? Half is dead, half remains alive.... Unlike a fairy tale whose premise is poetic reality in which nothing can surprise the reader, the uncanny story violates the observer's trust in reality. Life may then deceive by promising substance and delivering ghosts. The *doppelganger* sits at the dinner table" (1993, p. 335). Reading her words, I think of my own experience long ago with another kind of doppelganger at the dinner table.

Like Feigelson and me, most clinicians have personally experienced several kinds of ambiguous loss and surely see clients with such uncanny loss. For symptoms from long-term, drawn-out mourning, the ambiguous loss model adds a new lens to our current ways of working with loss and trauma. Whether we specialize in grief or loss, whether we work with individuals, couples, families, or communities, becoming familiar with ambiguous loss helps us be more effective practitioners. Let me explain why.

First, there are missing persons in *everyone's* life. Rarely is there absolute presence—or absence—in any human relationship. All of us at some time or place may have faced situations of ambiguous loss, personally or professionally. It is not therefore a condition that only our clients face.

Second, the loss of loved ones creates distress and trauma universally, in all cultures and religions. One needs only to watch the evening news to see this pain. But ambiguous loss adds another dimension of pain. We have the universal pain of loss, *plus* the often traumatizing ambiguity. Broadening our repertoire for helping people find resiliency with ordinary as well as catastrophic losses begins with understanding the traumatizing potential of ambiguity.

Third, regardless of discipline or professional training, therapists need a broader therapeutic vision. The ambiguous loss model allows us to work systemically and contextually at various levels of human interaction without ignoring individual symptoms. We can acknowledge *both* diversity and similarity as we assess and treat different people in different situations.

Fourth, because the cause of ambiguous loss is usually some external force or illness, therapists benefit from a model that looks beyond symptoms to strengths and resilience against that force. Through no fault on the part of the patient, ambiguous loss has no possibility of closure. Finding meaning in situations that defy logic and resolution—and there are many—is difficult, but it is possible if we look for resilience, not just pathology.

Fifth, in times of disaster and trauma, therapists need a treatment model other than PTSD and classic grief therapies to guide work with couples, families and communities when loved ones go missing. Notable exceptions to the standard of individual and medical models for treating posttraumatic stress disorder (PTSD) and grief are the work of Landau (1981), Landau and Saul (2004), Rolland (1994), and Walsh (1999), all of whom call for more family- and community-based approaches. I agree but add that traditional treatments for PTSD and loss after disaster miss a major trauma: that of ambiguous loss (Boss, 2002a, 2002b, 2004a, 2004b). Although ambiguous loss is also traumatic stress, the core issue is unresolved loss and the ongoing ambiguity that causes a pain that never lets up. The torture lies in being kept in the dark. With the ambiguous loss model, therapists have guidelines to work with children, youth and adults after such disaster.

Sixth, the model is easily taught and understood, even by clients, so in times of disaster and heavy demand, paraprofessionals and community leaders can be used to aid professionals. The psychoeducational quality of the theory (though the model is psychodynamic) means that we can help a larger number of people in times of unexpected ambiguous loss as well as in times of expected family life transitions.

Regardless of the kind of clinical work we do, considering these ideas about ambiguous loss expands our analysis and assessment for more effective interventions when loved ones either change beyond recognition or disappear altogether. How can we help individuals, couples, families, and communities stay healthy and resilient despite the strain of having to live with the uncanny nature of ambiguous loss? To answer this core question, I summarize the theory of ambiguous loss—what it is, why it matters, and how to intervene. As I train professionals to do this work, I use a contextual stress perspective with a focus on health and resilience.

THE AMBIGUOUS LOSS MODEL

We begin therapy first by determining who is perceived as family. In this way, we explicitly bring the client's psychological family into the therapy room. If family members are physically absent but psychologically present, or physically present but psychologically absent, we label the situation as one of ambiguous loss—the most stressful kind of loss due to the ambiguity. Knowing that the source of anxiety is external tends to mobilize resiliency as people realize the pathology is not theirs but rather lies in the outside situation.

There are two types of ambiguous loss: physical absence with psychological presence, and physical presence with psychological absence (See Figure I.1). Both types of ambiguous loss have the potential to disturb and traumatize relational boundaries and systemic processes.

In the first type of ambiguous loss, a loved one is physically missing—bodily gone. Catastrophic examples of such losses include missing persons and missing bodies in the context of war, terrorism, ethnic cleansing, genocide, or natural disasters such as earthquake and tsunami. In these cases, a loved one may be physically absent but kept psychologically present because his or her status as dead or alive is unknown. Without proof of death, family members don't know whether to close out the missing person or keep the door open for him or her to return. Family processes freeze and boundaries are unclear. People become preoccupied with the lost person and may think of little else. As a result, they may no longer function in their usual roles and relationships. More common examples of this type of ambiguous loss are absent parents in divorced families, absent biological parents in adoptive families, or babies lost or given up at birth.

In the second type of ambiguous loss, a person is psychologically absent—that is, emotionally or cognitively missing. Examples of this type of ambiguous loss include Alzheimer's disease, dementia, brain injury, AIDS, autism, depression, addiction, or other chronic mental or physical illnesses that take away memory or emotional expression. More common examples include excessive preoccupation with work and homesickness (often resulting from immigration). With this type of ambiguous loss, relational and emotional processes freeze; day-to-day functions and tasks don't get done. Roles and status become confusing. Often people don't know how to act or what to do.

Often we see both types of ambiguous loss overlap in one family or couple. For example, after 9/11, a woman I was working with in New York City had a physically missing husband as well as a mother who had Alzheimer's disease. Indeed, this woman said she felt twice abandoned. Young children may also experience both kinds of ambiguous loss when they lose one parent from a catastrophic event, accident, or illness and the remaining parent becomes depressed and preoccupied with the missing mate. After 9/11, several adolescents said that they felt as if they had lost both parents even though one was still present with them. I have seen the same dynamic when a parent becomes preoccupied with caring for an impaired or ill mate. The child ends up losing both parents, but no one notices because they are still there in the home.

HISTORY OF THE RESEARCH BASE

The first study of a situation of ambiguous loss with potential for high boundary ambiguity began in 1971 with families of United States soldiers missing in action in Vietnam and Laos (Boss, 1975, 1977, 1980a, 1980c). Subsequently, with colleagues, I studied families of missing children (Fravel & Boss, 1992), families with adolescents leaving home (Boss, Pearce-McCall, & Greenberg, 1987), and families of immigrants who were uprooting (Boss, 1993c, 1996; Gates, Arce de Esnaola, Kroupin, Stewart, van Dulmen, Xiong, & Boss, 2000). I also studied the other type of ambiguous loss—where someone is missing psychologically. In this area, the research centered on families where someone was psychologically missing from Alzheimer's disease or other chronic mental and physical illnesses (Boss, 1993d; Boss et al., 1988; Boss, Caron, Horbal, & Mortimer, 1990; Boss & Couden, 2002; Caron, Boss, & Mortimer, 1999; Garwick, Detzner, & Boss,

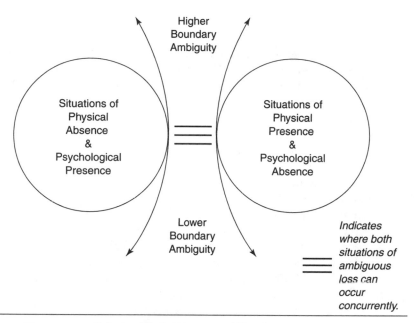

Higher
Boundary
Ambiguity

Situations of
Physical
Absence
&
Psychological
Presence

Situations of
Physical
Presence
&
Psychological
Absence

Lower
Boundary
Ambiguity

*Indicates
where both
situations of
ambiguous
loss can
occur
concurrently.*

Catastrophic and Unexpected Situations:

- war (missing soldiers)
- natural disasters (missing persons)
- kidnapping, hostage-taking, terrorism
- incarceration
- desertion, mysterious disappearance
- missing body (murder, plane crash, etc .)

- Alzheimer's disease & other dementias
- chronic mental illness
- addictions (alcohol, drugs, gambling, etc.)
- depression
- traumatic head injury, brain injury
- coma, unconsciousness

More Common Situations:

- immigration, migration
- adoption
- divorce, remarriage
- work relocation
- military deployment
- young adults leaving home
- elderly mate moving to a nursing home

- homesickness (immigration/migration)
- adoption
- divorce, remarriage
- preoccupation with work
- obsession with computer games, Internet, TV

FIGURE I.1 Catastrophic and unexpected types of ambiguous loss situations, which cause varying degrees of boundary ambiguity.
Adapted with permission from Journal of Marriage and Family, 66 *(2004), 551–566. Copyrighted 2002 by the National Council on Family Relations, 3989 Central Ave. NE, Suite 550 Minneapolis, MN 55421.*

1994; Kaplan & Boss, 1999). Theory was developed (Blackburn, Greenberg, & Boss, 1987; Boss, 1992, 1999, 2004b; Boss & Greenberg, 1984; Boss & Kaplan, 2004) with writings on measurement (Boss, Greenberg, & Pearce-McCall, 1990; Mortimer, Boss, Caron, & Horbal, 1992) and application for specific populations (Boss, 1983a, 1983b, 1993a, 1993d; Weins & Boss, 2006). Other researchers tested the theory with adoption (Fravel, McRoy, & Grotevant, 2000), divorce, addiction, autism, miscarriage, infertility, stillborn babies, foster care, adoption, incarceration, AIDS, brain injury, immigration, and cultural loss. This type of loss also includes lesbians and gays with unresolved family of origin loss. Carroll, Boss, and Buckmiller (2003) provided a review of these studies.

When I first began working with families of the missing in 1973, I thought that getting rid of ambiguity was the goal. I quickly realized that this was impossible. My goal shifted to trying to understand how people live well with ambiguity. Elsewhere, I have written in depth about the long process of research, theory development, and application (Boss, 1999, 2004b).[2] Here I review this process for clinicians.

In 1972, while training with Carl Whitaker and psychiatric residents at the University of Wisconsin-Madison, I observed a consistent pattern in the families treated in the family therapy clinic. These families were intact but the fathers seemed distant and absent. They were there but not there. They continually asked why we needed them in the session because "children were a mother's business." Indeed, in the early 1970s fathers were not expected to be part of child rearing, but children noticed and were distressed by the ambiguity. Based on clinical work, I first wrote about psychological father absence in the intact family. Later, I expanded the idea to a more general level so it could apply to any family member or person who is "there but not there." From 1975 on, I called the phenomenon *ambiguous loss*.

This broader lens considers the psychological family, and thus the subtle structural and perceptual processes of human relations and transitions that develop over time. I included the exits from and entries into the family and how these transitions of ins and outs are inherently stressful (Boss, 1980b). The boundaries of marital and family systems are blurred by the ambiguity and are thus harder to maintain at times of birth, death, separation, deployment, and even reunification. To understand how families remain resilient despite heightened ambiguity during normative and unexpected transitions, I studied the individual and collective perceptions of a family member's presence or absence. Research indicated that situations of ambiguous loss from, for example, dementia and war predicted symptoms of depression, anxiety, and family conflict (Boss, 1977, 1980c; Boss, Caron, et al., 1990; Caron et al., 1999; Garwick et al., 1994). A research-based clinical theory was developed that linked ambiguous loss with frozen grief, ambivalence, mastery, meaning, and hope (Boss, 1999, 2004b). As I continued to work with families of the missing—physically and psychologically—I realized that my awareness of a psychological family in a client's mind was critical to the success of therapy. Since 9/11, I believe this even more strongly.

THE CONCEPTUAL BASE: STRESS AND RESILIENCE

At the root of the ambiguous loss model is the contextual stress perspective discussed earlier, with an emphasis on resilience. What this means is that when there is a situation that cannot be fixed or an illness that cannot be cured, our therapeutic goal is to help the clients live with the inherent stress and anxiety by increasing their resilience. We cannot get rid of the ambiguity, but we can increase tolerance of ambiguity. Our therapeutic goals then are not about closure, as they are in classic grief therapies, nor do we view unresolved grief as an individual pathology as in the medical model.

The focus on the stress of ambiguity allows us to go beyond symptom treatment to build on people's individual strengths. In this way, we discover and reinforce (if appropriate) their ways of rebounding during troubled times. Viewing contextual stress, not a weak psyche or a dysfunctional family, as the source of symptoms gives hope to clients for some positive outcome. I want to clarify, however, that I do not recommend that therapists ignore pathology. Even in a model that prioritizes resilience and strength, therapists need to be aware of individual pathology. Physical and psychological symptoms need to be treated, especially if they are life-threatening. Suicidal thoughts, homicidal threats, violence, and addictions, for example, need immediate professional treatment. Individual pathology can result from ambiguous loss but also causes even more of it.

The conceptual base for the ambiguous loss model lies in family stress theory (Boss, 1987, 2002c; Boss & Mulligan, 2003). Ambiguous loss is an extraordinary stressor—a producer of uncanny anxiety and unending stress that blocks coping and understanding. It freezes the grief process and defies resolution. It understandably encourages denial of loss. It can lead to immobilization and more crises. The clarity needed for boundary maintenance (in the sociological sense) or closure (in the psychological sense) remains out of reach. Symptoms of pathology in individuals, couples, or families are often outcomes of the relentless stress of ambiguity. These symptoms do not necessarily point to a psychic weakness. The stress perspective with an emphasis on context and resilience provides a new lens for clinicians trained in the medical model but having to face unanswered questions.

Figure I.2 illustrates how the two types of ambiguous loss can immobilize but also lead to resilience. Part A of the diagram signifies the *ambiguous loss*, defined as a situation of unclear loss in which it is not known if a loved one is dead or alive, absent or present (Boss, 1999). How family members (individually and collectively) perceive the situation of ambiguous loss is tied to *boundary ambiguity* which means not knowing who is in or out of your family or relationship (Part C). A high degree of boundary ambiguity becomes a risk factor, which predicts depression, somatic symptoms, and family conflict.

The higher the incongruence between the psychological family and the physical family, the higher the boundary ambiguity in the family system. High boundary ambiguity is a compromise or risk factor for individual and relational well-being; it is a barrier to the family's management of their stress from ambiguous loss. Not knowing who is in or out of one's intimate circle immobilizes and erodes resilience (Boss, 2002c). From a sociological perspective, the family boundary is no longer maintainable, roles are confused, tasks remain undone, and eventually the family becomes immobilized. From a psychological perspective, cognition is blocked by the ambiguity and lack of information, decisions are put on hold, and coping and grieving processes are frozen (Boss, 1993a, 1999; Boss et al., 2003). Note that not all situations of ambiguous loss lead to high boundary ambiguity.

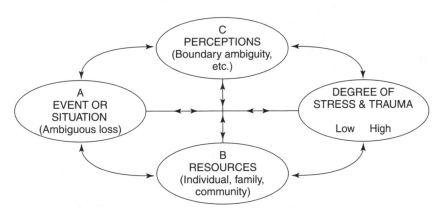

FIGURE I-2. Where Ambiguous Loss and Boundary Ambiguity Fit into the Family Stress Model
With permission, from Journal of Marriage and Family, 66 (2004), 551–566. Copyrighted 2002 by the National Council on Family Relations, 3989 Central Ave. NE, Suite 550, Minneapolis, MN 55421.

I must clarify here that the stress of boundary ambiguity can be seen as both objective and subjective. For example, no one would disagree that some events—a kidnapped daughter or a drug-addicted son, for example—are objectively stressful, but there are also subjective elements that determine the degree of stress and trauma experienced. These may be one's cultural context or one's psychological health. How boundary ambiguity is perceived is also influenced by the community in which one participates or lives (Goffman, 1974; Reiss & Oliveri, 1991). Subjective or objective, all these elements influence resilience. That is, stress is both a fact and a subjective experience, but the latter more significantly affects whether someone is brittle or resilient. The degree to which an event distresses someone depends heavily on perceptions (Boss, 1987, 1992, 2002c).

Despite family members missing either physically or psychologically, some people view their systemic boundaries as clear even though they may not appear so to some therapists. Aunts and uncles, for example, were often perceived as parent figures in the families that had lost a mother or father after 9/11. Such replacements by expanding the family boundaries are also common when a parent can't function due to mental illness or addiction. Grandmothers frequently become "mothers" in such cases. Culture and ethnicity play a major part in defining such family boundaries as more flexible. African-American families, for example, have more elastic boundaries (McAdoo, 1995) and a more communal focus on homeplace and family (Burton, Winn, Stevenson, & Clark, 2004).

THE TRAINING

How do we go from theory to practice? Typically, therapists are trained to think that if they are doing their jobs right, clients will get over their grief and do so relatively quickly. Healthy people find closure. But resolution after loss is rarely that absolute, and especially not when a loved one vanishes without a trace. When there is no body to bury, the situation defies closure, and individuals and families become symptomatic. Therapists are trained to see the larger picture and the external stressor of ambiguous loss.

To shape effective interventions, therapists need to assess the degree of congruence regarding both psychological and physical families among family members, especially parents and children. This means that instead of one best intervention for every couple or family, interventions are tailor-made based on the psychological and physical structure of one's intimate circle. With this in mind, the following provides the core of training for working professionally with people suffering from situations where loved ones are physically absent, psychologically absent, or both. The overall objectives, list of questions addressed, and outcomes give you a sketch of the training workshops.

Objectives and Outcomes for Training

The *overall objective* for training workshops is to inform mental health therapists, psychiatrists, clergy, medical practitioners, attorneys, and educators about a newly identified type of loss that has no closure and that is best treated systemically with family- and community-based approaches.

With this goal and the conceptual model in mind, the ambiguous loss training includes the following topics (which will be discussed over the course of this book):

- The psychological family
- What is ambiguous loss and how is it different from ordinary loss?
- What are the two types of ambiguous loss; do they ever overlap?
- How do you know if and when it's a problem?
- How do the causes and effects of ambiguous loss differ from those of PTSD?
- How do cultural values and beliefs influence how people cope with ambiguous loss? Are there religious, class, racial, and gender differences?
- To strengthen resiliency with ambiguous loss, what are the goals and guidelines for finding meaning, tempering mastery, reconstructing identity, normalizing ambivalence, revising attachment, and discovering hope?
- Self of the therapist

It is important to note that these topics are adapted to fit the needs of the professionals who attend. For example, in Tokyo, the focus was on ambiguous loss in three-generational families and the loss elders feel in the erosion of filial piety as more women enter the workforce. In Toronto, a workshop was aimed at professionals who work with couples doubly victimized by ambiguous loss due to current Alzheimer's disease and past trauma from the Holocaust during World War II. In Duluth, the workshop emphasis was on addiction; at the Albert Einstein College of Medicine in New York, on mental illness; at Texas Tech in Lubbock, Texas, on migration and immigration. In New Jersey, I gave a workshop for the chaplains who worked with the ironworkers and uniformed men and women who cleaned up the Ground Zero site. Most recently, in Australia, I trained professionals who work with the ambiguous loss of chronic illness, mental or physical, as well as professionals who worked with tsunami victims.

At the end of every workshop, and congruent with the goal and conceptualization, I expect two outcomes. First, by the end of the training, attendees are able to recognize ambiguous loss, understand its impact, and shape interventions and treatment for their specific clients who manifest symptoms of unresolved grief. Second, attendees are able to recognize and understand an ambiguous loss of their own, its impact, and its meaning. Paradoxically, for professionals who study ambiguous loss, the second outcome usually precedes the first. The two develop in a parallel process in which personal experience grounds the conceptual and therapeutic experience. When it comes to ambiguous loss, the professional outcome cannot be separated from one's personal growth.

Using a more inclusive model for clinical training, professionals from different disciplines can work more smoothly in healing teams. Depending on the situation and the need, teams may include couple and family therapists, social workers, psychiatrists, psychologists, trauma specialists, nurses, journalists, educators, and clergy. Using different approaches and skills, each person contributes toward a common goal—stronger families and stronger individuals. Although a multidisciplinary and multilingual team may add managerial complexity, teamwork is essential today to incorporate the conceptual complexity of the multiculturalism and diversity in couples and families—and in professional expertise.

Nuances in the Model

Any description of the training must address also the nuances of ambiguous loss theory.

First ambiguous loss is not always problematic for families or family members. How do we know when it is a problem? That question has both a structural and psychological answer. Ambiguous loss is a problem structurally when parenting roles are ignored, decisions are put on hold, daily tasks are not done, and family members are ignored or cut off. Rituals and celebrations are cancelled even though they are the glue of family life. Ambiguous loss is a problem psychologically when there are feelings of hopelessness that lead to depression and passivity and feelings of ambivalence that lead to guilt, anxiety, and immobilization.

Indeed, some people manage to live with missing loved ones without negative effects (Bonnano, 2004). Although further study is needed, the valence of outcomes appears to be influenced by attributions and belief systems—the individual's, the family's, and, perhaps most important, the community frame (Reiss & Oliveri, 1991). The old saying "What will the neighbors think?" has merit when it comes to determining whether loss has a positive or negative effect on a person or family. If the community thinks the loss resulted from an immoral act or a deficiency, the bereaved will experience greater guilt and less resiliency. Some of the survivors of 9/11, for example, believed that their loved one's being in the Twin Towers at the time of the attack was predestined; others thought it was their fault. With Alzheimer's disease and brain injury, I see similar variations. People may attribute the loss of their loved one as punishment from God or Allah, whereas others see it as a challenge to show more love.

Many who believe in God continue to trust in His will to see them through their daily lives. Others with religious faith may not see the event as predestined but still deeply trust that God or Allah will guide them through the current ambiguity. When their community also believes this, they are more able to move forward despite the lack of information and persistent ambiguity. In addition, certain personality traits appear to increase tolerance for ambiguity. These factors not withstanding, the most important predictor for resilience in the face of ambiguous loss is an individual's ability to learn how to hold two opposing ideas in their minds at the same time. Living well with ambiguity means that people have learned to live with conflicting ideas. A parent of a missing soldier says, "He is dead, but he may still be alive and come back someday." The daughter of a mother with brain injury says, "My mother is still here, but she is also gone." These are vexing truths. Yet many people for differing reasons can live with this uncanny tension.

A second nuance is that naming the ambiguity as an external culprit diminishes self-blame. After traumatic or painful loss, people often blame themselves. They ruminate on thoughts such as, "If only I had done this or done that, she would be alive today." Our therapeutic task is to externalize the blame, as family therapists Michael White and David Epston (1990) recommended. Dementia, brain injury, birth defects, mental illness and other forms of ambiguous loss represent a loss of dreams and an assault on the family and its members, but the situation is no one's fault. One would think this would have been obvious after the 9/11 terrorist attacks, but many family members were nevertheless immobilized by guilt, shame, or anger at themselves. "We had a fight the last night he was with me." "I wasn't there to answer the phone and all he got was my voicemail." After externalizing the problem, the next step is to increase tolerance (both in our patients and ourselves) for not having a definitive answer. As noted earlier, I do not dismiss the presence of pathology. I simply want to relocate it within the context of a situation that is far beyond normal human expectation. Although individual symptoms that require attention may appear, the root of the pathology—the ambiguity that wears down people with its persistent confusion—lies in the context outside the person.

The third nuance concerns us as therapists and the culture of psychotherapy in general. Many professionals believe that people who see an absent person as present or a present person as absent are irrational, even pathological. My work with families with a loved one suffering from dementia and my experience in conducting therapy with families directly affected by 9/11 have taught me once again that closure is a *myth*. It is a myth that unfortunately remains highly touted by many who view closure after loss as a criterion of normalcy. Despite our original training, we must shift our views about loss and take into account the psychological family. Some are already doing this as they shift to the idea of open systems in grief therapy (Rando, 1993; True & Kaplan, 1993; White, 1995).

Perhaps the reason we talk so much about closure is that we can't stand the pain. We assume pain is bad and must be eliminated. But when it comes to loss, especially ambiguous loss, pain often has a function (Cousins, 1979; Frankl, 1963). It leads to change, which in the context of ambiguous loss can be more challenging. The pain of loss can immobilize—or it can give momentum for change. In my experience, people choose change more readily when they can keep the door ajar.

We must take another look at this all-too-convenient concept of closure. Closure is not possible when a family member has in mind or body gone missing. Without verification of death or signs of life, a family's boundary understandably remains open; the inability to find closure and to resolve the loss is normal under such circumstances. Despite varying contexts, closure should not be expected or required when a family member is missing. Closure is *never* really possible even with a clear-cut death. Just ask someone who has lost a loved one in the most common of circumstances. Our hunger for closure is a byproduct of a culture that prizes knowing answers, fixing problems, and moving on. We need to temper our thinking on this point.

The myth of closure is paired with a set of norms regarding how we bring about closure. There is unfortunately a tendency to criticize and actually judge how families grieve their losses, both in terms of how long they take to get back to "normal" and also in terms of whether they grieve in a "proper" or "improper" way. With respect to the latter, I think of the memorial service for Senator Paul Wellstone in 2002, which was heavily criticized for being political when, in fact, only a fraction of the entire service was political in nature. The political talk, however, was all that was reported by outsiders who voraciously criticized this family's way of grieving. Should anyone have been surprised that a portion of the service was political? The Wellstones were, after all, a political family. It was their family's culture. For the two surviving sons and their friends, a political cry for carrying on their father's work was their way of grieving. Many in Minnesota are still not over grieving for their senator, and I think part of that is because their grief was interrupted and sullied by the shame and blame put on their memorial event. I suspected that a local community event would be needed if the community was to heal. This happened one year later, spontaneously, on the anniversary of the deadly plane crash, when all the theaters and concert halls in the Twin Cities explicitly dedicated their performances to the Wellstones. It was a night he and his wife would have enjoyed.

As therapists we have the opportunity to lead our communities in increasing patience for what may look like unorthodox ways and durations of grieving. Understanding this paradox helps: The more outsiders are critical, the more people withdraw and defend their right to keep on grieving in their own way. If some idiosyncratic ways of grieving become unhealthy or life-threatening, clinical intervention is necessary. Professionals need to give permission to let individuals, couples, families, and communities grieve as it suits them and yet also direct that grieving if it becomes unhealthy.

This brings me to the fourth and final nuance for training. There appears to be a universal human need to honor and bury one's dead, especially those we loved and admired. From Sophocles's Antigone, who defied King Creon in order to bury her brother, to more recent reports of mothers roaming deserted battlefields in Kosovo to find their dead, to children still searching in Southeast Asia for bodies of fathers whose planes were downed decades ago, the epics continue to illustrate the lengths people will go to retrieve the remains of those they love. Closure cannot happen when there are no remains to bury. At best, people find some sort of good-enough resolution with substitute remains. One family decided to bury a loved one's guitar to symbolize his body. This was an imaginative resolution and hopefully satisfactory for the surviving family members. But many families disagree over how and whether to do a memorial when a person is missing. Lacking a body, they simply do not know what to do, what rituals to perform or create, or what words to say.

The good news is that many can and do move on to some resolution in spite of never finding the missing person. As therapists we must be patient. We should never push for closure when the loss is ambiguous. The human need to find a loved one and bury him or her illustrates the intersection of cognitive and emotional processes in close human relationships—an uncanny circle of attachment and detachment. We need patience and full awareness when working professionally with this agonizing and complex process.

Nevertheless, loved ones continue to disappear or fade away. Ferries sink, airplanes crash, earthquakes bury thousands, children are kidnapped, and soldiers go missing in action. Less dramatically, but no less traumatically, loved ones slip into comas, are lost to Alzheimer's disease, or become vacant due to addiction. And family members continue to go to great lengths to find the remains of their loved ones or reconnect with their absent psyches. From my work with such families, the reasons for their tenacity vary.

First, the reason may be cultural. In United States culture, the valued and expected goals are to fix, cure, win, and solve. Living with loss is discouraged. Rather, one is supposed to get over it and do so quickly. If Becker (1973) is correct that death is denied in our culture, then ambiguous loss is denied even more fiercely. We all need to participate in more community efforts to break down the public and professional impatience for losses that are not clear.

Second, the reason for needing clarity may concern cognition and rationality. Without a body to bury, people feel confused about both physical and psychological losses. Cognition is blocked by the unfamiliarity of the situation. They can't begin to cope or grieve; they can't make decisions. Their assumption that the world is fair, comprehensible, and manageable is shattered by the terrible mystery of their loved one's status.

Third, a reason why people yearn for clarity about loss is that there are no supportive rituals without clear evidence of death. Families of the physically and psychologically missing are thus left to fend for themselves. After 9/11, some church officials allowed families to bury empty coffins or objects such as musical instruments, bowling balls, or photographs of the missing person, but for the most part, families were on their own in figuring out what to do. They should not have to be. Like families of the emotionally or cognitively missing from brain injury, dementia, chronic mental illness, or addiction, peer support groups and multiple family groups are very helpful.

Numerous surviving family members told me they had made decisions on their own for having a service without a body, but such shifts in their rituals were usually stimulated by support from people of authority—clergy, mayors, therapists, nurses, physicians, and elders in the community. Someone they respected had offered choices, patience, and symbols to help. The urn of ashes from Ground Zero that was used by many families in funeral rites for missing persons was one example. Yet differing perceptions persisted to complicate the makeshift rituals of burial. One young man said, "I choose to believe that part of my brother's body is in these ashes." But the wife of that same missing man did not believe this. Their differing perceptions over remains caused conflict that was eventually minimized at family meetings where such disagreements were talked over and normalized.

The fourth reason why people need clarity in loss depends on their attachment to the lost person. The goal of grieving has been to detach. Based on Freud (1917/1957) and Bowlby (1980), this means relinquishing the emotional bonds one had with the deceased in order to form new relationships with the living. Without a dead body to verify the end of a close relationship, it is difficult for people to let go and move on with new relationships. Whether the missing adult or child is beloved or simply an acquaintance may determine how persistently one holds out before acknowledging the loss and loosening the bonds by going on with one's life without the lost person. This does not mean forgetting them.

NEEDED RESEARCH

Although my clinical and research teams have increasingly discovered ways to transcend the traumatizing effects of ambiguous loss in various situations and with different populations, more research is needed. Testing will increase, I hope, as a result of this book. The process for theory development is, after all, never-ending, and it is best done as a collaboration between science and practice. What I have written in *Ambiguous Loss* (1999) provides a summary of the work from 1975 to 1999 and was the first step toward disseminating the theory so that it could be tried and tested by others. This book is the second step. It elaborates in more depth how to apply the theory of ambiguous loss. But the bottom line remains a call for continued research and clinical testing.

As I see it, the needs are threefold. First, more study is needed on the long-term effects of ambiguous loss and how resilience can be sustained. With the physically missing, anecdotal clinical evidence suggests that families across cultures appear to manifest remarkably similar family dynamics after ambiguous loss (Sluzki, 1990). Like the 9/11 families, Argentinean families of the desaparecidos (disappeared) manifested confusion in boundaries and family roles, denial of facts, and guilt if one dared to give up hope (Boss et al., 2003). The adult children of missing pilots shot down in Southeast Asia in the 1970s still manifest unresolved grief symptoms over 30 years later. Their families then had been told to be silent about their situation, which may explain why their grief processes were frozen. Researchers Cathy Campbell and Alice Demi (2000) found that many offspring of MIA pilots are still preoccupied with frequent intrusive thoughts of their lost fathers. Many are stuck emotionally, but some have found a way to move forward. Campbell, herself the daughter of a missing father, found solace through researching this topic and writing about it after her mother died.

For families of the psychologically missing, more research is also needed on resilience. The existing studies on addiction, Alzheimer's disease, and head injury focus mostly on negative long-term effects. For caregivers of those with dementia, for example, health is compromised. The Alzheimer's Association reports that spousal caregivers of Alzheimer's disease patients die at a rate 63% higher than their same-age cohorts (Schultz & Beach, 1999). What therapists and families need to know are the success stories, so that together we can more optimistically shape interventions toward re-silience and prevention of symptoms in the healthy partner.

Second, research is needed on situations in which both types of ambigu-ous loss occur simultaneously. I often see dual ambiguity when there is ad-diction or chronic illness combined with a family member missing from divorce or adoption. More study is also needed regarding the prevention of unintended child neglect after a parent's partner is missing physically or psychologically.

Third, more cross-cultural studies are needed to identify commonalities as well as differences in responses to ambiguous loss. Although diversity is emphasized and unique responses and coping strategies documented, we must also identify the common responses to common stressors such as am-biguous loss. Our clinical hunches thus far are that across cultures, harmful family secrets develop after ambiguous loss if there are no-talk rules and no interventions to encourage the sharing of perceptions (Boss et al., 2003; Imber-Black, 1993).

It seems that across situations and cultures, the ambiguity of missing per-sons blocks grief, seeds ambivalence, guilt, and relational conflict, and blurs family boundaries and processes. As if on cue, families of the missing argue over what to do, differ in their perceptions of the lost person's status, cancel family rituals and routines, and are often so preoccupied with the lost person that those present—especially children and adolescents—are ig-nored. Thankfully, because of the previous research, insufficient as it may be, and this new theory of loss, recent teams of therapists have become more alert early on to cues of resilience. They do not ignore symptoms that need immediate treatment, but are, with this broader lens, more able to help people regain resilience to live with the unsolved loss.

More than ever since 9/11, I am convinced that theory is useful to guide clinical work if we are to really help families stay strong in times of trouble. Without research-based theory on hand, we may lack the understanding of complex family processes and linkages that in times of urgency and uncer-tainty are even more challenging. With the theory of ambiguous loss as a guide, we could after 9/11 more readily recognize and understand the unique and terrible stress that families of the missing were experiencing. The ambiguous loss model helped us treat families of the missing, first in individual family meetings and then with multiple family groups in com-munity meetings. Without a guiding theory, we could not have been so inclusive in our work. From this experience and others with families stressed by dementia or brain injury, I am convinced that therapists need more theory and less specific strategy. The ambiguous loss model does not provide one right way for how to do therapy but instead offers a broader framework to guide specific clinical tasks for regular clinical work as well as for catastrophic emergencies.

CONCLUSION

Ambiguous loss is the most stressful loss because its incomprehensibility threatens health and resiliency. When people go missing due to human terror or natural catastrophes, or from the ravages of illness or accident, the anxiety from having no clear solution can immobilize. I am, however, optimistic: People can and do live well *with* ambiguous loss.

Part I

The Developing Theory of Ambiguous Loss

Chapter 1

The Psychological Family

In the summer of 2000, I emptied my parent's house. My father had died 10 years earlier, and my mother, now in simpler quarters, had left things as they were. I was emptying my father's dresser when I found his wallet. There was a driver's license, social security card, Medicare card, Lion's Club card, and then, a real surprise. Tucked deep in a secret pocket was a well-worn photograph of his hometown, Burgdorf, Switzerland. I saw the church where he was confirmed, the bluffs he so often told me about and where he and his brothers played, and below that, the house where he grew up. He had left this happy place, and all of his family, in 1929 when he came to America. He did not return until 1950, just before his mother died. I turned the old photo over, and saw that it was actually a postcard cut to billfold size. In elegant old-German penmanship, it was addressed by his eldest brother: "Paul Grossenbacher, Brooklyn, Wiskonsin, USA"— his address in 1931. My father had apparently carried this symbol of home and family for 59 years in his wallet until his death in 1990. I had always sensed my immigrant father's yearning for home and another family, but this treasure, secreted away in a wallet he always carried, reminded me that his psychological family—the one on his mind, the one he missed and longed for—was with him until the day he died.

After 3 decades of working as a clinician and researcher with families with various kinds of ambiguous loss, I have come to know that my father was not unusual. Ambiguous loss is ubiquitous. It is inherent in the experiences of human migration but also in family life transitions and in the unexpected catastrophes of trauma and loss. My work with New York families

25

after 9/11 confirmed what I had learned earlier with families of MIA soldiers and moved me to learn more about how to help survivors of all sorts
of traumatic loss.

To help people manage ambiguous loss, it is necessary to know first
about their psychological family. To understand my father was to know that
he had two families, the one he lived with and the other only in his mind.
To understand the families in lower Manhattan after 9/11 was to know that,
without evidence of death, they were going to keep the lost person present. In addition, most also had relatives in other countries and during that
terrible time, yearned for them. The primary methods of treatment after
9/11, however, were classic grief therapies and treatment for PTSD. Even
though thousands of families had the unique deficit of missing loved ones,
treatment for ambiguous loss was nonexistent.

The psychological family is intrinsic in the human psyche. It compen-
sates for loss, a basic feature of human experience. More than simply a collection of remembered ties, the psychological family is an active and
affective bond that helps people live with loss and trauma in the present.
Cut off from loved ones physically or psychologically, people cope by
holding on to some private perception of home and family. This psychological construction of family may coincide or conflict with official records
and the physical family one lives with, but who is viewed as being in the
family is of therapeutic importance. Whether we work with individuals,
couples, or families, this means that we as therapists need to be flexible
when defining family as well as when assuming the presence or absence of
family members. The myth of absolute presence or absence erodes when
we ask, "Whom do you see as your family?" A client's answer provides essential information that will shape assessment and therapeutic processes. If
we don't understand what family means to our clients, and whom they perceive as belonging to their particular family, even experienced therapists
may miss the source of unresolved grief symptoms. This is especially so
when no death has occurred.

LINKING THE PSYCHOLOGICAL FAMILY
WITH STRESS AND RESILIENCE

When people experience loss that has no closure, therapists are challenged.
How do we help clients change and move forward despite the fact that
they are experiencing an unclear loss? How do we help them live with the
trauma that continues with ambiguous loss? How do we help them find
clarity when there is none? Our recognition and affirmation of the psychological family is the first step in finding answers to these questions. The sec-

ond step is applying a conceptual model that knits together ideas from theories about loss, trauma, stress, and resiliency. To be able to do this in various situations, therapists need to understand how ambiguity complicates loss, elongates trauma, and threatens resiliency. The third step is for us to link ideas from theories of loss, trauma, and stress to guide interventions that will strengthen (not pathologize) clients who must, through no fault of their own, live with the ambiguity surrounding their loss. If their loss cannot be resolved, the therapeutic goal is to increase resilience for living with the stress of never knowing for sure where a loved one is—or whether he or she is absent or present.

The psychological family thrives when the only way to stay connected is in the mind's eye. This can have negative effects if life is put on hold. Preoccupation with missing loved ones, whether it is from disaster or illnesses like head injury or dementia, can immobilize, especially if there is absolute hope for reunification or recovery. If one leans too heavily on the inward construction of close relationships, the incongruence between psychological and physical reality can immobilize. The dissonance creates stress and weakens resilience. Disconnected from loved ones lost in mind or body, and then from present friends and neighbors, they are in a kind of limbo—blocked from coping or grieving, frozen in place, and thus brittle. Resiliency erodes.

Resiliency is a constant and positive adaptive trait. It is a basic part of our healthy psychological makeup and is needed throughout the life span. It is especially called for in cases of ambiguous loss. Resiliency is discussed further in Chapter 3, but here I will define it as the ability to regain one's energy after adversity drains it. It is more than "bouncing back," which implies regaining the status quo; rather, it means rising above traumatic and ambiguous losses by not letting them immobilize and living well despite them. Resiliency means flexibility, the opposite of brittleness, and movement, the opposite of paralysis.

When loved ones go missing physically or psychologically, the human capacity for survival is often frozen by the confusion that all too often cements into a rigid tenacity of hope that the missing will come back or recover. When the tenacity becomes preoccupation—all that an individual, couple, or family thinks about—their resilience is gone. This is the downside of the idea of psychological family.

There is, however, an upside, and this is the focus of treatment. The same psychological entity that can cause preoccupation and immobilization also becomes the motivator for change and forward movement. "What would your mother have wanted you to do?" "Would your brother have wanted you to do this or that?" Once recognized, the psychological family can provide the motivation and resilience for coping with what seemed like an untenable loss. Like my immigrant father who kept the idea of his distant family so close to him all of his life, many people hold close psychological ideations of family to provide warmth and support, albeit in imagined and remembered ways. The family in one's mind and heart can help overcome hard times. When we think about this family, we no longer feel so alone, even though we are not in physical proximity to anyone. Clinicians, clergy, and medical professionals will find psychological families a resource that can stimulate, not impede, forward movement and the ability to change—essential indicators of resiliency.

THE PSYCHOLOGICAL FAMILY AND DIVERSITY

The dissonance provoked by a loved one's blurred absence and presence has diverse effects depending on cultural beliefs, religious values, and personal tolerance for ambiguity. In cultures that value mastery over nature (Kluckhohn & Strodtbeck, 1961) and control over one's life (Zarit, Pearlin, & Schaie, 2003), the stress from never knowing whether a person is absent or present is especially high and can traumatize. That is, the more people value control and mastery, the more distressed they are when loss has no clarity or closure.

For clinicians to better understand the couple's or family's beliefs about mastery, we must ask more general questions that can apply to diverse cultures and religions. "How do you see your situation (of ambiguous loss)?" "What are your perceptions of what happened, and why?" "What are your views about what to do, how to proceed?" Much later, perhaps weeks or months, I ask each person, "What does this loss mean to you now?" "How do you see the missing person now?" There are vast differences in how people respond to these questions, but from my experience, the primary difference centers on their value of mastery versus their tolerance for ambiguity. Although more study is needed, I suggest that cultural values, religious and spiritual beliefs, and individual personality traits all influence the degree to which people can temper their need for mastery and tolerate ambiguity without experiencing debilitating stress and ambivalence (Boss, 2002c; Boss & Kaplan, 2004).

To shore up the individual psyche, knowing that we can't always have things our way is essential. In our conception of family, we learn that we cannot always control the ins and outs of loved ones who come and go across the life cycle. Hopefully, these ambiguous losses are those we expect—like growing up and leaving home or getting older. But sometimes human exits are shrouded in tragedy and trauma. I think of the millions lost globally in wars, terrorist attacks, catastrophic illnesses, and natural disasters. Whether in mind or body, their disappearances forever challenge the human need for certainty.

As one of those people socialized to value mastery and certainty, I have learned much about tempering these values from American Indian colleagues. For example, I learned about acceptance when the Ojibway women in Northern Minnesota shared with me their views of caring for an elder with dementia. Offended by my use of the usual caregiving term *burden,* and even the more innocuous term *stress,* the Ojibway preferred instead the term *spiritual acceptance,* as they saw caring for an elder with dementia as a privilege and the normal fulfillment of "the circle of life." This belief allowed them to balance taking charge with a spiritual acceptance to do the work of caregiving. I shall never forget that lesson.

The lesson was reaffirmed after 9/11. Many of the families I worked with in lower Manhattan after 9/11 were immigrants or refugees who did not assume mastery. Although they were stellar in resilience, they were accustomed to being buffeted about by external circumstances out of their control. They knew they were not in charge; they just wanted to do their job, support their families, and be out of harm's way. Their coming to America to escape terrorism and strife in their own countries and islands indicated a mastery that was, as with the Ojibway, clearly balanced with spiritual acceptance.

How does this relate to the psychological family? When loved ones are missing, one's need for mastery must give way to more acceptance if there is to be resilience. Specifically, this translates into being able to tolerate ambiguity or lack of closure. Keeping lost loved ones present in one's mind— without preoccupation—is a way to live with the ambiguity and lack of closure. The psychological family, for example, shores up resiliency as long as people are not frozen in place and can move forward in their present life setting, interacting with the family members who are physically with them now.

As a therapeutic goal, closure suggests mastery and control. It implies the need to close the door to pain of loss and ambiguity. Many are offended when professionals use the phrases "find closure" and "move on" because of their connection to the psychological family. They are understandably resistant.

Rather than labeling people resistant, professionals must realize that not all people in this world have mastery over their destiny. Many have learned resilience through spiritual acceptance. Given this, many from cultures other than our own reject the idea of closure on loss. They do not seek such absolute answers to loss. In my decades of work across cultures, I have come to think that only the privileged and mastery-oriented can value closing the door to loss and grief. The diverse myriads accustomed to having

little mastery over their destinies know they cannot shut out the pain of ambiguity. They have learned how to live with it. We can learn from them
how to find more balance between mastery and acceptance.

Rather than closure, most people worldwide must live with grief and loss
(Becvar, 2001; Boss, 1999). Although some mastery skills must be honed for
survival, ambiguity remains the norm. This is true for anyone who is faced
with ambiguous loss, even the more privileged. There is no closure for ambiguous loss and perhaps even for natural, expected loss. As a Swiss-
American and Calvinist, I struggle with my own needs for mastery and clar-
ifying loss by closing the door. As a researcher and psychotherapist, I struggle constantly to live more comfortably with the ambiguity of unanswered
questions, for they are inevitably part of the human experience.

THEORETICAL ASSUMPTIONS

An underlying assumption in this book is that the social interactions that
form the structure of a person's family may continue even when a loved
one is no longer physically present. A beloved mother's words are still
heard in the mind of an immigrant son who then passes them on to his children and grandchildren; long deceased, a favorite uncle's advice about
"never dating someone whose problems are greater than your own" is
passed down to subsequent generations. Through stories and sayings, the
longing is transmitted so that subsequent generations often take pilgrimages to visit these places lost to their ancestors. In mobile cultures, the people important to us may or may not be the people we live with physically.
The people we perceive as family may be an amalgam of biological kin
plus those dear to us (a lifemate, partner, noncustodial parent or child,
friend, coworker, neighbor, fictive kin) who are kept present psychologically. All are real players when it comes to therapeutic work.

Nearly 70 years ago, Willard Waller, a family sociologist, wrote: "The interaction of human beings with one another differs greatly from such simpler forms of interaction as, say, that of billiard balls on a table. The
interaction of human beings takes place in a cultural medium which is itself
the product of past interaction. It also depends upon the somewhat miraculous process of communication. It takes place in the mind, and all our
commerce with our fellows is mental and imaginative" (1938, p. 19). Although this idea of a psychological family was introduced decades ago by
Waller and other social psychologists (Berger & Luckmann, 1966; Hess &
Handel, 1959), the subsequent insistence on "hard data" restricted our focus
to the observable and quantifiable *physical* structure of couples and fami-

lies. This trend sent ideas about the social construction of reality (and incidentally also psychoanalytic ideas) into decline—until recently, when social
psychologist Kenneth Gergen (1994) reintroduced social constructionism to
contemporary therapists. Because the assumptions of early sociologists are
similar to what Gergen writes about today, the premise of a socially constructed family appears to have roots in both sociology and psychology.
This cross-disciplinary base sets the stage for a more contextual view of individuals, couples, and families experiencing traumatic and ambiguous
losses.

What, then, links this idea of the psychological family with the key topics of ambiguous loss, trauma, and resilience? The following assumptions
lay the groundwork for the connection.

First, loved ones who are physically absent are often kept psychologically present, especially when the loss is not verified by evidence of death.
Likewise, people who are physically present but psychologically absent are
often denied their affliction and expected to act as they always were, or
they are prematurely extruded from the system and treated as if they were
already dead or gone. What this means is that the more obvious physical
structure often differs from the construction in one's mind, causing tension
and stress in the family.

Second, some may interpret this idea of a psychological family as pathological, even hallucinatory. This psychological construct, however, is presented in this book as understandable and even useful in coping with a loss
that defies closure.

Third, when the status of lost loved ones remains ambiguous, keeping
them in one's mind allows time to seek more information and to prepare
for either a positive or negative outcome. It allows hope. Above all, it helps
begin the process of being able to hold two opposing ideas in one's mind
simultaneously. The person is coming back—but maybe not. The person is
dead—or may be alive somewhere.

Fourth, learning to live with ambiguous loss deemphasizes the idea of
closure. In dialectical processes, people keep physically absent family
members present in their hearts and minds. Psychologically absent members are kept present by including them in the action and touching and
talking with them even if they can't respond emotionally or cognitively.

Fifth, humans are social beings and ideally interact with the people and
community around them. Yet for many, the absent are present and the
present are absent. Few people have the absolute presence (or absence) of
people they love. As therapists, we must become aware of this more complex idea of family as we assess, treat, and intervene.

With these assumptions, we see that social interaction forms the structure of marriages, families, and other significant bonds both physically and

psychologically. Knowing this, we can more easily assess dysfunctional relationships. Treating the maladaptive interactions helps strengthen resilience for living with those never fully absent or present. In varying degrees, this is the situation in most human relationships. Rarely is someone we care about *fully* present, physically and emotionally. It is the unrelenting and extreme situations that can traumatize.

THE AMBIGUITY OF ABSENCE AND PRESENCE

People cannot heal until they and we know who the players are in the healing process. A beloved but deceased grandparent may remain the most important parent figure for a youngster; a wife may still be viewed as present long after the divorce, to the detriment of her husband's connection to others. Most important to the theme of this book is the fact that *the players in the therapy process are all the more obscure when the facts surrounding a loved one's status as present or absent, or as dead or alive, remain ambiguous.* Both client and therapist struggle with this situation, because the therapeutic set is challenged by a lack of information. With ambiguity, anxiety levels often go up for both therapist and client, and the therapeutic process may be compromised.

Whether present or absent, human beings deeply attached to one another become part of each other's significant life experiences. Whatever their physical relationship, they are no longer separate in the psychological sense. More than a half century ago, Willard Waller also wrote:

> In any ultimate sense, society exists only in the mind and the imagination. Experiences are significant only as they affect the mind and evoke the imagination; from the psychological point of view, the stimulus is only a stimulus in so far as it sets off a response.... Whatever produces a mental effect is important. As [sociologist W. I.] Thomas has put it, "If people define things as real, they are real in their consequences." Other persons are present to us less from the evidence of our senses than from the activity of our imaginations.... Social interaction is, therefore, in Cooley's phrase, ultimately an interaction of personal ideas in the mind. (1938, p. 20)

Today, Kenneth Gergen (1994, 2001) extends these ideas about reality and relationships for contemporary scholars, as well as clinicians. He also grounds his ideas in the assumption that relational reality is comprised of more than what can be objectively quantified or physically measured. The psychological family is an example of a phenomenon not easily measured.

CONCLUSION

As noted, the psychological family is the family that exists in one's mind—the people whom you want to be at your special celebrations as well as those you do not invite, those you talk with during stressful times and those you purposely avoid, those you want to be there for you in good times and bad and those you exclude or who come unbidden. Clients often tell me spontaneously who these people are, but other times I have to simply ask, "Who is family for you?" "Who is not?" Inherent in these questions is another: "Where is home for you?" The answers are often surprising. From them, I gain unique insight about who is present and who is absent, as well as any systemic incongruence and individual ambivalence about the apparent incongruence. Rarely have I found that documentable events such as birth, death, and even marriage guarantee or determine who is there for a person and who is not.

This raises the question that is central in this book. How do therapists take what are usually considered warning signals based on our training (immobilization from depression, anxiety, ambivalence, identify confusion, loss of hope, unresolved grief when there has been no death) and depathologize them, yet still consider these apparent incongruities worthy of therapeutic work and some sort of integration into the client's life? Although the effects of ambiguous loss are not necessarily indicators of personal pathology, they are nevertheless problematic and in need of understanding and validation from clinicians, clergy, and health professionals.

Whereas early family scholars wrote about the psychological family (Hess & Handel, 1959), contemporary family researchers have for the most part ignored it because it defies measurement. The dominant assumption in scientific positivism is that if a phenomenon can't be measured, it doesn't exist. Therapists too may resist the idea of a psychological family because their traditional training and psychometric instruments are geared to assess physical absence or presence (what can be seen and documented) rather than psychological absence or presence (which cannot). For cases of ambiguous loss, I recommend a more phenomenological stance. Without such a perspective, therapists (who assess and treat) and policy makers (who set limits for treatment based on official diagnoses) may inadvertently miss how to build and repair resilience in individuals, couples, and families after losses clear or ambiguous, ordinary or traumatic (for summary, see Boss, 1999).

Typically, therapists are trained to see the physical structure of relationships and to think that if they are doing their job right, clients will get over their losses and reattach relatively quickly to someone who is physically present. The myth is that healthy people find closure. Emotional resolution is rarely that absolute after the loss of a close attachment. This is especially so when a loved one suddenly vanishes (as in terrorist attacks or natural disasters), remains out of reach (as in immigration), or is lost psychologically from dementia, brain injury, addiction, depression, and other chronic illnesses. When loved ones go missing, physically or emotionally, a clinical approach for tolerating ambiguity rather than seeking closure is essential. The first step in this approach is understanding that there is a psychological family.

Chapter 2

Trauma and Stress

In this chapter, I limit my discussion to one unique kind of trauma and stress—that of having a loved one missing physically or psychologically. I peel the proverbial onion to discuss what ambiguous loss is not in order to clarify the difference between the therapy model for it and the more traditional protocols for trauma intervention. Ambiguous loss is not one particular event which leads to posttraumatic stress disorder (PTSD) nor is it one critical incident. Rather, it is an on-going *situation* that has no closure. The pain may go on forever.

Stress is defined as pressure on the status quo of a system. Like a bridge that is undulating from the pressure of wind or heavy traffic, the misfit between the pressure and the structure's support can lead to collapse. That is, the system is no longer in a steady state. Translated to individuals or families, this means that something created a pressure so great that it threatens a negative change (collapse; immobilization). If, however, one's supports are increased to meet the demands, we may be able to ride out the pressure and regain equilibrium—or, more correctly, a flexible equilibrium. That is resilience (Boss, 2002c).

Trauma, on the other hand, is a stress so great and unexpected that it cannot be defended against, coped with, or managed. The surprise element overwhelms and is part of why people are so quickly immobilized. Metaphorically, the bridge collapses. Supports can no longer absorb the pressure. Far beyond ordinary human expectations, the event stuns and immobilizes. Coping skills are frozen; defense mechanisms fail.

35

In different professions, trauma has different meanings. In medicine it is defined as a physical wound, in psychiatry as an emotional shock, and more generally as "a disordered psychic or behavioral state resulting from severe mental or emotional stress or physical injury" (*Merriam Webster's Collegiate Dictionary,* 2003, p. 1331). Today, trauma is viewed, however, as *both* a mind-body condition linking emotional and physiological responses (van der Kolk, 2002; van der Kolk, McFarlane, & Weisaeth, 1996). However it is defined, the trauma from ambiguous loss is *externally* caused. The disorder and pathology lie outside the client in their relational context and often is incurable.

In my work, I see combinations of stress and trauma. In many cases, the stress of ambiguity can traumatize a child or adult physically and emotionally just as a critical incident might. Having a loved one missing is like a continuously bleeding wound in the couple or family; having a loved one's mind missing, such as with dementia, is also an ongoing kind of relational wound. In both types, emotions are shocked, jarred, and stymied by the insolvability. For this reason, ambiguous loss is usually traumatic. If the stressor of ambiguity becomes unmanageable, it becomes immobilizing, critical, and thus traumatizing. If people are resilient, however, they are more likely to view the ambiguity as a chronic but manageable stress.

EXPANDING THE REPERTOIRE FOR TREATMENT

In addition to traditional and technical protocols for treating PTSD and critical incidents, I recommend the addition of family therapy and more community interventions. After traumatic ambiguous losses, for the sake of preserving resiliency in individuals, couples, and families, systemic approaches need to be included. Indeed, ambiguous loss, PTSD, and critical incidents all share a common conceptual root—that of trauma and stress—but the current insularity in treatment methods, dictated often by funding, hinders collaboration with family therapists.

Increasingly, when there is large-scale trauma, relational methods with families and communities are recommended (Boss et al., 2003; Landau & Saul, 2004; Sluzki, 1990). Disaster victims themselves call for more resiliency-based interventions (Norris, Friedman, Watson, Byrne, Diaz, & Kaniasty, 2002), and I would add that they must include familiar people, not just outside professionals. My goal in this chapter is to identify the common ground between conventional trauma interventions and conjoint/family therapies so that collaboration is more possible especially when loved ones are missing.

Although many therapists now acknowledge that we would benefit from training for PTSD treatment, I propose that professionals who treat PTSD and critical incidents would also benefit from more relational- and resiliency-based training. At minimum, treatment teams for critical and traumatic events should include professionals trained in family therapy, and community interventions that include children, parents, and grandparents. But right now, including family therapists as part of trauma treatment teams remains a relatively new idea to policy makers, training institutions, and providers.

With the trauma of ambiguous loss, human connections are severed, so it follows that treatment must also center on human connections. This means that protocols for individual and family therapy need to offer human relationships beyond that of the therapist or counselor as professionals can only offer a temporary connection. Survivors need to connect to someone familiar in their community, as such relationships are more likely to be ongoing. Even in individual therapy, I recommend interventions that take into account one's family and community. From my experience, such therapy can include various systemic combinations—a partner, spouse, friend, the immediate family, extended kin, coworkers, neighbors, and often spiritual advisers or elders. But always, it includes the psychological family. Within this self-defined family and community system, professionals can build on the knowledge that we are temporary. Clients and patients ultimately have to go home and live their lives with their own loved ones in their own communities. It is there—in their own homes and neighborhoods—where many people receive the ongoing human connection needed for resiliency.

I first learned that ambiguous loss was linked to trauma during the Vietnam era in the 1970s (Boss, 1975, 1980a). At the Center for Prisoner of War Studies in San Diego, I was studying families of soldiers declared missing in action.[1] In the 1980s I studied families with the second type of ambiguous loss—where the mind is missing (Boss et al., 1988; Boss, Caron, et al., 1990; Caron et al., 1999; Garwick et al., 1994). After 9/11, I studied ambiguous loss from terrorism and the agony caused by loved ones' vanishing physically without a trace. Nearly 3,000 innocent people disappeared that September morning while the nation watched on television in disbelief. But the relatives and friends of loved ones who never came home that night were numb with shock and helplessness. I thought of Fiegelstein's uncanny loss.

For the first few weeks after 9/11, people were sympathetic to the traumatized families yearning for the presence of their missing loved ones. Relatives wandered the streets of New York carrying photographs and posters of missing loved ones, asking, "Have you seen him?" "Have you seen her?" Their loss, so far beyond the normal range of human suffering, led to unorthodox behavior. At Ground Zero, a month after the attacks that collapsed the towers, I saw a young bride and groom, dressed in full wedding attire, her white veil flowing out behind them, moving toward the smoking rubble with photographer in tow. I wondered who in that pile was meant to be with them on their wedding day. It was surreal, but unorthodox behavior made sense in this terrible context. Reactions varied. Some people zealously avoided Ground Zero, whereas others made daily pilgrimages to lay flowers or light candles. Some people were suicidal or so traumatized that they needed hospitalization; most were just temporarily dazed and confused and were able to regain their composure enough to carry on with daily life. For all, however, what happened on 9/11 went far beyond normal human expectations and shattered everyone's view of the world as a fair and logical place. As with families of missing soldiers, and the families of loved ones whose minds are missing from injury or dementia, there was after 9/11 no satisfying way to grieve or recover. What professionals and the public did not realize, however, was that this state of traumatic numbness would go on for some time. Closure would not be possible with this unique kind of traumatic loss.

Most PTSD experts and grief therapists are not trained to address the trauma that the two types of ambiguous loss can cause. Rarely is ambiguity identified as a source of trauma. My goal, then, is to inform professionals and the general public about ambiguous loss to begin a discourse and ultimately prompt policy changes for broader treatment and intervention.

The aim here is to add a new theoretical lens—that of ambiguous loss—to the conventional repertoire of trauma treatments. Toward this end, I will discuss the similarities and differences between situations of ambiguous loss, trauma, and critical incidents and set the stage for more interventions with children, youth, and adults that take family and community into account.

STRESS AND TRAUMA

Keeping in mind the goal of resiliency and health despite the on-going trauma of ambiguity, it is useful to clarify the links between the stress and trauma fields and ideas about ambiguous loss, and then delineate the similarities and differences among the concepts and methods.

How Do Stress and Trauma Relate to Ambiguous Loss?

In a typology of stressors, none is as unmanageable and traumatizing as ambiguous loss (see Table 2.1).

The stress from uncertainty simply wears people down. Individuals feel helpless, hopeless, and depressed. They become ambivalent and anxious.

TABLE 2.1   Classification of Family Stress and Trauma

Source

Internal	**External**
Events that begin from someone inside the family, such as addiction, suicide, or violence	Events that begin from nature or people outside the family, such as floods or terrorism

Type

Normative **Developmental** **Predictable**	**Catastrophic** **Situational** **Unexpected**
Events that are expected during the life course: birth, puberty, adolescence, marriage, aging, menopause, retirement, and death	Events or situations not foreseen: a young person dies
Clear	**Ambiguous**
Facts are available; family knows what is happening and how things will turn out	Events or situations that remain unclear, facts about the status of a family member remain unclear
Volitional	**Nonvolitional**
Events or situations that are wanted and sought out: freely chosen job changes, college entrance, or a wanted pregnancy	Events or situations not freely chosen: laid off, fired, divorced, or abandoned

Duration

Acute	**Chronic**
Event that lasts a short time but is painful: broken leg	A situation of long duration: diabetes, chemical addiction, or discrimination and prejudice

Density

Isolated	**Cumulative**
One event that occurs with no other stressors; easily pinpointed	Events that pile up, one after the other, or situations that have no resolution; families worn down by multiple unresolved stressors

Adapted from Boss, P. (2002). Family Stress Management, *Second Edition. Reprinted by permission of Sage Publications.*

Family functioning suffers as decisions are put on hold, daily tasks are ignored, and fighting and rifts take place. Resiliency erodes as rituals and celebrations are cancelled. In such cases, individuals, couples, and families experience temporary shutdown. This is a crisis and, because it breaks down coping skills, it becomes traumatic as well.

When ambiguous loss is the stressor, therapists must remember that the source of stress and trauma lies in feelings of helplessness and confusion emanating from the context of ambiguity surrounding the individual. In this kind of context—incomprehensible, illogical, confusing, senseless, unjust, and outside of one's control—rational thinking about how to cope is blocked. Through no fault of their own, people experience trauma and stress because the ordinary facts about the absence or presence of loved ones are shrouded in mystery. No other loss is like this, and no other form of stress is quite so unmanageable.

PTSD: A NEED FOR CAUTION AND COLLABORATION WITH FAMILY THERAPY

PTSD is a medically defined disorder that arose from observations and research during World War II, the Holocaust, the Vietnam War, the fighting between Israel and Palestine, the Gulf War, the ethnic cleansing in the former Yugoslavia, and terrorism outside and inside the family. PTSD is defined as an anxiety disorder produced by an uncommon, extremely stressful event (e.g., rape, child abuse, assault, military combat, flood, earthquake, death camp, torture, car accident, head trauma). The key criterion for PTSD is *an experience that is beyond the normal range of human suffering*. The disorder is characterized by "(1) re-experiencing the traumatic event (e.g., intrusive thoughts), (2) numbing or feelings of detachment, and (3) a variety of autonomic and behavioral indicators of arousal including hyperalertness and other signs of sympathetic arousal, along the dimensions of generalized anxiety" (Goldberger & Breznitz, 1993, p. 727; see also American Psychiatric Association, 2000; Herman, 1992). The medical diagnosis of PTSD emerged in parallel research projects with Vietnam veterans (Figley, 1978) and rape victims (Burgess & Holmstrom, 1979), where individual responses were found to be similar. In 1980, the disorder was formally operationalized for research and clinical diagnosis in the *Diagnostic and Statistical Manual of Mental Disorders* (DSM) as PTSD (American Psychiatric Association, 1980). The treatment goal is to return the patient to health. Currently there is debate in the trauma field about expanding treatment for PTSD or advocating more community-based interventions. What is clear is that both are needed. Not everyone after a crisis or disaster develops PTSD (Bonanno, 2004). After a disaster, most people are stunned temporarily and manage to regain their coping skills and resiliency.

How Does PTSD Relate to Ambiguous Loss?

Loss complicated by ambiguity is a new challenge for most therapists, yet it is a situation experienced by many people. Indeed, ambiguous loss meets a PTSD criterion as an experience beyond the normal range of human suffering. In the DSM-IV-TR (American Psychiatric Association, 2000), PTSD is assessed and treated first as a mental disorder and second as an individual illness. Ambiguous loss, on the other hand, is a relational disorder, not a psychic dysfunction. It is the result of an externally caused stressor. Individual and relational symptoms may result, however, such as depression, anxiety, conflict, and somatization. The cause, though, is the ambiguity. Thus, treatment and intervention must include stress management along with relational and psychodynamic approaches. Unlike PTSD, where the traumatizing event is over but flashing back, ambiguous loss is an ongoing trauma. The assault never lets up. Yet, although they are different phenomena, the outcomes of both PTSD and ambiguous loss can paralyze relationships for a lifetime and even affect subsequent generations (Boss et al., 2003).

Currently, the PTSD diagnosis is being applied to treat victims of torture, rape, terrorist attacks, airplane crashes, school shootings, earthquakes, hurricanes, child abuse, and battering. PTSD therapy is also used preventively to avoid compassion fatigue by supporting professionals and critical incident teams who help such victims (Figley, 1995).

With some notable exceptions (Landau & Saul, 2004; Sluzki, 1990), most PTSD treatment is done with individuals, not families. Such individual treatment for trauma simply does not address the need for patients to go home eventually and live their lives with their families and intimate others. Of course, it is sometimes not possible to go home and find one's family again, and then, as in South Asia after the tsunami of 2004, community-based approaches should be used. Waters (2005) reported that both Eastern and Western trauma experts favor family- and community-based approaches to help survivors after nearly 300,000 adults and children were swept away. Bhava Poudyal, a Nepali psychologist, said, "The society [of Aceh] is very close-knit, supportive, and respectful of each other. Neighbors are taking care of each other, orphans are being taken in by other families" (p. 17). But Poudyal "worries that aid groups may 'take away people's resiliency, their meaning, and impose the PTSD model—which is new and medical for them'" (p. 17).

Neil Boothby of Columbia University, reported Waters, champions people's ability to go home and rebuild their communities and livelihoods together. Boothby said, "If a fisherman has a boat to fish and feed his family, that will have more effect on social functioning than any mental-health intervention . . . What heals people and helps them move on is solidarity and interdependence" (Waters, 2005, p. 18).

Although the conventional application of PTSD treatment is primarily individual and medical, many practitioners have adapted such treatments to more family- and community-based approaches (Boss et al., 2003; Landau & Saul, 2004; Sheinberg & Fraenkel, 2000). They are especially useful when the trauma is from relational loss.

CRITICAL INCIDENT STRESS DEBRIEFING: A NEED FOR CAUTION AND COLLABORATION WITH FAMILY THERAPY

Traumatic stress was used synonymously with a critical incident (Everly, 1989) and, according to critical incident stress debriefing (CISD) pioneers, may be immediate or delayed. (For an update, see Mitchell & Everly, 1993.) Critical incident stress is characterized by a wide range of cognitive, physical, emotional, and behavioral signs that result from a crisis event sufficient enough to overwhelm the usual effective coping strategies of individuals or groups (e.g., first responders: firefighters, police, soldiers, victims of war, terrorism, natural disasters). Such a crisis event represents a disruption in homeostasis (Everly, 1989; Mitchell & Everly, 1993; Everly & Mitchell, 2003; Mitchell & Everly, 2003).

The goal is early intervention, sometimes at the site of the crisis or disaster or nearby, with the rationale that giving opportunity for catharsis and verbalization with others leads to recovery (Everly & Mitchell, 1992). The original protocol is described as the Mitchell Model (1983). It initially had six technical stages, with a seventh added later: introduction, fact phase, thought phase, reaction phase, symptom phase, teaching phase, and reentry phase. The Red Cross also recommends a stage model, but with only four phases: disclosure of events, feelings and reactions, coping strategies, and termination (Armstrong, Lund, McWright, Tichenor, 1995). Such linear models, however, do not take into account human and cultural diversity in patterns and beliefs about coping. More will be said about this later.

Although the principles of CISD are sound, its original protocol was historically designed for the technical debriefing of emergency workers such as police (Mitchell, 1983). Today, the protocol has been updated for broader and more flexible application. For example, after the bombing of the Oklahoma City federal office building, many crisis workers were debriefed at the end of each day's work before they went home to their families. They were indeed vulnerable from the trauma of the sounds, smells, and pressures of their heroic effort to find the trapped people and missing bodies. The critical incident teams normalized the overwhelming stress experienced by the workers, firemen, counselors, pastors, and survivors of the blast. They helped support clergy and clinical professionals and their spouses who were helping survivors with the injured, dead, and missing.

In looking back, researchers say that in Oklahoma City, people found human connection to be the most healing, and they did come together as a community. But the family and community connections were primarily organized by the families themselves and had not been part of the official intervention protocol (Sprang, 1999). As with most disasters, treatment in Oklahoma had been funded primarily for individual and work group debriefing. Family therapy was—and still is—a relatively new idea for crisis intervention in the United States.

TREATMENT AND INTERVENTION

"The goal of all psychotherapy is to help people change in order to relieve their distress. This is true of individual therapy, group therapy, and family therapy" (Nichols & Schwartz, 2004, p. 381). This is especially true when there is ambiguous loss. The unequivocal aspects borrowed from PTSD treatment to treat the trauma of ambiguous loss involve the recognition and treatment of trauma symptomatology (as well as attention to professionals who may become secondarily traumatized). Major differences are apparent, however, as the original traumatic event continues. Ambiguous loss goes on.

The aspect borrowed from CISD is primarily the idea that telling one's story can be healing. Rather than following a structured methodology, however, I apply the narrative idea to family and community groups in their familiar settings and only with willing and voluntary participation. Not everyone will want to tell their story, but the premise is that listening is as healing as telling.

With the theory base for stress, trauma, and resilience just described, our methodology is based on these suppositions:

Methodological Suppositions

- The primary assumption is that for a relational condition such as ambiguous loss, a relational intervention is needed. The system may be a couple, a family, a community, or multiple families experiencing the same stressor. Therapists can take this systemic context into consideration even when doing individual therapy.
- Although symptoms that require medical or psychiatric attention are never ignored, there also needs to be focus on resilience, not just

pathology. Building upon resiliency enhances recovery for the majority of survivors.

- Treating just the individual adult or child is insufficient; an exclusive individual focus may erode parental and couple functioning and can be culturally insensitive. Trauma teams must therefore include family therapists, community-based professionals, and professionals or paraprofessionals who speak the language and know the culture of the survivors. Interventions can be tailor-made to fit individual, diversity, and cultural differences. With ambiguous losses from illnesses and disasters, meetings with multiple families in community settings may be more effective for building resiliency than clinical visits one at a time.

- Therapy is collaborative. Healing comes from a person's own resiliency, not just from trauma intervention. Therapists are just temporary connections in this process, so we must set the stage for linking patients and clients to where they live their lives. It is in their community that ongoing human connections build and sustain individuals and families when loved ones are missing.

- Finally, professionals who provide treatment and intervention for trauma must be culturally competent because the understandings of trauma as a disorder vary considerably. Leys (2000) argued that trauma does exist and varies within two camps: (1) one that endorses symptom relief and re-education, and (2) one that argues that beyond the symptoms, there are deeper meanings that emerge from one's family of origin as well as current relational context.

Like Leys, I am interested in meanings, not just symptom relief. But as we attend more to the vast diversity of norms and expectations among the people we see, there are also some common norms and expectations of health and decency. Both are important, so how do we find the balance?

When clients come from cultures different from my own, the therapeutic hierarchy flattens and collaboration becomes a necessity. I listen more. Sometimes, I ask an individual to bring in a family or community elder who can be like a cotherapist and inform me of cultural nuances. For professionals socialized in cultures that value individuality and self-sufficiency, this shift is a challenge. In times of disaster and crisis, those methods of diagnosis and treatment, which are based on finding closure, may be less effective than listening more to family members and elders who bring their own knowledge and survival experiences to the set. In times of stress and ambiguity, we set aside our own socialization and cultural assumptions and take into account those of the people we serve.

Today PTSD is also being reviewed as a condition that can result from a painful and traumatic cultural context, not just from an individual mental or physical weakness (Boss, 2002c). Cultural psychiatrist Laurence Kirmayer and colleagues (2000) recommended a more contextual approach to symptom diagnosis and treatment with more focus on cultural influences that can result in trauma disorders. Paradoxically it is from physicians that we are learning that the PTSD diagnosis is too medically oriented (Kirmayer et al., 2000; Landau & Saul, 2004; Sluzki, 1990). All emphasize the diversity in cultural meanings about stress, crisis, and trauma. They caution us about cultural differences in the meanings and manifestations of trauma as well as symptoms and adaptation (DiNicola, 1997; Kirmayer et al., 2000; Kleinman & Good, 1985; Wilson, 1989).

What Not To Do

Because PTSD differs conceptually and clinically from ambiguous loss, the assessment of and treatment for PTSD are insufficient when loved ones are missing. Some early practitioners advanced their work to the couple or family level (Figley, 1989; Herman, 1992; Matsakis, 1996), but many have returned to individual work. Today, therapy for PTSD is primarily aimed at the individual and rarely includes family sessions or community work. Although individual medical treatment is needed in some cases after a traumatic experience, it does not specifically address the patient's need to go home and resume life with mates and families. Indeed, the current critique of the PTSD diagnosis and treatment is that it is neither systemic nor contextual and that it is too focused on individual pathology (Kirmayer et al., 2000; Landau & Saul, 2004). In that case, PTSD treatment may miss the contextual cause of the trauma (having a loved one disappear) as well as the real cause of unresolved grief and immobilization.

How Do Stress, Trauma, and Critical Incidents Link to Therapeutic Action?

Some critical incidents become a lifetime of ambiguous loss—a lost person is never found, an accident causes permanent brain injury. A relationship is put on hold with no closure to loss. For this reason, the individual treatment methods therapists may ordinarily use are less effective with the trauma of ambiguous loss. Traumatized children should not be separated from parents (with the exception, of course, of situations where the parent is the perpetrator). However, systemic interviews are complex and require special training. Having a family therapist on the disaster team would be a real help. Ideally, disaster teams would be trained and aided in addressing the systemic ripple effect of trauma. Whether we do individual or conjoint therapy, however, the client's family would be kept in mind as part of the therapeutic context.

Trauma is the inherent core of PTSD, critical incidents, and ambiguous loss, but ambiguous loss is a relational stressor. It is not psychic pathology and it is not an individual problem. Relational interventions are needed to treat a relational problem.

Influences of Cultural Context on Therapy and the Therapeutic Relationship

Many people from cultures less individually oriented than the United States resist therapy and are frustrated when they are deemed sick by practitioners who miss what they have accomplished through family and community support. This means we have to take a second look at the concept of resistance. It can be ours, too.

After 9/11 in New York, I quickly learned that many of the spouses of workers gone missing were refugees and immigrants who had already successfully survived other traumatic losses in their homelands. The families of workers who serviced the two towers came from 60 different countries and spoke 24 different languages. Many came from Albania, Yugoslavia, Macedonia, and Russia; a small number came from East Asia. Many of the families of the Windows on the World restaurant workers emigrated from the Caribbean Islands, Mexico, Dominican Republic, and Central or South America, and thus spoke Spanish. Others were African or European. Most of these families had come to New York for a better and safer life, so their dream was shattered. Also, because they had uprooted, in their time of need they missed loved ones who were out of reach in faraway places. Their psychological family consisted of, in addition to the missing person, loved ones who had stayed behind and not immigrated with them. We knew that we needed an intervention that could help reconstruct the lost connections of family and community. With a wide array of ethnicities, races, socioeconomic levels, nationalities, and religions, we began our work. The first challenge was cultural competence.

What are the appropriate therapeutic goals for what *to* do when working with the trauma of ambiguous loss? How do we work with traumatized people from diverse cultures? The remainder of this book is aimed at answering these questions.

Chapter 3

Resilience and Health

To bounce back and even grow from the traumatizing effects of ambiguous loss requires immense resilience. Many people have this natural self-righting ability to get better—if given time. The challenge to us as therapists and medical practitioners is to be patient. Symptoms must, of course, be treated immediately, but resiliency is a process that takes time. Most therapists have been trained to look immediately for pathology, however, so the idea of looking for healthy resilience is relatively new.

DEFINITIONS

Health is defined here as the physical, emotional, and social well-being of individuals. It includes the absence of medical or psychiatric symptoms, as well as the absence of relational conflict or social isolation. On the positive side, health is defined as relational, as the ability to enjoy a positive connection with another person and with a community of others, such as one's family or friends (Walsh, 1996, 1998). Preventive health is the presence of resiliency in the face of stress and trauma.

Resilience has long been a word in engineering, but what does it mean in clinical circles? There is commonality across disciplines about what resilience means, but ideas about what the structure is and how we build resilience differs. Here the focus is on structures of human relationships—parent-child dyads, couples, families, friendship networks, and communities.

Individual Resilience

Coming from the stress perspective, I define resiliency as the ability to stretch (like elastic) or flex (like a suspension bridge) in response to the pressures and strains of life. This includes the normative stress from everyday hassles as well as the expected family transitions of entries and exits (birth and death) across the lifespan. It also includes the stress and trauma from unexpected crises and catastrophes. When crisis occurs (as opposed to just pressure, stress, or strain), resilience is defined as the ability to bounce back to a level of functioning equal to or greater than before the crisis.[1] Returning to the bridge analogy, stress means the bridge has pressure on it, strain means the bridge is shaking but holding, crisis means the bridge is collapsing, and resiliency means the bridge is bending in response to the stress on it but can absorb this pressure without incurring damage (Boss, 2002a). Flexibility is key, but there is more.

When there is ambiguous loss, *individual resiliency depends on the ability to live comfortably with the ambiguity*. A client's ability to sustain this comfort relies not just on his or her tolerance for ambiguity, but on the ability to live well with the ambiguity, now and in the future. Resiliency also depends on the maintenance of mental and physical health in the face of undue stress—stress beyond normal human expectations. As with a bridge buffeted simultaneously by wind and heavy traffic, resiliency must include being able to hold up over time under conflicting forces. With ambiguous loss it means thriving not just despite the pressures, but because of being able to manage having a loved one simultaneously absent and present. Resilience under such circumstances means being able to live well without having absolute certainty about a family member's absence or presence. It means flourishing and staying healthy mentally and physically despite having a child kidnapped, a parent with Alzheimer's disease, a spouse missing in action during wartime, or a child brain-injured from an accident. It means thriving during the inevitable ambiguities of absence and presence from life course transitions—a child growing up and leaving home or a frail elder leaving home for institutional care. Although some of these examples are more catastrophic than others, all represent some degree of stress, trauma, and ambiguity. The ultimate resiliency comes from being able to bend and flex and stay healthy in such times. It means not being undone by the less-than-perfect absence or presence of people we care about.

As I do, Hetherington and Blechman (1996) prefer the term *resiliency* to indicate process and movement over time. Their definition of resiliency in children and families is succinct and helpful for both therapists and researchers: "*Resilience, stress resistance,* or *invulnerability* refer to processes that operate in the presence of risk to produce outcomes as good or better than those obtained in the absence of risk" (p. 14). While the context surrounding a person may influence this process, resiliency provides the crucible in which people become stronger in difficult and uncertain times.

Family Resilience

Whereas individual resiliency is rooted in developmental psychology and pathology, *family resiliency,* a newer term, has its roots in family stress management and prevention. Family therapists Hawley and DeHaan (1996) reviewed the literature from these two streams of research and concluded that both theoretical approaches are needed to assess resilience.

Hawley and DeHaan integrated ideas about individual development with family processes over time to define family resilience; according to them, resilience is "the path a family follows as it adapts and prospers in the face of stress, both in the present and over time. Resilient families respond positively to these conditions in unique ways, depending on the context, developmental level, the interactive combination of risk and protective factors, and the family's shared outlook" (1996, p. 293). To work with families of missing persons, however, another element must be added to the definition: For families with ambiguous loss to sustain resiliency over time, there must be a tolerance for ambiguity, and also a comfort with it. In fact, some even come to see benefit in it (Boss, 1999). Being able to live comfortably (and without conflict) with unanswered questions is the real test of family resiliency.

When confronted with ambiguous losses, how do families do this? Some say spirituality helps living with not knowing; others say it is religious faith that helps. Still others say it is simply the family's optimistic hope that things will work out. Others are comfortable with ambiguity for reasons more philosophical and existential, living life as it comes, in the moment. What I have learned from the thousands of families I have worked with is that they attain resiliency in vastly different ways, and that each way can lead to the same end. Here we must be open to diversity.

What this means for clinicians is that not all people attain resiliency in the same way. What we hope for is that members of one couple and family have compatible views. This is not always the case, however. Too much incongruence among beliefs and worldviews within one couple or family blocks the process of resiliency. The incongruence can lead to family or marital splits. Building the teamwork necessary to keep moving forward during uncertain times may be one of our major therapeutic tasks.

For families to be resilient, they must first know who the team is. This brings us back to the psychological family. Rarely is there absolute absence and presence in anyone's family, so talking about how each family member perceives the missing person is necessary—as is talking about which persons make up the family. When there is ambiguous loss, reconstructing who the family is will often lead to conflict. Perceptions differ. In therapy, I try to normalize such disagreements. For example, as an elderly parent's gradual exit begins from dementia, congestive heart failure, or another illness—a process of leaving that can go on for years—the adult children may argue about where the parent should live and who should care for him or her. The usual family boundaries and roles are strained, as long goodbyes wear people down. Challenges to family resilience over time also come from normal human development and relational maturation (or lack there of), as well as from unexpected events such as unemployment and chronic illnesses. If families are to maintain the teamwork necessary for resiliency over time, members must continually reassess who is considered family. The ability to continually recalibrate family boundaries—psychological and physical—is essential for cognitive coping, stress management, and decision making, all essential to the process of resiliency over the life course.

It has been relatively recent that scholars have used the term family resilience (McCubbin & McCubbin, 1993; Walsh, 1998). Family therapist Froma Walsh, for example, wrote: "Individual hardiness is better understood and fostered in the context of the family and larger social world" (1998, p. 24). Family scholars have evidence of resiliencys being an entity of the family as a whole, but we still need further inquiry to determine more precisely when and how family resilience is more than the sum of the resilience of individual family members, as well as how therapists can support both.

HISTORY AND RESEARCH UPDATE FOR CLINICIANS

The history of resilience may shed light on why clinicians have been biased toward working with individuals. I will start at the beginning, when the idea of resilience (though not the term) was born, and then proceed to contemporary ideas that can inform our clinical work today. Note that ideas about individual resilience emerged from fields concerned with pathology whereas studies of family resilience emerged from fields concerned with prevention.

Resilience in Psychology

In the early 1970s, psychologist Norman Garmezy (1987) pioneered ideas about stress-resistance and competence in the face of difficulty. He was studying children at risk for pathology because they had schizophrenic mothers and was surprised that some of the children thrived, remaining healthy and doing well in school (1985, 1987). He and his colleagues then studied children in other high-risk contexts. In contexts of poverty, he also found stress-resistant children (Garmezy & Rutter, 1985). From these early findings, these researchers shifted to a focus on competence and no longer automatically expected pathology in high-risk populations. The search was now for health. Garmezy began *Project Competence* at the University of Minnesota to study at-risk children who nevertheless remained competent and healthy (Garmezy & Masten, 1986; Garmezy, Masten, & Tellegen, 1984). In more recent years, the term *competence* has been replaced with *resilience* (Masten, 2001). This shift to a resiliency focus continues today with research emphasis on assets, compensatory factors, protective factors, and competence in developmental tasks (Wright & Masten, 2005).

In addition to research, listening clinically to personal stories of ambiguous loss can shed light on resiliency and what it means. Helga's story is an example.[2] As a small child during World War II in Dresden, Germany, she spent many nights in the neighborhood bomb shelter as she and her mother and brother, grandparents, aunts, and cousins endured nightly bombing attacks. Helga remembers being frightened but enveloped by her extended family. Her grandfather built little beds in the shelter for all the children so they could sleep better during the bombing. Despite this less-than-ideal context for childhood, Helga did well. After the war, she left Germany to study abroad, married, had children, and much later divorced. In her middle years, her son went missing. Helga called me. She said not being able to find him was getting to be more than she could bear. We worked on gathering more information, but at the same time, we strengthened her other relationships with her remaining offspring and friends. When the boy's body surfaced in the river after the spring thaw, our sessions shifted to grieving and then planning a memorial. I encouraged her to invite her ex-husband into a session to explicitly discuss how they could do this for their son together. Though reticent at first, Helga brought him in to discuss how they could collaborate in memorializing and honoring their dead son. Together, as his parents, they became a team. It was a new idea to them, for they hadn't seen each other in years. In spite of being a child of war, and the stress of divorce, and the tragedy of one son gone missing and later being found dead, Helga remains healthy and accepting about life. Her relationship with her remaining son has deepened, and she continues to make creative contributions to her community. For me, Helga is an excellent example of resiliency.

Garmezy would have called Helga competent while today, we call such people *resilient*. Across disciplines, it is now agreed that it means more than coping or overcoming. Resiliency means *thriving* under adverse conditions—in other words, maintaining one's physical and emotional health and one's spirit for living life with joy. This is a tall order for people who have experienced the trauma of ambiguous loss, but resilience does exist and is increasingly the focus of scientific study.

Contemporary psychologists have studied how people stay resilient across the lifespan with risk factors such as poverty, homelessness, divorce, physical illness, and mental illness (Cowan, 1991; Hauser, 1999; Hauser, DiPlacido, Jacobson, Willet, & Cole, 1993; Masten, 2001). Developmental psychologists increasingly see resilience as a process and now favor the term *resiliency* to indicate development over time (Hetherington & Blechman, 1996). For example, in Hauser's (1999) longitudinal study of clinical and nonclinical adolescents (now mature adults), he found that hospitalization for mental illness as teenagers did not predict which adolescents would become healthy adults 35 years later. Many turned out to be competent and healthy later on. Hauser found that attributing a positive meaning to the earlier experience of institutionalization accounted for the adult health and resilience. Studies like this give hope, especially if resilience can be nurtured by clinicians and learned in psychoeducational groups. Wolin and Wolin (1993) used the term *survivor's pride* and found that if something bad happens to a person, a positive meaning or attribution could, as the saying goes, turn lemons into lemonade. (I will revisit this idea of meaning in Chapter 4.)

Resilience in Sociology

In sociology, the pioneer in resiliency (though he also did not use terms like resilience) was Aaron Antonovsky from Ben Gurion University of Negev in Israel. As a medical sociologist, Antonovsky thought that clinicians needed an approach broader than simply treating specific illnesses and diseases if they were to be effective with the modern world's health problems. His broader approach was to identify psychological, social, and cultural resources that people use to resist illnesses. If patients saw their world as understandable and manageable, they possessed what he termed a *sense of coherence.* In his research, Antonovsky (1979, 1987) found that a sense of coherence was the major factor in determining how well patients would manage stress and stay healthy. Antonovsky's work influenced clinical thinking about the need for *agency,* a sociological term referring to one's ability to master a situation or problem and, I would add, clients' or patients' faith that they *will* be able to do so. Because agency relates to self-determination and the dignity that comes from being able to help oneself to get better, clinicians should do what they can to remove any barriers that block agency. At the same time, they must prepare the person for *not* being able to do so. Some illnesses or situations have no answers or cure. The human desire for mastery and personal agency must, then, be therapeutically tempered.

I thought of Antonovsky's concept again recently when I saw a client, a corporate executive, whose elderly mother had died 2 weeks earlier. She was immensely distraught. "It doesn't make sense that I fell apart over a 92-year-old parent's death, does it?" I told her it did make sense. "She was your mother, you loved her, and now she is gone." My task was to normalize the effects of her loss—the crying, the confusion, and her lack of energy—so that she could see her world once again as coherent and manageable. Indeed, she could not cope or manage her own situation because she did not understand the normalcy of her grief. The missing piece in the puzzle was that she (and her boss) did not think it made sense to grieve over losing a parent so old.

Where do such absurd ideas come from? Usually from a view of the world that makes people think they can control all things, even their own emotions about the loss of a parent. Such ideas also come from a culture that overemphasizes mastery and productivity, thus devaluing connections to the very old. What we forget is another kind of resource—human attachment. When we lose our elders, we grieve not because we have lost a person at the height of their productivity, but because we no longer have them with us. When a workplace values productivity at all costs, complications of grief can develop.

With this woman, my goal was to bolster her resilience, or her sense of coherence, to use Antonovsky's term. More than personal agency, a sense of coherence is a worldview that indicates one can eventually find some understanding in a distressing outcome. She was a mature businesswoman who was deeply distraught by the loss of her elderly mother, and her boss thought she should get over it. Once she knew it was normal to be grieving even a 92-year-old parent, she understood what she needed to do. She had to give herself time and space to grieve the death of her elderly mother, for the workplace would not give it to her. She made the decision to take a long vacation. With time for grieving taken volitionally, she also made a new and deeper connection with her husband and eventually with her siblings. When I last saw her, she said that she now felt better at work having consciously allowed herself time to grieve. As a manager, she said she now knew that even competent executives must take time out to grieve their losses and also know that it is all right if it is never really over. She had developed a more coherent worldview—one that allowed her to integrate loss more comfortably into her work life.

Resilience in Family Studies and Family Therapy

The earliest pioneers in family studies for the strength versus pathology approach were the family stress and coping researchers. Unequivocally, Rueben Hill (1949) is known as the father of family stress research. In his studies of family separations during WWII, Hill (1949), a sociologist who began the field of family studies, found that flexibility and adaptability were key for families to stay healthy. Later, after the Vietnam War, Hill was a consultant to the Center of Prisoner of War Studies, where he mentored a second generation of family stress researchers: Boss (1975, 1977, 1980c, 1987, 2002c), Boss and Greenberg (1984), Figley (1989), and McCubbin (1979). As noted earlier, Figley (1985) later moved away from family studies to individual psychological approaches. McCubbin and McCubbin (1993) continued the family studies approach by studying family resilience in medical settings. My own work continues Hill's original emphasis to develop theory to guide family interventions for distressed and traumatized families.

Although units of analyses differ, those of us who work directly with families must pay attention to what both psychology and family studies are finding. I agree with Hawley and DeHaan, who say that "of particular importance are the influence of developmental transitions on resilience and the identification of potential risk factors at the family level of analysis. Family science has a rich heritage of exploring the influences of development and identifying precursors of pathology . . ." (1996, p. 295). Both individual and systemic study is needed. After all, individuals do not live in isolation. They have relationships outside of therapy that predate and postdate our work with them. Because of the need to focus on both individual and relational issues, the cross-fertilization between psychology and family therapy is essential to strengthen the validity and effectiveness of clinical work.

Although there is now substantial support for the existence of a phenomenon called family resiliency, questions remain for further study. Clinicians could contribute by using their observations to generate new hypotheses about how and when family resiliency helps individuals stay healthy. Clinicians may also have valuable ideas about when family, community, and culture can get in the way of individual resilience and health. Researchers need these ideas. At present, however, research suggests that resiliency is both an individual and a family phenomenon. For this reason, I continue to take into account both the individual *and* his or her family. This is essential for working with children, but I also do it with adults. Like the family of former President Ronald Reagan, which came together to support Mrs. Reagan during his decline from Alzheimer's disease, the whole is greater than the sum of its parts. I can only surmise that what the family offered Mrs. Reagan during those years of ambiguous loss was the warm support and help she needed to stay resilient and healthy.

Whether in our practice, we treat individuals, couples, or families, the resiliency paradigm is now becoming prominent. What we have learned is that there are many families, like the Reagan family, that not only endure but also get stronger as family members lean on each other to sustain their resilience with illnesses and disabilities that so brutally can take away a mind.

Research Update for Clinicians

In his encyclopedic review of loss, trauma, and human resilience, Bonanno (2004) reviewed the research evidence about resilience and made three important points:

1. *Resiliency is more than recovery.* With resiliency, normal function never really gives way. The person has the ability to maintain a stable equilibrium no matter what. Bonanno defined resilience as "the ability of adults in otherwise normal circumstances who are exposed to an isolated and potentially highly disruptive event, such as the death of a close relation or a violent or life-threatening situation, to maintain relatively stable, healthy levels of psychological and physical functioning" (2004, p. 20). Bonanno went on to emphasize (as Walsh, 1998, did earlier) that resilience is more than the absence of psychopathology. According to this line of thinking, resiliency is not part of the recovery after crisis (Boss, 2002c). Instead, it is mostly continuous healthy functioning with regenerative growth and positive emotions (Bonanno, Papa, & O'Neill, 2001).

   What these various definitions mean for clinicians is that not everyone requires the same intervention after ambiguous loss. Resilient adults and children may require no intervention. In fact, they may be impeded by our good intentions. Treatment should instead be targeted toward the most vulnerable—those who are immobilized and traumatized—to prevent chronic and delayed reactions (Bonanno et al., 2001; Boss, 1999; Stroebe & Stroebe, 1991). Cognitive-behavioral treatments that help clients understand and manage their anxiety and fear associated with trauma-related events are the most effective (Resick, 2001).

   This brings us back to the discussion about treating CISD and PTSD. The idea that everyone exposed to a violent or life-threatening event needs debriefing is false. The originator of CISD himself said this (Mitchell, 1983). Mitchell and Everly (2003) and Miller (2002) also criticized the blanket debriefing protocol for workers after 9/11. Researchers say debriefing is at best ineffective (Rose, Brewin, Andrews, & Kirk, 1999), and at worst, it impedes natural recovery processes in the people who are naturally resilient (Bisson, Jenkins, Alexander, & Bannister, 1997; Bonanno, 2004; Mayou, Ehlers, & Hobbs, 2000). According to the PTSD Alliance (2005), almost 70% of Americans will be exposed to a traumatic event in their lifetime, but only 20% of them will go on to develop PTSD. The majority are resilient.

2. *Resilience is more common than we thought.* Grief therapists have traditionally been trained to pathologize both underreactions and overreactions of grief after loss. On the other hand, trauma therapists have been trained to focus only on negative reactions, no matter how mild or extreme. In both cases, resilience has been overlooked. (There are of course exceptions—e.g., Landau & Saul, 2004). According to Bonanno, the vast majority of people exposed to loss and trauma "do not exhibit chronic symptom profiles . . . many and, in some cases, the majority show the type of healthy functioning suggestive of the resilience trajectory" (2004, p. 22).

The traditional focus on pathology was perhaps influenced by Bowlby (1980), who defined the expression of positive emotions after loss as defensive denial. Middleton, Moylan, Raphael, Burnett, and Martinek (1993) found that 65% of self-identified grief therapists believe that the absence of grieving stems from inhibition or denial; Osterweis, Solomon, and Green (1984) said it was personality pathology (Bonanno, 2004). What the empirical research shows is this: "Resilience to the unsettling effects of interpersonal loss is not rare but relatively common, does not appear to indicate pathology but rather healthy adjustment, and does not lead to delayed grief reactions" (Bonanno, 2004, p. 23). Current research backs up the claims of Wortman and Silver (1989), who said that there was no basis for the assumption that the absence of grief is pathological or that its absence is always followed by delayed grief reactions.

According to Bonnano and Keltner (1997), there is, in fact, solid prospective evidence that resilience to loss is enhanced by positive emotion. What they found, however, is that those who did well after loss were ready to accept the death, believed in a just world (Boss, 2002c), and had instrumental support. Although early on after the loss there were some yearnings, emotional pangs, intrusive thoughts, and ruminations, they did not endure or interfere with daily functioning and affect in resilient individuals (Bonanno, 2004; Bonanno, Wortman, & Nesse, 2004). What this tells us is that Bowlby was wrong about people who experience loss and trauma without negative emotions. I have seen this often with family caregivers of Alzheimer's disease patients.

The ambiguousness of their loss allows them a gradual process of grieving so they have shed all their tears by the time the patient dies. They may even express relief as they can now tend to their own needs and rebuild their own health and emotional well-being. This is resiliency, not pathology.

3. *There are multiple and sometimes unexpected pathways to resilience.* For some people, repression is a functional way of coping (Bonanno, Noll, Putnam, O'Neill, & Trickett, 2003). For others, laughter and optimism build resilience (Bonanno et al., 2003). Still others benefit from self-enhancement (eg. actions or beliefs to become less vulnerable) (Bonanno, Field, Kovacevic, & Kaltman, 2002). Hardiness for some can buffer extreme stress (Kobasa, Maddi, & Kahn, 1982). What is clear is that although more study is needed, pathways to resilience vary by development, genetics, environment, gender, and other risk/protective factors yet to be determined. Practitioners could help researchers uncover more information by sharing their clinical hunches and generating hypotheses about resiliency after trauma.

Community as Source of Resilience

In parallel with emphasis on the commonality and unexpected sources of resilience, therapists have recently defined resilience as a complex relational process that must include community (Boss et al., 2003; Landau & Saul, 2004). Although more studies are needed to determine if and how community resources, values, and connections help people heal, recent clinical reports the Oklahoma City bombing, 9/11, and after the South Asian tsunami have supported the idea that a *sense of community* helps individuals and families heal. Much earlier, Speck and Attneave (1973) proposed that community-based therapy with extended family groups, which they called *network therapy,* would be more effective than individual therapy. Attneave's American Indian background undoubtedly influenced her then-innovative approach. Personally and professionally, she believed that one's community or tribe could help heal one's marital or family troubles—a belief held by almost all indigenous peoples. What worked in primitive times may not always work today, but clearly in contemporary cultures that promote independence and self-sufficiency, treatment has swung too far away from family and community approaches. Studies continue to test the effi cacy of community interventions (Saul, 2003) and what Landau calls *link therapy* (Landau, 1981; Landau & Saul, 2004). While we wait for further evidence of the efficacy of such community approaches, I remain optimistic about the community's being a major resource for building resilience in individuals and families.

CAUTIONS ABOUT RESILIENCY

In addition to acknowledging the advantages of the resilience approach, we must also be aware of the pitfalls.

First, remaining resilient is not always desirable, especially if it is always the same persons who are expected to bend. People with less privilege and power or agency—for example, people of color and women—have become great adapters to the whims of others. They are expected to give in to those with higher agency and to fit in without making waves. Resiliency, therefore, is not itself always a sufficient therapeutic goal. Sometimes fighting back, insisting on radical change, or going into crisis is better than continuing to endure, for example, abuse and injustice. In such cases, we must be supportive of a person's refusal to continue being adaptive. This requires our being cautious about resiliency and what looks like strength. Rather than focusing on, for example, how people can thrive despite oppression, we should also be looking for ways to reduce discrimination and poverty. Resiliency is not always the ideal outcome (Boss, 2002c).

We may recognize and support the resilience of a child of war, for example, but at the same time, we should do what we can to eliminate traumatic loss and violence for children and their families. We must be cautious about adopting a resilience model that simply supports the status quo. Of course, we will not reach utopia, but we cannot assume that war and poverty will always be with us and that there is nothing that can be done about this. We must not be content with human resilience as the only answer. Although the essential criterion of resilience is health, we must also promote the health of a society and environment in which humans can thrive.

Second, even with a focus on resilience, we must attend to symptoms that need medical care or psychiatric treatment. Years ago, my teacher, Carl Whitaker, told me that when he saw an alcoholic in the family, he saw only his liver and the damage the alcohol was doing to him medically. I had been voicing my concern about my lack of medical training, and he said this to make me see that we each brought something valuable to our cotherapy work. He said he saw my lack of medical training as an advantage in family therapy because I could see the whole family and the whole person first without being preoccupied about damage to internal organs. His vote of confidence, however, did not mean I should ignore the medical, but rather that both views were needed. Today, I frequently ask depressed clients, for example, to get a medical consultation to eliminate possible physical or hormonal causes of their symptoms. Sometimes a cigar is a cigar and not a psychological or relational issue.

Third, although therapies that build resilience can be called "strength-based approaches" they are not synonymous with solution-focused therapies. When there is ambiguous loss, I do not believe our therapeutic goals should be to produce *solutions*. The therapeutic goal is more often to adapt, approximate, find a way to walk through the woods in the dark, and even thrive doing it. Being resilient means learning to live with unanswered questions. Not finding solutions is not failed therapy.

With these cautions about resiliency in mind, we must remember that if we focus only on pathology and symptom diagnosis, we miss the very buoyancy that makes it possible for people to move on. Despite the lack of solutions for definite absence and presence, individuals, couples, and families stay afloat in unique and wonderful ways. Indications of resilience come from unexpected places and still surprise me.

PRINCIPLES FOR THERAPEUTIC TREAMENT AND PREVENTIVE INTERVENTION

With ambiguous loss, increasing the comfort and resiliency of individuals, couples, and families is the therapeutic goal. Walsh (1998, 2003) has developed a family resilience framework to guide assessment and intervention, targeting key processes that promote resilience in three domains of family funtioning.

1. Belief systems (making meaning of adversity, positive outlook, transcendence and spirituality)
2. Organizational patterns (flexibility, connectedness, social and economic resources)
3. Communication processes (clarity, open emotional expression, collaborative problem solving)

Using her typology to organize the following therapeutic principles, I list what I do clinically to build and support family resiliency after ambiguous loss. Overall, the goal is to decrease risk factors and strengthen protective factors for the remaining family members, as well as for the family as a whole. There is no hierarchy in the order of this list, and some items under certain headings could also fall under other headings.

Belief Systems

People's beliefs are paramount in determining their brittleness or resiliency under stress. The same holds true for dyads and family systems.

Balance perceptions with facts. Perceptions matter, but they are not all that matters. There are, indeed, some facts that we as therapists must heed—for example, laws against child abuse, incest, battery, and homicide. If individuals and families perceive these acts to be normal, they must be corrected. We must also heed facts about structures that complicate human relationships (adoption, divorce, remarriage), as well as facts about impending separation or loss (military deployment, immigration, terminal illness, bankruptcy, unemployment, mental or physical illness). Such events require therapists to consider facts along with perceptions.

Be tolerant of clients who have spiritual and religious views that differ from your own. A healthy spiritual life provides resilience regardless of one's religious faith or lack of it. In studying palliative medicine for malignant brain tumors, Strang and Strang (2001) found that Antonovsky's sense of coherence explained how patients handled their failing health. These researchers found Antonovsky's concept helpful because it more broadly ". . . integrates essential parts of the stress/coping model (comprehensibility, manageability) and of spirituality (meaning)" (p. 127). This more inclusive way of thinking is also useful in our practices, where we treat people with various beliefs about religion and spirituality. Spirituality that enhances resiliency is not defined in an absolute way.

Reattribute the cause; externalize the blame when appropriate or take responsibility. Guilt, shame, and self-blame make people brittle and block resiliency. The goal is to reattribute the problem to an external source to relieve self-blame and guilt. Situations in which this is appropriate include those involving, for example, mental illness, or having a family member who is kidnapped. Of course, there are exceptions. For some things, the goal is to take responsibility and alter behaviors to prevent the bad thing from happening again. Examples here are being a neglectful or *absent* parent, and abusing drugs and alcohol. In these cases the therapist must reattribute the problem to the client's personal behavior and the client must make a commitment to changing.[3] This is akin to the Alcoholics Anonymous model, which teaches people to take responsibility for their actions.

Reframe and relabel events that cause guilt and shame. Guilt and shame are not only inherent in ambiguous losses but also are used in methods of torture and ethnic cleansing to intentionally dehumanize victims. In Kosovo, for example, the soldiers themselves not only raped many of the Albanian Kosovars but also forced the sons to rape their mothers and the fathers to rape their daughters. The overlay of incest on the trauma of rape was meant to produce immobilizing guilt and shame that would last for generations. And it did, unless victims could gradually reframe what had happened (torture) and relabel it as not being incest. The process is speeded up if the therapist states this reframe explicitly. For example, a therapist told of the resiliency in a family where the son had been forced to rape his mother. She said that progress toward the reunification of mother and son came only after she relabeled the forced rape as torture—and not incest. This statement from an authority figure (the therapist) to the mother and son—and the rest of the family—helped lift their guilt and shame.

Rethink power and control. Believing one has more power and control over life may build feelings of security and confidence. Changes one can make to lower the chances of being raped or mugged, for example, build resilience. But clinicians must also be cautious about this approach, because all the best intentions to avoid harm may still fail to prevent a traumatic loss. When I work with traumatized people, I do not suggest that there may be something they could do to avoid this problem in the future.[3] The client, raw with trauma, hears only blame and is further victimized by any suggestion of a need to change. Clinicians must first listen, empathize, and validate the trauma. Much later, once the person is less traumatized, we talk about some tools for empowerment against future trauma. For example, a client might adopt better health habits and do more exercise or meditation to help prevent heart disease. Or she might take a class in self-defense and practice walking in a more assertive way and in a clear direction before she walks into a parking lot. This is not blaming the victim but rather preparing people who have been traumatized to feel more empowered. Sometimes, however, feelings of mastery become unrealistic and must be tempered (see Chapter 5).

Encourage optimism. When under pressure, optimism is useful for both therapist and client. Thinking one can survive or make it out of a tough spot actually helps survival and resilience. Seligman has written extensively on how to teach people to have a more positive outlook (Seligman, 1991; Seligman & Csikszentmihalyi, 2001; Wallis, 2005).

Reconstruct hope. In the early aftermath of ambiguous loss, denial of permanent loss is often helpful. As time goes on, however, people must gradually shift to a new version of hope. That is, they must find new hopes and dreams. People need a bit of time to come to this, so I at first support their hopes for a return to the status quo, even if this seems unrealistic. In the early days after 9/11, most of the family members we worked with believed their loved ones would come walking up the sidewalk again. I suggested that therapists not interfere with that hope, because for the moment it was all they had to keep them going. Until they found a new positive hope (and this takes time), they needed the illusion of a good outcome a bit longer. The children, too, needed some thread of hope in those early days. Had we interfered by labeling the temporary denials as pathological hallucinations, we would have interrupted the natural process of resiliency, which was to defend against a sudden and horrific loss.

Support varying ways to find justice. When people think they deserve fair and just treatment from others and then do not get it, they feel hopeless and angry. Lerner (1971) told us not to evaluate the fairness of the situation, because often it is not fair. Rather, we must learn to react with appropriate feelings and actions. This is cognitive coping. From this perspective, the traditional justice of being right may not be as critical for resiliency as taking the high road and finding a new way to feel justice. When traditional methods of justice (such as the courts) are not available or helpful to your clients, help them find justice in living a healthy and productive life despite what was done to them. Joining a cause to right the wrong can help.

Help the family regain its pride. By using therapeutic strategies that strengthen problem-solving and decision-making skills, pride can be restored even after a traumatic loss. I think of the pride people and communities exude when they find ways to live well despite great trauma and loss. The first steps in doing this, however, should be modest, so that success, however small, is assured. Armour (2002) refered to *small successes* in her research on treating families of murdered children. With a few small successes, individuals and families are gradually able to regain their pride and competence. I think of New York City, a population of over 8,000,000 traumatized by a terrorist attack in 2001, which in 2003 responded to a citywide blackout by finding their way home in the dark, helping one another in their neighborhoods and communities, and having remarkably no looting and few incidents of crime. This was indeed resiliency that grew from previous pain and loss.

Reduce stigma, discrimination, and prejudices. Discrimination and stigma erode resilience. They narrow the options for coping and adaptation, and they always reflect a power imbalance. A person who is stigmatized or discriminated against does not have access to the same choices and resources for resiliency as others. Pride is eroded and successes come harder. Telling people they are second-class, tainted, or a bad seed can decrease resiliency across several generations. Gender constraints for both women and men are also problematic. According to Walsh (1998):

> Women have been reared to assume the major role in handling the social and emotional tasks of bereavement, from the expression of grief to caregiving for the terminally ill and surviving family members, including their husband's extended family. Now that most women combine job and family responsibilities, they are increasingly overburdened in times of loss. Men, who have been socialized to manage instrumental tasks, typically take charge of funeral, burial, financial, and property arrangements. They tend to be more emotionally constrained and peripheral around times of loss. Cultural sanctions against revealing vulnerability or dependence block emotional expressiveness and their ability to seek and give comfort. These constraints undoubtedly contribute to the high rates of serious illness and suicide for men after the death of a spouse. (p. 197)

Organizational Patterns

People's organizational patterns also play an important role in determining brittleness versus resiliency. The main principle here is that organizationally separating traumatized children or adults from loved ones is a barrier to the natural tendency for human resiliency (Boss et al., 2003; Landau & Saul, 2004; Saul, 2003; Sluzki, 1990; Walsh, 1998). This overriding principle is, of course, valid only when the trauma is perpetrated by a nonfamily member. The family- and community-based approaches used after 9/11 broke with the tradition of individual treatment by not separating traumatized children from their families. Other organizational principles follow with this overriding principle in mind.

Connect clients to familiar people. Isolating oneself when traumatized by ambiguous loss is not conducive for health. But connecting to others while under duress requires strong social skills. Often in therapy this can be taught by role playing to prepare the client for real-world connections and finding their own community. Such strategies also help develop agency and thus resiliency. Such cognitive coping strategies can be learned (Seligman, 1991; Turnbull, Patterson, Behr, Murphy, Marquis, & Blue-Banning, 1993). This may explain why cognitive therapies and psychoeducational interventions are effective for trauma recovery. Community and family meetings are an example of such therapeutic connection after loss and trauma (Boss et al., 2003; Landau & Saul, 2004). Whether you are a caregiver working alone or a 9/11 survivor, knowing you are not alone helps sustain and rebuild strength.

Build community. Encourage clients to actively participate in shared endeavors and projects. The most recent advances in thinking about resilience (though they stem from an old idea from indigenous cultures) conceptualize resilience on the community level. Psychologist Jack Saul, director of the International Trauma Studies program at New York University, wrote about fostering community connectedness to promote a lasting recovery after trauma. He suggested that professionals can best foster mental health after major traumatic events (always a test of resilience) by linking to or tapping into the community's competencies and resiliency (Landau, 1981; Saul, 2003). Regrettably, in lower Manhattan, where children were directly exposed to the multiple stresses of 9/11, mental health professionals and funding agencies did not see the community's parents, for example, as resources to help the children regain their resilience. Despite being kept out of the loop by mental health professionals and funding agencies, these downtown Manhattan parents organized and initiated community projects including improvisational theater performances about what they had witnessed, talkback sessions between actors and audience, a community narrative archive, and informative meetings for parents about how to deal with their underlying feelings of grief and fear (Saul, 2003).

Expand the therapeutic set. Call in whomever the client considers family. This may include close friends as well as biological family members. When, for example, there is chronic mental illness, head injury, addiction, or dementia, the dynamic of one family member's being elected as the family caregiver is not unusual. All too often other family members stay away. This only doubles the loss and ambiguity for the caregiver and patient. My approach is to have the whole family participate in one or more sessions using a speakerphone or conference call for those far away. By expanding the boundary to include more family members than the caregiver, they can work conjointly to create a team plan, each taking their turn to do their part in the work of caring. In my experience, the common response is relief, not resistance, as the family members who were not helping often feel guilty. Usually these family members are glad to make some contribution, even if it is long-distance bookkeeping or periodic visits to relieve the caregiver on site. Sometimes resistance will come from the in-home caregiver, who will ask me not to bother other family members even though her own health is suffering. When she says, "Oh, my son and daughter are so busy," I point out that if something happens to her, the patient will have no caregiver at all, and that she must now bring in other family members to help to protect her own health.

Sometimes the therapeutic set includes public policy advocacy. Families have become the case managers for the chronically ill, the dying, and the traumatized. As managed care restrictions increasingly force family members to care for their ill relatives at home, ideas about ambiguous loss become important to the health of family caregivers. If physicians are to prevent the development of a second patient, they must empathize more with the caregiver. They frequently note the depression of caregivers, but their depression may have more to do with the ambiguity surrounding their loss than with the caring work or the illness itself (Boss et al., 1988; Boss, Caron, et al., 1990; Caron et al., 1999; Kaplan & Boss, 1999).

Use systems thinking, but with care and fairness. The systemic experience of the partner of an alcoholic or brain-injured mate is not balanced. One partner is ill and the other is trying to adapt, albeit in a dysfunctional way. Using the old theory about the overresponsible caregiver and the underresponsible patient insults both partners. The assumption of balance in human systems (e.g., overfunctioning/underfunctioning) was criticized in the 1980s as a misuse of systems theory. The reality is that when one person has an illness or condition, the other must adapt to it. The idea of balance and a "mutual couple dance" is wrong because both partners are being pushed around by the illness. Each is affected in a different way. One might say there are now three entities in the couple system, with the third being the illness.

Reconsider the value of termination at the end of therapy. From a resilience and health perspective, challenges will arise throughout the life course. These are not a result of personal pathology but rather of situational contexts. Because of developmental changes, maturation, and contextual shifts, a client may want to come back for a few sessions months or years later. Within reason, I keep the door to therapy open for such periodic checkups or treatment. Like a family practice physician, I often see the second and third generations of the same family. One can only do this ethically by maintaining boundaries and thinking about individuals as actors in a larger social system that also influences them.

Communication Processes

Processes of communication are also critical in determining individual and systemic resiliency. Without effective communication processes, coping and managing processes break down and resiliency becomes brittle.

Talk explicitly about how to reduce stress individually and relationally. Talk together about avoiding predictably tense situations (staying out of danger zones) and accepting what is unavoidable (e.g., having a mentally ill family member). If clients are still distressed, help them learn and practice how to resist and manage stress (cognitive coping). Meditation and relaxation skills help, as do physical exercise, laughing, and good health habits. Many have found the Serenity Prayer, written by Reinhold Niebuhr, helpful: "God, give us grace to accept with serenity the things that cannot be changed, courage to change things that should be changed, and the wisdom to distinguish the one from the other" (Sifton, 2003). Although this approach to stress management is especially useful in recovery from addictions, it can also be a useful basis for discussion for lowering stress from loss and trauma. Whatever basis for communication is used, it is the process of discussion (not rumination) that promotes resiliency.

Communicate empathy, not sympathy. Therapeutically, giving protective, sentimental sympathy may actually reinforce traumatized clients' views of themselves as victims longer than necessary. More effective are therapeutic empathy, sensitivity, and compassion for misfortune. We must also monitor who else is influencing them—friends, neighbors, relatives—to make sure that others are not reinforcing the victimized thinking. I have seen this occur in families that are labeled by the community as losers, as well as in church congregations that shun a person after rape, unwed pregnancy, or the exposing of secrets about sexual abuse. With ambiguous losses, people should not offer victims the well-meant sympathy of "Time will heal," because it might not. The lack of closure may last for a lifetime. But we should offer opportunties to reconstruct their victim narrative to one of resiliency. I often begin with a simple statement of empathy such as, "I am sorry that you have to live with such pain and stress." The goal is to validate and communicate empathy, so that gradually, resiliency is regained.

Talk about anger: It's not always a bad thing. Anger is an appropriate response to the frustration and stress of ambiguous loss. Clients are less likely to act out these feelings in inappropriate ways if they can accept their anger and use it to find their strength to move forward again. Anger can be a positive motivator for making necessary changes. Professionals, of course, must become comfortable with angry feelings, their clients' and their own, in order to communicate that anger may have some positive function.

Interrupt ruminations. The goal is to help clients learn how to distract themselves from obsessive rumination about a traumatic or unclear loss. Continuous rumination builds victimization, not resilience. It also predicts depression, especially in women (Beardslee, 2003).

Commiserating with other victims is not always productive unless there is forward movement. Sympathetic responses from well-meaning friends and family can eventually be destructive. Choosing the people one communicates with is, therefore, critical. Communications centered on "woe is me" must shift eventually to "How can I move forward with my life despite what happened?"

Teach cognitive coping. Communicating stoicism does not guarantee resiliency. People need problem-solving skills such as how to seek help from others (Boss, 2002c; Turnbull et al., 1993). Encourage people to seek information, as information about one's situation is empowering. Being aware of choices remains a core idea for agency and for building resiliency. Discussing choices for making end-of-life decisions, for example, is more useful for adult children than fighting at the bedside of a dying elder. Cognitive coping may also involve some intentional denial, conscious ambivalence, "positive illusions," or "selective biases" (Walsh, 1998, p. 182). These methods of cognitive coping are helpful especially over the short term.

Let others know the success experiences. To build confidence and resiliency, help clients communicate their successes to their friends and community. This requires increasing success experiences as well as finding a relational network with whom to share such successes.

Listen to individuals and families. When clinicians ignore parents and when attempts to communicate, however clumsy, are thwarted, families often take it upon themselves to make things better in their own way, as did the families that started the National Alliance for the Mentally Ill

(NAMI), the Downtown Families of 9/11, and the Families of the Missing in Kosovo, to name a few. It would be better, however, if family members, especially parents, were included as part of the healing team from the start. To build on rather than thwart resiliency, we must hear the narratives of the affected parents and children.

Encourage dialectical versus absolute ways of communication. Holding two opposing views at the same time means one cannot talk in absolutes about the missing person's absence or presence. What I have learned from working with families of the missing is that they feel they have to struggle more with the social norms that push for closure than they do with the loss itself. Until recently, the prevailing notion was that mourners should get over their loss and do so relatively quickly. After Senator Paul Wellstone's death in 2002, there were some bumper stickers that read, "He's dead, get over it!" Such blatant absolutist communication is a brutal barrier to human resiliency.

These therapeutic principles are key for supporting and building resiliency in clients after the trauma of ambiguous loss. For all, a practical recommendation to consider is to minimize language differences between therapist and clients. With the diversity of our clientele today, we must be proficient in a second language, work toward becoming so, and committed to training professionals who already have multi-cultural language capabilities. If traumatized people cannot understand the language of their therapist and vice versa, the awareness of the problem and their choices for easing it are blocked. Cognitive coping is impossible when people literally can't understand each other. Using a translator is also problematic. We cannot espouse resilience and at the same time do nothing to improve our multi-cultural communication skills.

CASE STUDY

Sometimes people must learn what resilience is not before they can learn what it is. Through trial and error, they learn what works and doesn't, but the therapeutic concern must always be about the costs to individual and family health in this process.

Peg and her husband had grown up in rural America in the 1940s and 1950s, during a time and in a place where girls were expected to marry right after high school graduation. At 19, in the middle of her sophomore year at a nearby university, Peg gave in to the hometown pressure and married her high school sweetheart during semester break.

In the beginning, her young husband did not drink excessively. He liked to pitch softball and skate. He was stunningly handsome. But when his big break came to join the business world, the three-martini luncheons began to take their toll. Within a year, he showed signs of addiction and the young couple's life together changed. The man Peg married was no longer there.

Peg's way of coping was to carry a book in her purse so that when a social evening turned raucous, she could find a quiet spot and read until her husband was ready to go home. She thought she was the perfect wife, resilient to the end. She was, after all, going to make this marriage work. When her husband was late for dinner, she would keep his meal warm in the oven—until their junior high son finally said, "Mom, don't you know he isn't coming home?" She went into the bedroom and sobbed. The truth hurt, but the boy was right.

For 15 more years, Peg continued being overly flexible, bendable, and what she thought was resilient. Why? There had never been a divorce in her family, and as several locals said to her, "Why are you upset? He doesn't hit you. Lots of guys drink." In that cultural context, what her husband was doing was normal. She also lacked knowledge about addiction and naively thought that trying harder to be a good wife would help stop the drinking.

Eventually Peg sought respite at a nearby university. Her studying and her husband's drinking became complementary: He drank; she studied. When he didn't come home until late at night, her anger and disappointment motivated her writing. Reading remained an escape. When she began attending Al-Anon meetings, she realized that her way of coping was doable but preserved the status quo. Many of the women in her Al-Anon group truly could not opt for change because of religious reasons. It took a while before Peg realized that she was not bound in this way. But the idea of giving up came hard.

What finally prompted Peg to decide to divorce was her failing health. Her back froze up and the pain was paralyzing. The doctor suggested it was her commuting to school, but the truth was that she felt helpless about what to do. She was married, but not married. She had a husband, but didn't have a husband. Numerous times, the orthopedist hospitalized her and put her in traction for weeks at a time. The children now had two missing parents. She pleaded with her husband to go for treatment, but he refused except after DWI arrests when the court demanded it. Nothing changed.

Given the norms of her community, it was probably no accident that Peg waited until her children were in college and she was financially independent before she found the courage to seek real change. She participated in a five-day residential Al-Anon family program. The psychoeducational and interactional programs brought her to an important turning point.

With psychoeducational lectures, discussions, and therapy, Peg learned what she needed to do. She had been most conflicted when her husband repeatedly told her that if she left he would kill himself. Those threats had kept her in the marriage for 15 more years. When she asked the counselor how she could leave without tragedy, he rolled up his sleeves and showed her the scars encircling his own wrists. She gasped. He told her this is what he had done when his wife left him. Then he said something she never forgot: "What makes you think you can keep people alive?" These powerful words changed her perceptions of resiliency forever. She could not rescue her husband; instead she had to take care of her own health.

From that time on, Peg understood that true resilience was more than stoicism and endless adaptation. Psychosomatic symptoms were indicators that change was necessary. She had not been resilient but rather just stubbornly persistent in thinking she could fix things if she worked harder. Dealing with the ambiguous loss of addiction, Peg had to learn what resilience was *not* before she could see what it *was*. More will be said about this case later in the Epilogue.

Part II

*Therapeutic Goals
for Treating Ambiguous Loss*

Chapter 4

Finding Meaning

Therapists at my workshops frequently ask, "Isn't tolerance for ambiguity simply faith in God?" The answer is that yes, it is for some people, but the correlation between religious faith and tolerance for ambiguity is, in my experience, far from perfect. People with strong religious beliefs often show little tolerance for ambiguity; people with little religious faith may have a higher tolerance. For this reason, I see the search for meaning after loss, clear or ambiguous, as a journey that occurs in a diversity of ways. In my practice, I pay less attention to specific religious beliefs and more attention to the more global beliefs and values that affect one's overall tolerance for ambiguity, regardless of the match (or mismatch) between client and therapist beliefs.

Finding meaning in loss is not necessarily important to all people, but when life and well-being are threatened, it becomes a therapeutic issue. How clients find meaning varies greatly. Some find it through cultural beliefs (e.g., the Latin *destino,* meaning destiny, or the Germanic *Schicksal,* meaning fate). Others find it through a spiritual acceptance of nature and the circle of life. Still others find meaning in a philosophy of life that helps them live more existentially—that is, in the moment. Finally, many find meaning through religious spirituality.

A growing body of research indicates that both religion and spirituality are positively related to health (Hill & Pargament, 2003; Miller & Thoresen, 2003; Powell, Shahabi, & Thoresen, 2003; Seeman, Dubin, & Seeman, 2003), but how this process works is not yet clear. Some researchers hypothesize a direct link between religious beliefs and health, whereas others propose that there is an intervening variable—*meaning.*

73

The search for meaning is essential to guide therapy, because when there is no solution to the problem, as with ambiguous loss, meaning shapes how and whether people cope or are overwhelmed by stress, as well as how and whether people grieve or refuse to grieve. The meaning one attributes to the ambiguous loss also determines whether there is hope or hopelessness. In sum, because of its inherent tie to hope, meaning deeply influences human resilience, health, and survival.

THE SEARCH FOR MEANING

What does *meaning* mean? It means being able to make sense of an event or situation. It means that one can eventually find some logic, coherence, or rational reasoning about what has happened. Human experience is meaningful when it is comprehensible to those who are having the experience. Thus, meaning is both personal and phenomenological.

Without meaning, people cannot really know what the problem is. Without that knowledge, there is no cognition; without cognition, they can't cope and make decisions to move forward. They feel empty. As I work with clients, I am often reminded of T. S. Eliot's *The Hollow Men:* "Shape without form, shade without colour, Paralysed force, gesture without motion."

With ambiguous loss, the problem is labeled as the ambiguity. It blocks cognition and paralyzes the coping process. People understandably have difficulty making sense out of what they are experiencing and the ambivalence they are feeling. Without meaning, actions are robotic; life is colorless. This is akin to what sociologist Max Weber called *anomie,* a phenomenon he associated with the increased likelihood of suicide (Weber, Parsons, & Tawney, 1930). Certainly the frozen grief is associated with depression (Boss, 1999).

Neuropsychologist Victor Frankl[1] theorized that "striving to find a meaning in one's life is the primary motivational force . . ." (1963, p. 154). Making sense of one's life, no matter how dismal or horrific, is the key to human survival. For example, when a person loses hope in some future goal, such as seeing a loved one again, life no longer has meaning, and it is then that the will to live gives way—physically, emotionally, and spiritually (Frankl, 1963). Said another way, without meaning, human resilience is gone.

It appears then that a lack of meaning is dangerous to one's health. Today, empirical research supports what Frankl observed personally in the Nazi concentration camp. Researchers Kiecolt-Glaser and colleagues (1985) and Seeman and colleagues (2003) have found empirical evidence for the link between mind, body, and spirit regarding health. Going a step further,

Powell and colleagues (2003) linked religious spirituality to the reduced risk of death.

This chapter explores the link between the search for meaning and the health and resilience of those experiencing ambiguous loss. The question is how to help people find some positive meaning in their trauma and loss, no matter how nonsensical or horrific. But to answer the question of how people find meaning in the traumatizing incomprehensibility of ambiguous loss, we must first define another type of meaning—the collective meaning that comes from one's family or community.

The Collective Meanings of Family and Community

Because meaning is found relationally, we must consider the idea of context and how an individual's search for meaning may be influenced by talking with family or friends.[2] Again, for many people, the family is more than a biological or legal entity. It may be a broader community of others who suffer from the same kind of loss and trauma, or it may be a friendship network or community that empathizes and provides relational and spiritual support. In such supportive contexts, people can more easily find meaning for the irresolvable losses they must live with.

According to Berger and Luckmann (1966), all meanings are created and maintained through social interaction. Rituals for example are the social constructions in one's culture (Imber-Black & Roberts, 1992). Because meanings are socially constructed and are expressed relationally through language, symbols, rituals, and hopes, it follows that interventions are most effective if they include family and community perceptions. This is because the meaning that one's larger community has for a particular predicament influences individual, couple, and family meanings (Reiss & Oliveri, 1991). Meaning influences the action or inaction—individually and relationally.

In family research, ideas about relational meaning are found in such concepts as Reiss's family paradigms (1981), Antonovsky's sense of coherence (1979, 1987), and Boss's boundary ambiguity (1977, 1999). Patterson and Garwick defined family meanings as: "the interpretations, images, and views that have been collectively constructed by family members as they interact with each other; as they share time, space, and life experience; and as they talk with each other and dialogue about these experiences. They are the family's social construction, the product of their interactions; they belong to no one member, but to the family as a unit" (1994, p. 288). Such references to the existence of a relational construction of meaning remind us again that family is more than a physical entity. It is also a psychological unit based on personal relational perceptions and experiences that shape the meanings we give to a particular traumatic event or situation. Additionally, there may be a relational identity, worldview, and meaning that represent the collective thinking of the family in one's mind. This too may influence meaning for the individual.

With ambiguous loss, the family's identity becomes confused because one of its members is neither in nor out of the system, and the family's worldview may be shattered, especially if they are accustomed to certainty and solving problems. For all these reasons, ambiguous loss is a major challenge to the family's ability to make meaning out of their distress.

Just as inner strength can save people from outward fate, so too can a family's inner strength protect them from the outward forces that create ambiguous losses. Therapists can discover a family's inner strength if they listen more to the collective discourse and observe the systemic interactions. We must not repeat the mistakes of previous therapists who may, for example, have interviewed only the mother to understand her child's symptoms. We must instead see family members within their "family worlds," and hear each family's "conversational voice" if we are to understand the various meanings of a person's illness and care (Garwick et al., 1994; Pollner & McDonald-Wikler, 1985; Reiss, 1981). Ambiguous loss from illness as well as disaster is best understood within a family and community context.

In the 1990s, researchers and therapists increasingly began to go into families' homes, into what Hess and Handel (1959) called the "family world." Today, Jane Gilgun (Gilgun, 1994; Gilgun, Daly, & Handel, 1992), Judith Stacey (1998), and Linda Burton (Burton & Jarrett, 2000) have joined Hess and Handel in reaffirming that people should be studied where they live their lives and with the people they care about in their communities. The "real" world of individuals, couples, and families is not found in our clinical offices or in the researcher's laboratory but rather in settings where they naturally interact in daily life. If we cannot go to the home or community to do our work, then at least we must ask about and view individuals within their larger social context.

Being influenced by the worlds outside of our offices is also a reality for professionals. In Kosovo a man shared his story of how he found meaning in his mother's suffering during World War II by becoming a professional investigator for war crimes. His mother survived rape and torture, but lost 20 members of her family in the Nazi extermination camps. His story was hard to hear, but I could see he was explaining to me how he made some meaning out of the terror in his mother's life. When he finished talking, I asked if his mother's experience had influenced his choice of work. "Yes," he said, "I do this work in honor of my mother." Then he added with emphasis, "Yes! To honor my family, I try to help today's victims." It was evident that this man's difficult work with victims of rape and torture had a positive meaning for him because he was doing it in honor of his mother and lost relatives. Such meaning gave him the resilience to do this difficult work (see *A Village Destroyed*, 2001, by Fred Abrahams, Eric Stover, and Gilles Peress).

THE PHENOMENOLOGY OF MEANING*

If we are to understand personal meaning, we must assess both the external and internal context of the person. Whereas the external context may be assessed rather objectively, the internal is much more subjective. Helping clients find meaning, therefore, also requires the perspective of phenomenology, which values the subjective.

In situations that have no clear resolution, perceptions provide the main window for intervention—what to build on, what to reframe, what to externalize, what to change, and what hopes to revise. With this in mind, I reemphasize what Merleau-Ponty in 1964 called "the primacy of perception," as well as how perceptions mediate stress and trauma (Boss, 1992). Because perceptions are influenced by subjective experience, not just objective data, the following discussion is meant to pique your interest about adding phenomenological thinking to your clinical repertoire. Understand that this way of thinking is compatible with social construction and narrative approaches.

Phenomenology as a Clinical Perspective

Phenomenology is a theoretical perspective that views truth as somewhat relative, but not with all things and not at all times. Phenomenology, then, is the critical study of perceptions.

What is real is based on perceptions, not just on factual and quantified data. Reality, therefore, can also be in the eye of the beholder and in the time of their experience. Phenomenological experience often clashes with what we call "hard" data. As a Midwesterner, I tell this story to illustrate:

Are cows pink? "No," said the realist, "they are black and white or brown." But those of us who have had direct experience with seeing cows know they can be pink. At sunset, when the sky over a country field is rosy and glowing, cows are indeed pink. At that moment and in that particular

---

* Portions of this section are adapted from the chapter, "The Use of Phenomenology for Family Therapy Research: The Search for Meaning," from *Research Methods in Family Therapy*, published by The Guilford Press. ©2005 The Guilford Press.

context, the description of pink for cows is true. This is the phenomeno-logical perspective (Dahl & Boss, 2005).[3]

Artists, musicians, and poets have for ages recorded their interpretations of human relationships using the phenomenological approach. They have always known that truth is relative. As clinicians, we too must be aware of multiple truths, especially when the traumatizing phenomenon is ambiguous loss. When people go missing and bodies can't be found, when loved ones have a mind-robbing illness or any illness with no clear diagnosis, we need to listen to all views. Differing perceptions are stimulated by the phenomenon of ambiguity.

In the sociological context, phenomenology originated more than a century ago in Europe by Edward Husserl, and was brought to the U.S. as other scholars escaped from Europe during the Nazi attempt to annihilate the Jews.[4] Because of the Holocaust, the University of Chicago became the new base for phenomenology. Among the theories that emerged were Erving Goffman's (1959) dramaturgical model and Berger and Luckmann's (1966) sociology of knowledge. Others were labeling theory, existential sociology, sociology of the absurd, symbolic interactionism, and ethnomethodology. Although these perspectives differed from each other, they are for the most part interpretive inquiry. There is emphasis on cultural and political contexts that influence meanings (Dahl & Boss, 2005). What does this mean for therapists? After 9/11, for example, we did indeed work with immigrants and refugees from 60 different countries who spoke 24 different languages. There is no way we could know all that there was to know about each client's cultural context and religious beliefs. We had to listen more and talk less. Meanings were found through collaboration.

With a phenomenological perspective, therapists can utilize subjective information for more effective intervention with a diversity of individuals and groups. Taking a less dogmatic posture about objective truth, we listen more to discern each person's perception of what happened, and we notice the degree of disagreement among the individuals in a couple or family. What are their thoughts about the person who is missing psychologically or physically? Is there disagreement in a couple or family about the lost person's status? Are there perceptions of negative attribution (guilt, blame, shame)? By focusing on perceptions and subjective meanings, the window for intervention is opened. Knowing what the ambiguous loss means for a particular person or family, we can intervene and treat more effectively. When it comes to meaning, each crisis or loss is a different phenomenon; each must be interpreted differently. Random samples of distressed persons or families may not always give us the best answer about how to intervene with a particular person or family.

Working more phenomenologically lowers the hierarchy in therapeutic work in that the client is also a source of knowing. From this perspective, we as therapists can be more effective with persons from cultures, religions, and lifestyles that are unlike our own. The following eight assumptions about phenomenology can guide us in being more sensitive about how we know what we think we know, what we think we need to know, and where we locate ourselves in the therapeutic process. These three categories were introduced in Dahl and Boss (2005), and are expanded here for therapists working with ambiguous loss.

How We Know What We Think We Know

1. *Knowledge is socially constructed and therefore inherently tentative and incomplete.* Truth remains relative and ultimate truth is illusive. The scientific method does not negate this assumption. What this means for therapists is that no matter how well trained and experienced we are, there are instances when we don't have an answer—nor may anyone else. In the absence of facts, the multiple perceptions of family and community members are essential for the social construction of meaning.

2. *Because knowledge is relationally constructed, objects, events, and situations can mean various things to various people in a group.* A catastrophic illness or a terrorist act can, for example, mean "punishment from God" or "a challenge from God to show one's love in a new way." Such conflicting views often occur in one couple, in the same family, or even one person.

   Therapists must elicit the perceptions and views of various people to get the total picture of a particular individual, couple, or family. Although this makes the organizing of a therapy session more complex, in the end it eases the work. It helps us understand the diversity of gender, generation, sexual orientation, ethnicity, and culture inherent in a particular case. In addition, it helps to elicit multiple views of the situation. For example, with divorce and remarriage, it is difficult to get agreement in couples' reports about existing child custody arrangements (Rettig & Dahl, 1993). Asking a couple how many children they have can yield discrepant reports because women often count miscarriages, stillborns, and babies given up for adoption. Such discrepancies often indicate that there were ambiguous losses in the psychological family.

3. *We can "know" through both art and science.* Important knowledge can be gained from stories, songs, and art. For example, richly detailed family of origin stories abound in the embroidery of Hmong refugee women, who, with needle and thread, recorded their families' harrowing escapes from Southeast Asia. Another example is Pablo Picasso's painting *Blue Family,* which shows parents and child in cold blue color, arms around only themselves, all eyes downward, and no connection

between family members. This painting depicts the same phenomenon
described by researcher David Reiss (1981) as a "distance sensitive family." Reiss illustrated distance with an empirically based technical drawing of small separated circles, whereas Picasso painted on canvas what
he felt were symbols of distance and a lack of familial connection. Both
scientist and artist depict the same phenomenon, but from their own
experience, within their own discipline, and through their own modes
of expression.

What this means for clinicians is this: Sometimes after the trauma of
ambiguous loss, the use of music, film, art, or literature can help begin
the therapy, with more cognitive approaches used later. In multiple
family or community settings, music and art can be stimuli for discussions about a common ambiguous loss. The process of facing one's
own traumatic loss sometimes begins more easily when it is once-
removed from one's own experience. Listening to Dvorak's "Going
Home" or seeing the drawings of children after 9/11 helped ready people for their own processes of grieving. Knowledge from both art and
science are critical, but in my experience, artistic truths cut deeper into
one's psyche than the more cognitive information. Both, however, are
necessary for healing trauma and loss.

What We Think We Need to Know

4. *Common, everyday knowledge about relational and family worlds is
   epistemologically important.* Phenomenologists are intensely curious
   about everyday, "taken-for-granted" routines and life-cycle rituals, not
   just relational dysfunction. That is, we are not just curious about epi-
   demiological or diagnostic data but equally curious about ordinary relational life (family dinners, dating, family reunions), as well as the
   rituals that every culture and religion mark in some way (marriages,
   births, deaths).

   Understanding what a couple or family's everyday life is like is necessary for therapists working with trauma and loss. Without knowing
   how clients manage everyday hassles and stressors, we lack knowledge
   about their indicators of resiliency. How do they hold up under stressful and traumatic conditions (Boss, 2002c; Boss et al., 2003)? Therapists,
   of course, are not expected to study nonclinical families, but we can
   read the work of others who study couples and families who remain
   resilient despite trauma and loss. I highly recommend professional peer
   groups to keep up with the research, another way to strengthen professional resilience.

5. *Language and meaning of everyday life are significant.* Rather than referring to the science of linguistics, "the study of family discourse high-

lights how language serves to assign meaning to objects and social conditions" in everyday life (Gubrium & Holstein, 1993, p. 653). The family's language offers information that is symbolically rich in meaning
and information. In sum, we should listen more to what the family says
and how they say it.

From qualitative analysis of couple or family conversations, we see
that there are indeed collective themes and patterns that can be identified and are helpful in treating relational dynamics (Blumer, 1969; Garwick et al., 1994; Patterson & Garwick, 1994). As the primary symbol of
human interaction, the couple or family's language ideally should be
studied where it takes place naturally. In-home family therapy is an opportunity to observe in the natural environment. Although it may be increasing in some areas, it is often not possible for therapists to get away
from their offices to observe and interact with couples and families in
their natural settings. However, we can at least encourage clients to invite the people who are naturally in their lives into some sessions. We
can also learn from the research of others. Developmental psychologist
Linda Burton (2001), for example, spent time in high-risk neighborhoods to study childcare patterns and taught me that professionals cannot generalize about such families. Liebow (1967), Henry (1971), and
Stacey (1998) also studied families in their natural settings, and as with
the Ozzy Osbournes on TV, resilience appears in unexpected places.

If we remain isolated in our own professional worlds and do not in
some way connect with people in their natural community settings, we
do not have all the knowledge we need to see resilience when it
emerges in clients. To know health and resilience, we need to go
where families live their lives.

Where We Locate Ourselves in the Therapeutic Process

6. *We are not separate from the phenomenon we observe and treat.* Our
   feelings, beliefs, values, and responses (about things like equality, mastery over nature, or individualism) influence the questions we ask as
   well as our interpretation of symptoms and responses. Who we are and
   what we believe influences our work.

   Subjectivity is part of who we are. For this reason, a continuing and explicit process of self-reflexivity and self-questioning is a necessary part of
   phenomenological therapeutic work. Reflections are critical during and
   after treating people with the trauma of ambiguous losses. Not only does
   self-reflection help us understand more deeply who we are and thus
   strengthen our own resilience, but it also leads to necessary midstream
   changes that may be needed for more effective or ethical treatment.

7. *Everyday knowledge is shared and held by therapist and patient alike.*
   Common, everyday knowledge is often devalued in professional circles
   even though that is where we may find indicators of resilience. According to Gubrium and Holstein (1993), all persons, common and celebrated, researcher and participant, therapist and client, are considered
   epistemologists. What this means for therapists is that we can learn
   from listening to clients' stories, observing their interactions, and noting
   their feelings (and ours). We contribute to the process by asking questions because the client, not us, can best describe the phenomenon
   they believe is causing their distress. Although an inherent power differential exists, we engage in a collaborative process to find meaning in
   their suffering. We do not negate what ordinary people are saying.
8. *Regardless of approach, bias is inherent in all therapy.* Alvin Gouldner,
   a sociologist of the rebellious 1960s, foreshadowed postmodernism
   when he said that the social sciences were not value-free and that traditional practice and assumptions of objectivity and neutrality were in-
   consistent with emerging social conditions. I believe he saw the need
   for equality in diversity. Gouldner called for a reflexive science that
   was self-consciously self-critical. He insisted that we "raise our flag"
   early in our work to let others know explicitly our values and assumptions (Gouldner, 1970). In the early 1990s, we saw this "raising of the
   flag" by clinical scholars using hermeneutics and critical theory (Goldner, Penn, Sheinberg, & Walker, 1990; Hare-Mustin, 1978; Imber-Black
   & Roberts, 1992; Walters, Carter, Papp, & Silverstein, 1988; Welter-
   Enderlin, 1996).

   For therapists today, this means not slipping back to a time of absolute views. The resulting hierarchy would considerably narrow our
   effectiveness in a multicultural and multiracial society. In therapy and
   supervision, rather than pretending to be objective, I state what I believe but value what others believe even if it differs. The content of our
   beliefs and values, at least for purposes of therapy, is less important
   than our being open and straightforward about them to the client or
   trainee. Of course, in some cases, a referral is needed for a better therapeutic or supervisory fit.

To summarize these eight assumptions, the phenomenological approach
considers how we learn about our clients' condition (truth is socially constructed and includes reactions as well as scientific data), what we need to
know about them (everyday knowledge as well as diagnoses of dysfunction), and collaboration (flatter hierarchy). The people we serve are indeed
a source of our knowing.

All three categories inform meaning and the sources of resilience. The
process is therefore a collaborative one. The knowledge of the people we

treat must never be ignored; it can only enhance our professional effectiveness in strengthening their health and resilience.

WHAT HELPS FIND MEANING?

Victor Frankl (1963) stated meaning could be found in three ways: by per-
forming some act; by experiencing a value such as nature, the arts, religion,
or love; and by one's attitude that suffering is not always preventable. I
agree with Frankl. Actions, values, and attitudes are all needed in the
search for meaning, but the sense of purpose in this process is hinged to
action. Resiliency necessarily implies movement. What therapists need,
however, are specific strategies that can help clients find meaning despite
ambiguous loss. Whatever your discipline, the following techniques offer
you a useful repertoire for your particular work. In my own practice, I prepare myself to use all of these ideas, but I first observe and listen to determine which are relevant for a particular case. Assuming that there will be
some commonality and difference across families and communities, I build
on the previous phenomenological assumptions with the following list of
what helps people find meaning in the trauma of ambiguous loss.

- Naming the problem
- Dialectical thinking
- Religion and spirituality
- Forgiveness
- Small good works
- Rituals
- Positive attribution
- Sacrifice for a greater good or love
- Perceiving suffering as inevitable
- Hope

Each of these items is fully discussed under "Guidelines for Intervention"
(page 90). The guidelines there, and throughout this book, are not hard and
fast rules but rather theoretical guidelines for the specific work you do with
people traumatized by ambiguous loss.

WHAT HINDERS?

It is also important to know what blocks the process of finding meaning
after traumatic loss. We must be aware of barriers at the outset because they
will sabotage or block therapy and interventions. In my experience, the following barriers occur often with ambiguous losses and must be overcome

in order to find meaning and resilience. I give examples of how each barrier could be overcome, but these are just suggestions. Using the ideas presented here, you may devise your own ways to deal with these barriers in your own professional work. Religious and secular interventions will, of course, differ, but they can nevertheless incorporate these same general ideas.

Hate and Revenge

Whether in divorce or at war, people who are suffering from ambiguous losses and harbor passionate hatred and desire for revenge are not yet ready to find a positive meaning. Hate and revenge make people rigid and thus block resiliency. I tell a story of extreme hateful feelings, but the ideas can be applied to warring couples as well.

My greatest challenge came in postwar Kosovo, in the area of Pristina, where longtime enemies, the Serbs and Albanians, coexisted in the same region in a brittle détente. In the room where I gave a workshop to professionals and family leaders, the hate and rage were palpable. It was not until the second day that discussion began. An Albanian woman stood up and said, "And now, I have a question. No one else might ask it, but I am a strong woman, so I will. You said trust begins with sharing honest feelings. So I ask this. What should I do with the hate?" This was from a mother who had witnessed her daughter being shot 17 times by the Serbs. My answer to her courageous question was imperfect, but it was a start: "The hate may not go away, but you might be able to balance the hate with some positive feelings. This will take great strength. You will not forget your anger and pain, but you can find a way to live without being paralyzed by such feelings. They block your real strength. Try holding two opposing ideas in your mind." I held up my two fists. "This one is the hate, and I know you don't want to let that go right now." I held up my other fist. "This side represents strength and resilience. It can gradually grow upward to balance the hate side. Strength means taking care of your other children, taking care of your own health, connecting with others, and participating in treatment groups for posttraumatic stress. Gradually this resilience side can get stronger— stronger even than the hate side." I shifted the lower fist to move up gradually to surpass the level of the fist that symbolized hate. Because of language constraints, they saw what I meant better from this demonstration than from my words.

I concluded, as I would with a contentious divorcing couple: "Your real strength now, real resilience, lies in moving beyond your hate. Try to develop a side of you that outweighs the hate, because hate is an emotion that eventually erodes health and well-being. Above all, it is not good to raise children in an environment of hate." In Kosovo, however, I had gone too far. The response was, "Why not? How else will we get our children to know the evil things done to us?" I should not have been surprised by this challenge because I often get it from fighting couples as well. But whether it is conflict in the family or between religious and ethnic groups, I stand by my view: It is not good for children to be raised in an environment of hate and desire for revenge.

Nonetheless, hate continues. I use a metaphor in therapy. It is like climbing a mountain to get to know your enemy. You start with one step at a time. Small steps. Find some common ground, even if it is something small. Go slowly. When you feel you are ready, move to another step. Later, perhaps, you can share a greeting or some food together. By connecting to one person, rather than to a group, we often can lessen hate more easily. Even if we cannot forget, we can forgive. This is another quality of resilience.

Therapists can't take the pain away from traumatized people in conflict, but we can offer options and ways to balance the hate with resilience. Perhaps the best contemporary example of how to reconcile with an enemy is South Africa's Truth and Reconciliation Court, which offers innovative meetings of the victim's family and perpetrator to offer the truth about the missing person's fate and in some cases the location of his or her body, something the family members want more than revenge (London, 1995). In exchange for truth telling, the perpetrator often goes free, for the mother and father now have the information they yearned for to clear up the ambiguity of their son's status as dead or alive. They now have the comfort of knowing where the remains can be found. Such answers are indeed not perfect, but they do provide a much better option than continued hate and revenge.

In more common therapeutic situations, I adapt these ideas for warring couples or families where the children are being ignored or torn apart. Even here, truth and reconciliation methods work.

Secrets

Family secrets shape meanings (Imber Black, 1993), but when loved ones are missing the secret can severely skew family interactions and relationships. Because keeping secrets about loss and trauma require rigidity, resilience is blocked. For example, therapists discovered parents who, a year after 9/11, still had not told the children that the other parent was probably dead. The intervention then became helping them to give up the secret.

The little girl who was told without explanation the day after 9/11 to call her aunt "Mommy" was finally told the truth; the teenagers who were told their father was working in another state were finally told he was killed in the World Trade Center attack. Carlos Sluzki (1990) found the same phenomenon of secretiveness in a case he worked with in Argentina. He used symbolism therapeutically to label the aunt and uncle with paper badges as "honorary Mom" and "honorary Dad," who now committed themselves to be parents for these children whose real parents had disappeared.

The therapeutic goal of opening secrets should be centered on the long-range shifting of perceptions and meaning so that the grief process can begin and the family can reconstruct itself knowing the truth about the situation. Of course, this strategy is inappropriate if there is a chance that the absent person could return. In cases of divorce, incarceration, hospitalization, foster care, adoption, and even desertion, I recommend telling children and teenagers about the ambiguity of the missing person's status and then helping them to find meaning as best they can depending on their age.

With ambiguous loss, rather than keeping it secret, I recommend simply telling children and other relatives that the whereabouts and status of the absent person are unclear. This can be done in a clinical session or at home. Family members, young and old, struggle with the lack of information, but they accept the truth of ambiguity better than later finding there was a secret. Children ultimately tend to see the cover-up as betrayal. For this reason, I encourage parents to be truthful. "I don't know where your mother is. I don't know whether your father is dead or alive. I know that your knowing we don't know is terribly stressful, but I didn't want to tell you anything that isn't true. Meanwhile, I will take care of you until we get more information." Not all information needs to be shared, however. I don't recommend, for example, revealing details about torture, rape, or abuse to children. When they are older, they may want a fuller story.

Violent and Sudden Death

Finding meaning is difficult when loved ones have met violent deaths or disappearances. Armour, a social work researcher, found that families of murder victims resist finding meaning but, importantly, express "an intense pursuit of what matters" to them (2002, p. 378). What matters is often seeking justice. That may not sound like meaning, but it is meaningful action. I saw similar reactions in families with persons with sudden head injuries after violent auto accidents, many of them made even more senseless by the fact that the accident was caused by a drunk driver. Such traumatic losses are real challenges to loved ones, and although they never reach a *rational* meaning, actions in pursuing something that "matters to them," often in the honor of the killed or wounded person, are resiliency. With meaningful action about something that matters, there is hope for a new future and better health.

Ultimately, meaning may emerge in the pursuit of something else that matters (Armour, 2002). Working with families of victims murdered in the terrorist attacks of 9/11, I found that finding meaning through actions such as rituals and artistic expression worked better than asking them to find meaning in the abstract. Actions speak louder than words and may be more therapeutic when grief and rage paralyze.

Disillusionment

Frankl (1963) identified the three stages of disillusionment. The first was clinging to the hope that things might not be so bad after all. The second was a mind-numbing apathy and emotional death. The third was the recognition that a new meaning had to be found if the suffering was to end. I see this same dynamic in clients who were sexually abused, battered, or raped in war or in more familiar settings, sometimes within the family. In therapy, we determine at what stage they are and move from there toward meaning and hope. The process is like a Möbius strip. Without hope there is no meaning, and without meaning there is no hope. (This is addressed further in Chapter 9.)

THERAPY METHODS AND GUIDELINES FOR FINDING MEANING

Finding meaning is especially difficult when the loss is shrouded in ambiguity. In such cases, asking clients to understand is beyond reason. That their view of the situation will never make sense is valid, but even this is a kind of meaning. When the ambiguity can't be changed, the window for therapeutic change lies in helping clients change their perceptions. By shifting from self-blame, guilt, or feelings of revenge to more positive interpretations, people are more likely to find meaning, resiliency and health.

Our purpose as therapists is not to take the pain of ambiguous loss away but rather to make human existence with it more meaningful and therefore hopeful. The reality of human relational life is, after all, adapting to change, not stasis. With ambiguous loss, change must be made without the benefit of clear information, so the dialectical, systemic, and narrative approaches are basic to all interventions for treating the trauma of ambiguous loss.

These three core approaches do not exclude other approaches, but they are privileged in shaping intervention for this unique kind of loss.

Narrative

Although psychoeducational approaches are also used to infuse information for perceptual shifts, ultimately the communal sharing of narratives helps people to find meaning. Interacting with others, clients develop flexibility and resilience as others encourage new ideas and change. This is needed for the meaning-making process. Anderson and Goolishian (1992) called the narrative approach *interested inquiry*; White and Epston (1990) called it *reauthoring lives*; Friedman and Fanger (1991) called it *positive possibilities*; and Lipchik (1993) called it *balancing the both/and for change*. All are relevant with ambiguous loss.

In our family meetings after 9/11, parents, adolescents, and children told us that hearing and telling stories about the missing person helped begin the healing process (Boss, 2004b; Boss et al., 2003). The narrative traditions we used in these family meetings merged ideas from European "talk therapy" with tribal storytelling traditions. Utilizing the diverse training and cultural beliefs of the therapists on our team, plus the diversity of the families, we merged ideas from Sigmund Freud, Melanie Klein (1984), and Nelson Mandela (2002) to promote resilience. We began the family meetings by asking the adults, teenagers, and children to share a story about their missing person and encouraged family members to listen to each other's differing views. If destructive "no-talk" rules had begun to develop at home and children thought they couldn't talk about their missing parents or relatives for fear of making others cry, storytelling during the community family meetings broke the impasse. Adults, too, had difficulty telling their story to the children for fear of making them cry, but in a group setting it was easier to find support and thus overcome the reluctance to speak or express feelings. Teenagers often preferred different ways of expression. For example, three adolescent girls—the daughter and nieces of a missing worker—offered to sing several songs about courage and overcoming loss. As they sang a capella for the parents and children in the union hall, I could see from the sidelines how their vocalized story soothed singers and listeners alike (Boss, 2004b; Boss et al., 2003).

Dialectical

When working therapeutically with families facing ambiguous loss, the both/and approach is essential. In the absence of clear information, we cannot say, for example, that a person is dead or not dead, or here or not here. With both/and thinking, people can understand more easily that a loved one on a respirator, but brain dead, is both gone and not gone, or that the person with Alzheimer's disease is both here and not here. Such situations call for dialectical interventions. Surprisingly, family members pick up this way of thinking quite readily once they know about its possibilities for living with such painful situations. Whatever your clinical discipline, I recommend the both/and approach for finding meaning, as there may be no other way to gain the resilience needed to deal with ambiguous loss.

Systemic (Family and Community)

Just as resilience is a process that continues over the life course, finding meaning is a process that occurs over time. Since the terrorism in Oklahoma and 9/11, the ongoing bombings in Israel, and the war in Iraq, professionals are learning that the spouses and children of the surviving traumatized victims are major components in trauma treatment. The mate and family also need help—preventive help. They need information about how to build and sustain resilience enough to live with and care for a loved one who is traumatized. But couple and family work is rarely provided. A critical incident worker after 9/11 asked me how I could stand all those children in the room where I was working with families of the missing. Clearly, not everyone is suited for systemic work. But, as I have repeatedly stressed, treatment and intervention for the trauma of ambiguous loss must include couples, families, and the community. In times of trouble, it will be the community's assumptions that help a family and its members carry on with day-to-day actions and problem solving. The community frame (Reiss & Oliveri, 1991) influences family and individual perceptions. If meanings are shared, the stress of ambiguity and uncertainty is more easily managed. Using a community approach thus helps people to maintain strength despite troubled times.

Most helpful after 9/11 was grouping multiple families together in a familiar community setting—in this case, the union hall. Sitting in circles so that they could hear each other's stories and form connections through common experience, the bereaved began to connect. "Did that happen to you, too?" Those frozen with confusion and rage talked more easily with others who also had missing family members. Many eventually exchanged phone numbers and continue to meet to this day. Grandparents offered help. Multiple family meetings proved to be a highly effective intervention for helping the remaining parents and their children move on with their family and community lives. Together the widows helped each other find new hope for their future and their children's futures.

The Therapeutic Relationship

The idea of meaning is central in therapy after loss and trauma because without meaning, there is no hope. Without hope, apathy fills the void. Because of this, the therapy and therapeutic relationship must shift to a more collaborative endeavor between therapist and client. The perceptions of clients and patients count as knowledge, too. The therapist should listen to the clients' interpretations of the problem that brought them to therapy. Assessment includes not just symptom diagnosis but also the phenomeno-logical interpretation of each person's experience of therapy as well as of the traumatic experience.

Concretely, what this means for the therapeutic relationship is that the heal-ing hierarchy is flatter. It means that as therapists, we have more variables to consider—the diagnostic facts plus the clients' versions of their stories. Also with more phenomenological approaches, we do not limit ourselves to one person's view, and we consider developmental, cultural, and environmental contexts. From the perspective of social construction, meaning is collabora-tively constructed and reconstructed as relationships and perceptions change (Gergen, 1994). With ambiguous loss, the goal of intervention is the joint cre-ation of meaning, through discourse, symbolic interactions, rituals, and the telling and reframing of stories amongst loved ones and community in a safe setting.

Gergen (1994) suggested that the goal of therapy is transcendence beyond the narrative. What does this kind of transcending movement mean for the therapist? We do not set as a goal a point where families will reconstruct a true reality of their ambiguous relationships. This is not possible. Instead, we help them find meaning—or meaningful action—to reconstruct new hopes and dreams for their future. As Gergen wrote, narrative constructions "remain fluid—open to the shifting tides of relationship" (1994, p. 249). Indeed, being able to shift when there is ambiguous loss is essential for resilience.

Guidelines for Intervention

Although there is no hierarchical order to this list of guidelines, naming the source of stress is the first step.

Naming the Problem

Labeling the problem as ambiguity helps people begin their coping process. Knowing what the problem is, they are better able to move for-ward, make decisions, and gradually make sense of what they are experi-encing. Frankl said it another way: "Suffering ceases to be suffering as soon as we form a clear and precise picture of it" (1963, p. 117). Paradoxically, finding a precise name for the paralyzing stress people with ambiguous loss endure is a way to give them more understanding, and thus resilience, so that they can move forward despite uncertainty.

Novelist and poet Ray Bradbury wrote about things that can't be solved but nevertheless can be witnessed and celebrated. While he was referring to earth and universe, I write about ambiguous loss, a thing that cannot be solved but also is not witnessed or acknowledged through ceremony or rituals of burial. An essential part of the witnessing, then, is the therapist, the clergy, and medical professionals. In the absence of official frames, professionals can label what the mate or family is suffering as ambiguous loss. Once the phenomenon they feel has a name, they can begin the process of finding meaning in it. The unanswered questions they must live with can begin to make sense.

Dialectical Thinking
I begin with a cognitive approach, suggesting that it is possible to hold two opposing ideas in one's mind at the same time: The missing person is gone, but also still present. Adding psychodynamic approaches, we talk about what is irretrievably lost and grieve that part. We then talk about what is still present of that person to celebrate—his or her ideas, work, the symbols of the person's life, the rituals the person loved and would want continued, and sometimes the physical features now seen in others. For many people, this is a new way of thinking and a real test of resilience.

In 1974, when I worked with the families of missing pilots in Southeast Asia, I learned that meaning would not emerge from a winner-take-all competition to declare who was absolutely right and who was absolutely wrong. Meaning does not emerge in such contests. When people are viewed as either angels or evildoers, the search for a positive meaning is lost in the rush to absolutes. The meaning of ambiguous loss that promotes growth and resilience comes instead from a confluence of perceptions that eventually lead to the same end—learning to live with the ambiguity in a positive way.

After 9/11, there were numerous examples of naturally resilient family members who, without the benefit of therapy, held two conflicting ideas about missing family members. For example, the father of an electrician who worked in the World Trade Center said, "My son has been missing so long now, he's probably dead, but I feel he's here with me and always will be." Six months after the attack, a young mother said, "I am moving forward now with my life, for the sake of the children, but I'm not ready to give up hope of finding my husband, his body." Such dialectical thinking indicates a resilience that begins the healing process even while confusion persists. The only way out of the emotional dilemma of not having a body to bury is to recognize the persisting importance of both ideas: "I must move on and organize life without my loved one, but at the same time, I can hope." Incidentally, the father's son was never found. And only the torso of the young woman's husband was found. For her, that clarity brought solace.

Religion and Spirituality

Many people find meaning after the trauma of ambiguous loss through faith in God. Others find meaning as emerging from a spirituality that allows an acceptance and comfort with ambiguity. Still others find meaning through nature or the arts—places where opposing truths often coexist. Many say they find meaning in traumatic loss by listening to the music of Bach. For me, it is Mahler who brings meaning to the paradox of absence and presence.

Being able to help clients connect with the spiritual part of their lives can be beneficial in therapy (Kersting, 2003). But how do we discuss ideas about religion and spirituality with clients who come from cultures or religions unlike our own? What should we as therapists do ethically, let's say, in a public hospital, school, or clinical setting with no denominational affiliation? Even if we are not trained as religious teachers or spiritual counselors, is it ethical to have prayer during a sessions, help clients find ways to pray outside of sessions, lead spiritual journeying, discuss ways of forgiving, or use Biblical texts to reinforce healthy mental and emotional habits or interactions?

Although I am cautious about overstepping professional boundaries, I have used some religious approaches in my practice at times. For example, with two brothers who were deeply religious and were suing each other over the family business, I reflected on the Old Testament stories of Cain and Abel. What did that story mean to them? How did they see their story ending? Talking about Cain and Abel was a way to externalize their conflict over property and move the discourse to a more symbolic level. Tempers were calmed. With female clients who see power as unfeminine, I refer them to the strong women of the Bible, such as Deborah and Ruth, who exemplify female empowerment. In such contexts, referring to religious stories and even specific texts can be helpful and appropriate.

An idea that frequently comes up in therapy is forgiveness for a loss that has occurred. Depending on the couple or family's beliefs and values, I may again refer to spiritual stories or parables from the East or West. In Kosovo, where loved ones were kidnapped in the late 1990s and retribution was on most everyone's mind, I asked Albanian Muslims if the concept of forgiveness was in their religion. They said it was but were aghast that forgiveness might become a therapeutic goal. They were just beginning to see the meaning of living in peace with former enemies.

In more ordinary settings of training and supervision, I ask about perceptions of death and the meaning an unclear loss may have. With trainees and supervisees who are Hindu, Christian, Jewish, Muslim, Mormon, Unitarian, and atheist, the training seminars are rich and interesting. Rarely do any of us know about all of these religions, but we can respectfully ask questions and listen for meanings. As supervisors or therapists, our ethical task is to provide a safe environment for such discourse. Because theology is not my area of expertise, I often refer supervisees and clients to their own spiritual communities for answers to their religious questions. I do the same with other questions (e.g., legal and medical) where I am not trained to answer. This is for me a matter of ethics.

Professionals who see clients or trainees from other cultures and ethnicities may want to include in their network of collaborators some clergy as well as native healers or shamans familiar with native interventions, such as the sweat lodge, for spiritual healing.[5]

In the U.S., many find spirituality and religion helpful in shoring up resilience (Dingfelder, 2003; Dittmann, 2003; Kersting, 2003). While researchers call for more study and improved measures, it appears that religious beliefs and spirituality can have positive effects for some people. In my experience with ambiguous loss, I see that religious and spiritual beliefs often increase people's tolerance for unanswered questions and thus promote their resilience. But I have also seen cases in which religious beliefs do just the opposite.

As a therapist, I work with the hypothesis that spirituality and religious belief can promote resiliency and health, but I stay open to variations in beliefs—which indeed I see. It is clearly not my task to proselytize or to denigrate but rather to hear people's perceptions about what their situation means to them, and then build on the positive aspects of their interpretation for health and resilience.

Forgiveness

Frankl laid the groundwork for linking forgiveness and meaning. In the Nazi concentration camps during World War II, he said he experienced kindnesses as well as brutality. Based on his experience, Frankl reconstructed his view of humanity around the competing ideas of *indecency* versus *decency* rather than on concepts of race, ethnicity, or nationality. In this way, he found that he could forgive most of his captors. Frankl explained, "There are two races of men in this world, but only these two—the 'race' of the decent man and the 'race' of the indecent man. Both are found everywhere; they penetrate into all groups of society. No group consists entirely of decent or indecent people" (1963, p.137). I find these ideas helpful in doing therapy with survivors of trauma and loss who are focusing on one religion or race as a defining quality of the enemy or as the enemy itself. By gradually reconstructing one's thinking about revenge and the evilness of everyone in a particular group, forgiveness and a positive meaning for moving forward are possible. I recommend clients start this process with very small steps.

Small Good Works

Losses often don't make sense. Armour (2002), who studies families of homicide victims, recommended small good works. In Kosovo we talked about the pain of seeing loved ones kidnapped by the enemy and still not knowing their fate. What is a small good work or a small good step for such tormented wives and mothers? One mother spoke up: "Coming to this workshop was that for me." The next day she shared other ideas she had thought about overnight. She could help other families with murdered or missing children do the same—do some small positive act. Maybe say "hello" to a mother from the other side.

I confess that this process of finding positive meaning is painfully slow. A great deal of patience is needed. Also, trauma survivors are not always likeable. They tend to be hypervigilant and regularly fluctuate between depression and rage. Professional countertransference abounds (see the Epilogue). For now, I emphasize that it is especially important to be fully present and patient when working with survivors of ambiguous loss. We start small, very small.

Rituals

Rituals are designed to help people find meaning in loss. However, the loss rituals in any religion are for the clearly dead. Once when I discussed ambiguous loss on Canadian radio, a woman from the Yukon wrote, "Our society has rituals in place for those who are dead, but none for those who are dying bit by bit before our eyes." Family members of loved ones missing psychologically or physically are painfully aware that there are no rituals for ambiguous loss. Our task as therapists is to help families to create them. Because rituals, social and religious, give meaning to loss, our therapeutic task is to help people revise the old rituals to continue without the missing person. Rituals are understandably confusing for families when there is ambiguous loss, but this therapeutic work is central in finding meaning. I shall never forget the Goldstein family. A cotherapist and I had met with them in their home to discuss the tension over Grandmother's wanting to go to Florida to visit her sister. Her husband was still alive, but with advanced Alzheimer's disease. If she took a vacation, he would have to be placed in a nursing home while she was gone. Her grown sons thought she was being disloyal, but a grandson spoke up for her. He thought she was working too hard and needed a vacation. After nearly 2 hours, this four-generational family agreed that Grandmother should go to Florida, and that her leaving was not disrespectful of her ill husband. The family stress was eased. It was noon, and a family member said food was ready and invited us to eat with them. Then, from the back of the room, came a loud voice from the grandmother's brother-in-law, an elderly man who had said nothing during the family session. "There will be no sitting shivah here. My brother is still alive." He was right. My cotherapist and I left, and the family ate alone. This experience demonstrated not only the ritualistic meaning of sharing food but also the need for therapists to be alert and sensitive to the fact that family members know best what certain actions mean in their culture.

Positive Attribution

The meaning attributed to a stressful situation such as ambiguous loss can influence outcomes negatively (by creating barriers to healing) or positively (by increasing the desire and momentum for life-enhancing change). For example, if the loss is attributed to an act of God versus to one's own fault, the outcome may be less devastating. On the community level, if what the missing person did was perceived as heroic (as with soldiers and firemen), families seemed to frame the loss more positively. An attribution that is viewed as positive on the individual, family, and community levels is indeed conducive for living with ambiguous loss and buoying resiliency over the long haul. Our therapeutic task is to discover each person's perception of what caused the loss and to mediate the negative attributions as much as possible. (This does not negate taking responsibility when one makes a mistake). Wolin and Wolin (1993) used the term *survivor's pride* to describe one's positive attribution when something bad happens.

Sacrifice for a Greater Good or Love

When people perceive their suffering as a sacrifice for someone they love, it has meaning for them and thus is more bearable. A woman may sacrifice herself to save her children; a soldier may give up his life to save his buddies. For the survivors, seeing someone's death as a sacrifice for the greater good allows for transcendence that strengthens resilience. After 9/11, for example, seeing lost relatives as heroes helped people cope because it helped them understand the situation: "Of course he would fight the hijackers in the plane. That is who he was. We are proud of him." Frankl also wrote about meaning gained through sacrifice. He wrote about not wanting "to die for nothing," suggesting that one's death and suffering should at least have a purpose, such as saving the lives of others if you cannot save your own (1963, p. 133).

To extend the idea of sacrifice, just as there is meaning in suffering to save others, there is meaning in moving forward to honor a loved one. As an expression of love, for example, a new mother whose husband is missing pushes herself to care for her newborn despite her misery. She says she does this only out of love for her husband—and their child. Her love for him gives her the strength she needs to care for the baby and move forward. For some, resilience emanates from love of a religious deity, but for her and many others, the love that strengthens resilience comes from feelings for another person (see Chapter 9).

Perceiving Suffering as Inevitable

To further extend the idea of sacrifice, finding meaning does not mean avoiding suffering. This way of thinking may be foreign to people socialized to master their own destinies and have things their way. When there is ambiguous loss, one's destiny is clouded. The uncertainty can cause suffering. Psychologists are learning more about ways of thinking about control over suffering (Dingfelder, 2003; Wright, 1997). Applying ideas from Eastern thinking to understand suffering in people with depression and mental illness, these researchers proposed that a belief in something permanent (as opposed to change) hinders happiness and increases suffering. In other words, a belief that life has to be the way we are accustomed to having it relieves suffering less than a perception that life changes and that one can adapt. In Buddhist writings, independence and self-sufficiency are barriers to resilience and relief of suffering, whereas in more Westernized cultures, they are values. We strive for self-sufficiency and self-esteem. It may be that focusing on self can make a depressed person feel worse because the suffering is perceived as personal failure. With less self-focus, the depressed person, like the Buddhist monk, can view suffering "as an inevitable part of the human condition" (Dingfelder, 2003, p. 48).

There is, however, a caution in this strategy. When I work with clients, I must be sure that their suffering is truly unavoidable. Sometimes they are in denial (as with addiction) or prefer not having the facts (avoiding genetic tests for illnesses that will be fatal; Boss, 1999). Helping clients reframe their suffering in a more positive light is *not* helpful when there is ambiguity from illnesses that can be treated or other situations that can be ameliorated with treatment and intervention. Determining whether a situation is amenable to change is essential. Helping clients reframe their suffering as inevitable is thus limited to situations that are truly unavoidable, without a cure, and without resolution.

Hope

Finding meaning must include some hope for the future—hope that one can see a loved one again, or be free of pain, or simply find home and family again. When such hopes are dashed, one's meaning in life is also lost. This is when clients are at their most vulnerable. As therapists, we must help people discover new hopes and increase self-care to prevent life-threatening illnesses. To help with the isolation and despair of hopeless situations, I ask a client to bring someone to therapy with them—a friend, a relative, a pet—so that they strengthen their connections in real life outside the therapy office. When hopes are dashed and dreams are lost, our primary task is to help people discover new hope for the future. Having hope for one's future is the culmination of all other strategies for treating loss and trauma. More will be said about this in Chapter 9.

CONCLUSION

Overall, when a loved one's absence or presence remains a mystery, meaning and purpose are essential to find the health and resilience one needs to move on with life. After 9/11, some survivors believed that their loved one's being in the Twin Towers at the time of the attack was predestined or God's will. Many who believed this continue to trust in God to see them through their travails while they move forward with their lives. Other survivors appear to have high levels of tolerance for ambiguity due to inherent personality traits. But the most critical key to resiliency is the ability to hold two opposing ideas at the same time. Whatever path is taken, the search for meaning is much more difficult when a loss is unclear. The capacity to find meaning in ambiguity requires a systemic both/and approach. Sheer self-reliance is not enough to find meaning in such cases.

As clinicians, we must study our own perceptions and meanings from our professional work as well as our personal experiences. We, too, must trust in something or someone outside of ourselves in order to let go of the—dare I say—arrogance that makes us believe we must have all the answers all the time. In this age when solutions to problems are expected, we as well as our clients are struggling to find meaning in uncertainty and ambiguity.

Chapter 5

Tempering Mastery

When we ask how people remain resilient with chronic stress and traumatic loss, their answers are colored by their views of the world and how much control they feel they should have to manage their lives *their* way. This control is illustrated by a concept called *mastery,* a consistent moderator of stress and trauma (Pearlin & Schooler, 1978; Pearlin, Menaghan, Lieberman, & Mullan, 1981). How and if one copes is influenced by a person's beliefs about the value of mastery (the ability to manage one's life) and his or her agency (the ability to exert power when needed to manage one's life). Our resiliency is also influenced by mastery. For example, feeling able to manage one's life can alleviate depression and somatic stress symptoms even when ambiguous loss is long-term. But to maintain resiliency with the ambiguity and uncertainty, we must temper our need for mastery.

Ironically, I began this chapter as my 91-year-old mother, who taught me about mastery, was being recommended for hospice care. A survivor of hard times, she epitomized the use of mastery for resilience and told my three siblings and me as we grew up that if we worked hard enough, we could do anything. In her version of Calvinism, work was equated with moral fiber and would assuredly be rewarded with success. Now, with advanced congestive heart failure, she was working hard to simply master her breathing.

When an elderly parent's health declines, one's sense of mastery erodes as soon as we know we can't change the course of the disease. For me, that time had come. I told my mother that the doctor said her kidneys were now also failing. I was not surprised when she asked, "Well, what can we do to fix this?" I told her the doctors said there was nothing more they could do. She became very quiet. I told her she was doing a good job. She smiled. We both knew she would die soon, and she wanted to do that well, too. But resigning to death is difficult for people accustomed to overcoming problems. With great reluctance and a shaking hand, I signed the papers for my mother's hospice care. Lessons for tempering mastery come at the most unexpected times.

The inability to cure illness and resign to death has always been part of the human trauma from loss, but today both subjective and cultural attitudes influenced by a vast technology tend to strengthen our beliefs in mastery without the caveat that we can't always fix a problem. Feelings of failure can immobilize. If we are socialized and conditioned to value mastery dogmatically, without the caution of tempered moderation, we are poorly prepared to maintain resilience when things don't go our way—or problems have no solutions.

What I have learned from my own experience and from working with many kinds of ambiguous losses is this: The more highly people value being in charge and having things their way, the more distressed they become when a loss has no resolution or closure. Although I value mastery and agree with researchers that it prevents depression and health problems, I also see a need for moderation. We must learn to temper our need for mastery if we are to have resiliency, especially with ambiguous losses.

WHAT IS MASTERY?

Leonard Pearlin, medical sociologist at the University of Maryland's Stress and Health Program[1] defined mastery as having a "sense of control over one's life" (1995, p. 12). His research scale on mastery includes items such as, "I can do just about anything I really set my mind to do"; "There is really no way I can solve some of the problems"; "I have little control over the things that happen to me" (Pearlin & Schooler, 1978, p. 20; also, Gaugler, Zarit, & Pearlin, 2003; Pearlin et al., 1981; Pearlin & Pioli, 2003; Pearlin, Pioli, & McLaughlin, 2001). When I first read this scale, I heard echoes of my mother's Calvinistic advice—work hard, and you can solve your problems and do anything you want to do.

Pearlin's concept of mastery is not the same as self-efficacy and locus of control. Whereas self-efficacy "focuses on the control one exercises over the performance of specific tasks" and locus of control "emphasizes the source of the forces affecting one's life," mastery is "control over such forces regardless of their source" (Pearlin, 1995, p.16). It could be illness or terrorism. Based on this understanding, plus decades of research with people stressed by caregiving for illnesses such as AIDS and Alzheimer's disease, Pearlin clarified the connection between chronic stressors, social forces, and health. Specifically, he provides the base for linking meaning and mastery as he documents how different people attribute different meanings to the same event due to differences in mastery skills, real or imagined (Pearlin, 1995).

Pearlin proposed that mastery is a powerful moderator of stress for two reasons. First, having a sense of control by itself reduces feelings of vulnerability to threatening conditions and, in so doing, also reduces the fear of threatening conditions. Second, mastery can act as a self-fulfilling prophecy. That is, when people feel that they possess control over a threat, they tend to act accordingly and may be more successful in overcoming that threat. Pearlin (1995) calls mastery a liberating quality that frees people to be more experimental and forceful in dealing with life's threats. Given this, a mastery orientation can seed resiliency as it enhances "the scope and vigor of coping" (p. 17).

Valuing mastery too much or too little and ill-timed mastery can however weaken resiliency. That is, insisting on fixing an impossible situation in a particular time frame is paralyzing and can be destructive. An example of too little mastery might be an elderly man who turns to alcohol instead of seeking help for a wife who has Alzheimer's disease and has developed bedsores. An example of too much mastery might be parents who insist that their brain-dead child must be kept on life support even though decades have passed. Try as they may, these family members cannot repair their ambiguous losses. But they can temper their use of mastery to fit time and place.

According to Pearlin (1995), a sense of mastery consistently alleviates depression and somatic stress symptoms. Suggesting resiliency, Pearlin sees mastery as "interventions that people engage in spontaneously and naturalistically on their own behalf" (p. 22). For clinical work with ambiguous loss, this means normalizing people's need for mastery but also helping them temper their needs to higher, lower, or better-timed mastery.

How Does Mastery Relate to Ambiguous Loss and Resiliency?

Based on the research of Kiecolt-Glaser, Dura, Speicher, Trask, and Glaser (1991) and Pearlin (1995), living with a persisting stressor without the moderation of mastery can be dangerous to one's health. In addition, although outcomes vary, personal stress can proliferate into relational stress—family conflict, divorce, and marital conflict (Boss, 2002c; Pearlin, 1995).

Although therapists and researchers have for decades agreed on the dangers of people feeling out of control and without options, there has been little mention of ambiguity as the culprit. The point of this book is that the dangerous condition of helplessness is often induced by situations beyond our control. In such cases, people can only temper their needs for mastering a problem by learning to live with never knowing definitive absence or presence. The point of this chapter is that helplessness is exacerbated when the standard of control is mastery *without moderation*.

I was reminded of untempered mastery just recently in New York as I talked to a young journalist. He asked, "Why aren't we over 9/11 yet?" My answer seemed simplistic: "Because you are trying to get over it." I explained: People can't "get over" such traumatic loss; instead, we need to learn to live with the loss and ambiguity. Seeking closure and getting over it are understandable desires for ending the suffering and getting back to normal, but having it *our* way is unrealistic. Ideas about mastery in a can-do city are forever tempered by 9/11, but the tempering has also strengthened us.

THEORY BASE

To provide you with a new theoretical lens for working with ambiguous loss, I link together concepts from psychiatry, sociology, social psychology, and family therapy. Specifically, earlier theories from sociology and medicine show us that a sense of mastery (as opposed to helplessness) and a sense of coherence and manageability are essential to shield people from depression, somatic illness, and other damaging effects of stress. As noted earlier, in situations of ambiguous loss, people who value mastery too highly are less resilient. Although we all need to retain some level of mastery to avoid helplessness and illness, with ambiguous loss, mastery needs to be modified to retain health. Social psychologist Seligman's ideas merge here with those from sociology and psychiatry.

Martin Seligman (1992) defined learned helplessness as a situation where mastery is extinguished. He found that trauma can be reduced if it is possible to learn that the pain can be controlled; trauma persists if there is uncertainty about whether pain can be controlled (Seligman, 1992). When people are exposed to uncontrollable events and they are unable to remove themselves from the distress (as is the case with ambiguous loss), "Such learning undermines the incentive to respond, and so it produces profound interference with the motivation of instrumental behavior" (1992, p. 74). What this means is that motivation for change is blocked by feelings of helplessness. One's mastery orientation for future stressors is also blocked because, according to Seligman, learned helplessness "produces cognitive distortions" about one's ability to be effective (1992, p. 74).

Seligman, like Frankl and Antonovsky, found that of all the variables that lead to psychosomatic illnesses, one's "exertion of will" instead of "a fatalistic surrender" to the environment may be the most powerful (1992, p.184). Seligman summarized: "The expectation that an outcome is independent of responding (1) reduces the motivation to control the outcome; (2) interferes with learning that responding controls the outcome; and, if the outcome is traumatic, (3) produces fear for as long as the subject is uncertain of the uncontrollability of the outcome, and then produces depression" (1992, pp. 55–56). This means that although some people are more prone to depression and anxiety than others, the perception of helplessness and being out of control can lead to depression and anxiety in even the strongest of people. Such feelings are inherent when there is ambiguous loss.

As you may have noticed, there is a theoretical confluence between Seligman's ideas about helplessness, Pearlin's ideas about mastery, Antonovsky's sense of coherence, and Frankl's meaning making. To these, I add the concept of ambiguous loss because it is a serious challenge to all of the former. Ambiguity fosters the chain of helplessness, incoherence, unmanageability, meaninglessness, and lack of mastery. Together, they severely block resiliency and health.

Methodological Suppositions

How do we temper mastery for resiliency and health? Seligman (1992) suggested that, when the controllability over aversive events has predictability between effort and outcome, there are anxiety-reducing consequences. This indicates that our methods of intervention and treatment should be aimed at predictability, but this is impossible with ambiguous loss. Clinically, I see families where a loved one is comatose and no one knows if or when the person will wake up; I see families with mental illnesses that manifest with no predictability; I see families of the physically missing who have no information at all. Finding predictability with ambiguous loss is impossible, so how do we intervene?

For treatment, tempering one's sense of mastery means softening what mastery (and helplessness) means. People start at different places, and their sense of mastery is influenced by culture, gender, class, and health status. The poor and underprivileged have little control over their lives. But rich or poor, the people who suffer incurable illnesses say they feel more distressed by the loss of control over their lives than from the illness itself. In many cultures, women have less mastery over their lives than do men, yet African-American women tell me they often feel pressured, to the detriment of their health, to live up to the cultural expectation of being always strong.

Being male, however, does not always guarantee mastery either. Race, class, and health status may trump gender.

WHAT HELPS TEMPER MASTERY?

Accepting the inability to solve problems or ease pain can be difficult for professionals. With ambiguous loss, the goal changes—both for clients and the professionals who work with them. When the preferred solution is impossible, the goal instead is to temper one's need for mastery. This means being able to accept an imperfect situation. It requires immense flexibility and the belief that one is choosing to accept and live with the ambiguity rather than continuing to perceive oneself as being the helpless victim of it. Whether the needs for mastery stem from race, class, health status, socialization, religious beliefs, or psychological predisposition, clinicians need to assess the capacity of clients—and ourselves—to live with ambiguous losses. The overall goal is learning to live well despite the lack of closure and imperfect absence and presence. Following is a list of what helps to temper mastery. Each item is discussed in depth under "Guidelines for Intervention" on page 107.

- Recognizing that the world is not always just and fair
- Recognizing where views of mastery originate
- Externalizing the blame
- Decreasing self-blame
- Identifying past competencies
- Managing and making decisions
- Increasing success experiences
- Softening attribution
- Accepting (sometimes) what will not change
- Having (sometimes) a sense of invincibility
- Knowing the exceptions
- Reconstructing rituals
- Mastering one's internal self

WHAT HINDERS?

As mentioned earlier, if people value mastery too highly, they become brittle and without resilience. Nevertheless, human beings need some degree of predictability between effort and outcome in their lives and their relational environment if they are to maintain hope for the future. Our therapeutic goal is to moderate expectations of mastery that are too high or too low. This does not mean devaluing mastery but rather moderating it. The barriers are:

Too Much Mastery

Seeking perfection is often the manifestation of too much desire for mastery and control. Perfect absence or presence are rare under ordinary circumstances; with ambiguous loss, they are surely an unattainable goal. Seeking absolute absence or presence hinders the process of learning to live with ambiguity and thus weakens resiliency.

Too Little Mastery

Being passive or fatalistic is often a manifestation of too little desire for mastery and control. Waiting for a miraculous intervention instead of mobilizing active coping strategies is unrealistic and may lead to depression and health problems. Active coping, which implies some use of mastery skills, is optimal for health and resiliency.

Ill-timed Use of Mastery

In the early stages of life-threatening illness or disaster, it is useful to actively seek out cures and solutions. Mastery-oriented skills and behaviors are useful to discover every possible means to solve the problem. As time passes, however, one needs to re-assess the probability of a cure or solution and gradually shift to more acceptance of the situation.

Belief That One's Efforts Will Always Result in the Desired Outcome

Although optimism is highly valued, there is little resilience in a belief that one's efforts will always guarantee the desired outcome. With ambiguous loss, going through life without a "Plan B" sets one up for disillusionment and feelings of failure. Believing that one's investment will lead to the desired outcome prevents the tempering of mastery and is a barrier to resiliency.

Belief That Bad Things Cannot Happen to Good People

We can hope that good things will happen to us if we work hard and are moral, but there is no guarantee this will be true all the time and for everyone. If we rigidly hold onto the assumption that bad things happen to only bad people, we end up blaming the victim—ourselves or others who are experiencing the misfortune of ambiguous loss. Believing too strongly that bad things never happen to good people prevents tempering mastery and is a barrier to resiliency.

Blaming Oneself or Others for Not Being Able to Solve the Problem

Blaming oneself or others in one's relational network for the ambiguous loss blocks one's natural social support system from being mobilized. Blame becomes a barrier between the individual and the other people they care about. Self-blame becomes a barrier to tempering mastery and resiliency because it paralyzes an individual with guilt and shame.

THERAPY METHODS AND GUIDELINES FOR TEMPERING MASTERY

To temper mastery, stories should only be told voluntarily in the company of familiar and trusted others. That is often one's family or community. A too rigidly scripted format for debriefing that keeps individuals away from their loved ones, and child and parents separated, will lower mastery and thus increase feelings of helplessness. The people experiencing the trauma should help select the people they want to tell their story to, as well as the time to tell it.

For tempering mastery after ambiguous loss, I recommend using narrative means (White & Epston, 1990). Although reconstructing cognitions through storytelling helps people adjust their relational methods of problem solving, decision making, role assigning, and formulating expectations after loss, the narrative approach also provides a much-needed experiential component. What this means is that we also use the narrative lens for tempering the meaning of one's relational experience after trauma and loss. Dickerson, who recommended a broader lens than just cognition when using the narrative approach, stated that "the narrative metaphor situates experience within meaning systems that come from larger cultural narratives. So, the narrative approach then is not cognitive-behavioral so much as it is experience/meaning-performance of life story" (2004, p. 340). It is this more experiential view of the narrative approach that I recommend for tempering mastery during ambiguous loss.

Therapists should use this discourse to determine each individual's expectations for mastery and control, to determine people's perceptions of options/choices, and to determine the collective view, if there is one. This will shed light on whose views carry the most and least weight in swaying an individual's perception of blame as well as choices. In other words, such discourse can reveal any power dynamics that need to be tempered if someone is being made to feel helpless and cornered. In such cases, we can increase mastery by listening for evidence of resiliency and competence in people's stories—by charting and making explicit their past experiences that illustrate mastery and competency. When stories illustrate ill-timed efforts at mastery or too much persistence at trying to solve the problem, it is useful to have people tell their story in a new way by imagining how they could have perceived and managed the situation differently or how they might manage it in the future. The main goal is to demonstrate successful mastery—the ability to temper it to maintain resiliency and health.

Through the use of storytelling and narrative discourse, we can determine individuals' and families' beliefs and values about being in charge and having control over their destinies. Did they ever live with ambiguity before? How did they manage? How did they stay in charge of their lives when finding a solution was not possible? Generally, if people's past history has been one of learning to live with ambiguity, it is easier to do so the second time around. Accustomed to ambiguity and uncontrollability, others learn from their stories of survival and growth.

Increase Human Connection, Not Separation

After trauma and loss, the feeling of being connected to loved ones is essential for healing. Treatment should never interfere with such connections. Crisis and grief counselors need to include relational networks, or the victim's *natural social network* (Groopman, 2004). The best approach, then, is to join a familiar and trusted community group—family, close friends, and familiar clergy.

To avoid relational splits between mates and family members, mediate the conflict about the ambiguous loss. Increase tolerance for conflicting views about the absent person. Help them restructure roles, rules, and boundaries, but maintain flexibility in case the absent person returns. Conflicts and family splits can be avoided only with patience from family members and professionals about understandable disagreements in perceptions during this stressful time of ambiguity. When answers about the status of a loved one are not forthcoming, or remain blurred, the therapeutic goal is to help couples and families stay together despite their different perceptions about the ambiguous loss.

The Therapeutic Relationship

What this means for clinicians is that our clients' perceptions matter. We need to ask how they see their ability to manage the trauma of ambiguous loss. Do they think they can change its course? Do they feel they still have some mastery over their situation? Have their perceptions of mastery changed over time? Has their meaning of it changed? Does their culture or environment influence their sense of mastery? People in poverty or without language skills, for example, experience less power and control over their lives. Perceptions of powerlessness also may stem from family of origin issues or from past traumas that keep a person in a victimized state rather than in an empowered mode. Regardless of whether they are based on things real or imagined, perceptions about mastery can help shape intervention individually and relationally.

Professionals also must temper their need for mastery when clients face untenable situations of loss. After 9/11, I found journalists, TV producers, executives, and even therapists who were impatient and even irritated with the families, friends, and coworkers of the missing because they could not find closure. The lack of closure made many therapists feel as if they had not done their job well. I was asked repeatedly, "Why can't these people see there's no one alive anymore?" That's the point! They were not able to *see* a body, so they had no clear evidence of death. They kept hoping for a miracle. And now and then, someone did turn up alive—in the hospital or in a foreign country—just enough times to keep hundreds of families hoping.

It is often difficult for me to understand why there is so little empathy for clients who refuse closure until I realize that the discomfort of not knowing and not being able to master a situation is rarely discussed in professional training. Yet unanswered questions are a constant part of the clinical issues we see—with traumatized people, uprooted families, the newly fired and unemployed, with family caregivers for incurable illnesses or conditions. Our own discomfort when a client's problem has no solution is rarely addressed. Our training instead has been to cure or heal. If we too rigidly hold on to this perspective, our inability to take away a client's pain is considered a therapeutic failure. Tempering mastery means considering that much in our work, and in life, remains unknown and unresolved.

Our own self-study is the first step in tempering mastery. To increase empathy for clients' lack of mastery, we must recognize our own situations of imperfection. By studying ourselves and our own relationships first, we are better able to empathize with clients and understand their distress. More is said about self-study in the Epilogue.

Guidelines for Intervention

Following are recommendations for helping people temper their sense of mastery to avoid feelings of helplessness with outcomes of depression and somatic illnesses. Although this list assumes some commonalities across couples and families, your specific interventions must be tailor-made to fit the diversity in your particular practice.

Recognizing That the World Is Not Always Just and Fair

Many people in our culture believe that the world is just and fair (Lerner, 1971; Lerner & Simmons, 1966). That is, they believe that they have control and mastery over what happens to them, including from the external environment. According to Festinger (1957), for us to hold this belief, we must also believe in an objective fit between effort and outcome—and in the viability of this fit for *all* people. When this belief in justness and the assumption of mastery is accepted, people who suffer loss can be viewed as somehow deserving what they get. Furthermore, if we believe that good people are expected to master any event that happens to them or their loved ones, the inability to heal or solve a loss is viewed as failure and deserving of blame. Therefore, our first task in trauma intervention is most often to say to survivors that the loss—and the ambiguity—are not their fault.

Recognizing Where Views of Mastery Originate

Context, environment, and culture matter in tempering mastery for living with ambiguous loss. When people have already been robbed of their power by some outside force (torture, rape, incest, abuse, poverty, stigmatization, prejudice, second-class status), insisting on an admission of powerlessness is not fair. For example, North American Indians are often reluctant to do this and use sweat lodges rather than 12-step programs for addiction treatment. In Minnesota, there are now separate treatment strategies for women, adolescents, and North American Indians, all with less emphasis on relinquishing power and more emphasis on cognitive empowerment. Such shifts in treatment approaches indicate that the professional community is also tempering their value of mastery.

Context includes the impact of diversity, so gender and racial differences must be taken into account when assessing a client's sense of mastery. Pearlin and Schooler (1978) measured mastery and found that in comparison to women, men reported higher psychosocial resources that gave them greater resilience and resistance to life's stressors. For the most part in this world today, men still have more agency than women, especially if the women are at-home caregivers for children, the sick, and the dying. Instead of asking already-disenfranchised people to surrender power, I begin with small issues such as giving them choices about times to come to therapy or asking them whom they wish to include.

The broader issues are: Where do ideas about fatalism and *destino* originate? Which came first—mastery or fatalism? Do clients' fatalistic beliefs prevent them from coping, or does their lack of resources foster a fatalistic belief system as an adaptation? Although a fatalistic belief system may be functional in the short term when a loss occurs and nothing can be done to reverse it, the same belief system may be dysfunctional in the long term because it reinforces the status quo. People may survive, but their circumstances will not improve if there is no openess to change.

Believing that one's family or community has mastery over a situation of loss aids the process of developing active behaviors to manage the event or stimulate a revolution in the family that will change things (Boss, 2002c). With fatalism, professionals must be aware that such views can originate from cultural and situational circumstances beyond the individual's control or psyche.

Externalizing the Blame

Regardless of worldview, it is helpful to individuals, couples, and families if a professional can attribute their feelings of helplessness and lack of mastery to an external culprit—in this case, the ambiguity surrounding their loss. After the trauma from ambiguous loss, people often say, "If only I had done this or done that." Our therapeutic task is to externalize the blame. The next step is to shift one's view of fault for not having done a good enough job.

Decreasing Self-Blame

Another way people can moderate their sense of mastery is by shifting their view of self-blame. A young widow in New York told me that she blamed herself for not waking her husband at 6 A.M. on the morning of 9/11 when his alarm didn't go off. Because he left late for work, he found himself inside the Trade Center when the tower collapsed. For the first 2 years, she blamed herself, despite the fact that her husband had set the alarm clock incorrectly. When I spoke with her on the second anniversary of 9/11, she had tempered her view. She said she no longer saw her husband's death as her failure to wake him up but rather as his desire to have just one more hour with her and the family that fateful morning before he was killed.

Identifying Past Competencies

Look for evidence of past resiliency. Just as a person's past history of feeling helpless may make it difficult to maintain hope, a person's past history of tempering mastery makes it easier to do a second time. Stories of past competencies may come from the client or from others. This is the advantage of group work. I also recommend having grandparents and other elders present in a narrative intervention group so that they can add their stories of competent coping. If the group has no stories, I gather them from literature. For example, I have used the story of two old Inuit women who survived abandonment from their own children in an Arctic winter (Wallis, 1993). We also learn from others who have successfully weathered what we are now experiencing. For example, when I was caring for my mother in her declining years, I learned much from friends and colleagues who already had done long-distance caregiving and had done it well, without deleterious effects to their own health. Although we can learn from our own experiences, we also learn much from hearing about the experiences of others who have gone before us with the same kind of ambiguous loss.

Managing and Making Decisions

The ongoing trauma of ambiguous loss wears out people. Their sense of mastery, individually and as a couple or family, erodes not only because of psychological reasons but also because of the sheer physical exhaustion that comes from feeling one has no control. Clinical issues then legitimately include time- and stress-management issues, as well as how to get more help, more support, more sleep, and more recreation. Peer groups or multiple family groups may be useful. Homebound caregivers can be empowered by social and informational groups, but we may need to meet with their family in order for the caregiver to be relieved by others to attend such groups and have such outings.

Increasing Success Experiences

After loss and trauma, it is essential to gradually replace responses that fuel helplessness with empowering behaviors. When people learn that trauma is clearly uncontrollable, "fear gives way to depression" (Seligman, 1992, p. 74). With ambiguous loss, the situation is inherently uncontrollable, and depression is often an outcome. Encourage activities that can be easily mastered—small steps that help people regain a feeling of competence. To increase success, isolation should shift to social connection, helplessness to believing one can do something to change things, and confusion to a trust in the world as coherent and manageable. The goals of recovery and empowerment are to find and construct options, information, social support, and some new hopes and dreams (Boss, 2002c).

Softening Attribution

What people perceive to be the cause of their traumatic loss affects their view of mastery versus helplessness. Rigid and harsh attributions must be softened. Depending on their ethnic or religious backgrounds, people may attribute loss and trauma to God's will, fatalism, or bad luck. They may too rigidly believe they had no influence in what happened or in its prevention, or they may too rigidly see themselves as the whole cause of it. Although attributing loss and trauma to destiny can interfere with social and environmental change, a more accepting belief system often fosters resilience in people with little access to resources (Kagitcibasi, 1983)—or clear information (Boss, 2002).

Accepting (sometimes) What Will Not Change

We must never be sanguine about poverty and people without resources. Nevertheless, when there is no rescue from the suffering, as with ambiguous loss, people need stories about how others have accepted powerlessness over adversity. By acceptance, I do not mean giving in but rather deciding with volition to accept the situation. Acceptance then, is a kind of tempering one's need for mastery. In narrative therapy, we need to differentiate stories of helplessness from stories of acceptance. If people decide to accept and live with ambiguous loss, they are no longer passive victims of ambiguity. They are no longer helpless. Making decisions about how to memorialize a missing person, for example, is acceptance, not helplessness. Problem solving for survival is also resiliency. Sometimes, if it is conducive to health, acting out what one thinks his or her fate may be can also be a way to temper mastery.

As noted earlier, people without resources are accustomed to having little mastery, and people of means and privilege are accustomed to having things go their way. Both have to temper their value of mastery, but in different directions. With the poor, we may coach them to use community services and networks more. With the privileged, we may help them redirect their management skills and shift their desired outcome. For example, when a young woman died of breast cancer, her sister, a corporate executive who excelled in mastery, wrestled with her inability to save her sister's life. Ultimately, she found a way to help—not her sister, but other women. She organized and still today manages the most successful annual fund raising event for breast cancer research in the upper Midwest. She tempered her need for mastery by shifting her managerial skills toward a new meaning of hope.

We need stories of how people survive dangerous situations by staying in charge of some part of life. Sadly, many films and stories today are about heroes who win all and bad guys who lose all. Real life is not that absolute. Good guys suffer too, but hopefully they learn to be resilient by redefining what it means to win and overcome. It is not always aggression that wins out. This was beautifully illustrated in the film *The Pianist* (Polanski, 2002). The protagonist, a gifted professional pianist, accepts the need to hide from the Nazis and secretly lives in vacated apartments where he cannot make a sound without alerting others to his presence. Under the most horrific of circumstances, the pianist survives because he stays hidden, but at the same time, he remains in control of a part of his existence: When he couldn't play a real piano, he imagined one and played notes in the air.

Having (sometimes) a Sense of Invincibility

In other cases, people need a sense of invincibility. The soldier going into battle and the cancer patient beginning chemotherapy, for example, need a sense of mastery if they are to cope with their situation. Although it may not be helpful to deny our mortality and failures in everyday life, when people are facing overwhelming odds it does become helpful. Denial of the threat of death and reliance on one's skills and hope can promote safety in battle. For prisoners of war or the oppressed, passivity may be a lifesaving choice, but even then, we encourage some small action that sustains mastery. Prisoners of war tap messages on the walls between cells to maintain a network of communication for life support; a hostage kept for years in solitary confinement purposely misses the urinal just to get back at his captors. Others, as years of captivity drag on, build houses or manage farms in their minds. Others memorize the Bible. Such actions, real or imagined, help to sustain human mastery—and thus hope—in the most confining and inhumane situations.

Knowing the Exceptions

When there is addiction, an exaggerated sense of invincibility is not conducive to recovery and health. To shape treatment strategies and interventions, therapists must first assess clients' beliefs and values about how much control they have over their lives. In many cases, mastery over addiction is gained by admitting powerlessness over it. There are, of course, exceptions. For people who are already dependent, stigmatized, or victimized by external forces, admitting powerlessness may not be effective. Instead, the focus may need to be on finding power. When I visited with North American Indians from Barrow, Alaska; Duluth, Minnesota; and Montreal, Quebec, they told me about treatment that uses a more contextual view—finding self mastery over addiction by reconnecting to one's tribal community.

Reconstructing Rituals

When there are no rituals to help normalize the trauma from ambiguous loss, we help clients to create one that corresponds with their beliefs and values. For example, when people don't have a body to bury and the religious institution's rules are that there can be no funeral without a body, we help clients to be creative and assertive about creating a new ritual. It can also be helpful to ask religious groups or authorities to be more flexible about rituals in such times of disaster. In New York after 9/11, many were.

Authorities who keep the rituals must temper their need for mastery to help people cope with missing loved ones.

Mastering One's Internal Self

When the outside world is unmanageable, as with ambiguous loss, learning how to manage one's inner world is helpful and stress-reducing. One's subjective sense of control is more important than one's objective control of the situation. When a situation can't be changed realistically, we can reinterpret it in such a way that it is no longer perceived as immobilizing (Mandler, 1993). In other words, a positive interpretation can change negative arousal. Shifting mastery from trying to control one's environment and the people in it to controlling one's inner self is a redefinition of mastery that must be added to the coping repertoire for ambiguous loss.

At MIT, Western scientists and Tibetan Buddhists are collaborating to learn more about mastering negative stress (Dingfelder, 2003). Whereas research psychologists study the mind by observing others empirically, Tibetan monks spend their lives studying their own minds. Their meditative knowledge provides them with a unique type of resilience—inner mastery. The Buddhists do not view negative emotions as inevitable but rather see such stress-producing emotions as preventable. Western psychology tends to focus on emotional control *after* a person is already feeling the negative emotions, whereas Buddhism emphasizes preempting negative emotions *before* they emerge. This is called mindfulness meditation (Ekman, 2003).

The preemptive nature of meditative techniques to master stress has relevance for learning how to live with ambiguity and loss. The commonly accepted idea in psychology, based on a Western view of mastery, is that we need to know what the problem is before we can cope with it (Lazarus, 1966). But with meditation, people learn how to resist taking in distressing thoughts before they even know that there is a problem. Assumptions that people can't cope without knowing the facts need to be adjusted, especially for situations of ambiguous loss. Buddhists and many other spiritual thinkers are neither traumatized nor stymied by unanswered questions.

The following anonymous Zen story illustrates how our need for control can cause trouble if we are rigid and without resiliency in our way of thinking. A man was enjoying himself on a river at dusk. He saw another boat coming down the river toward him. He yelled to tell the captain to watch out and turn aside, but the boat just continued its course toward him, faster and faster. He stood up in his boat, screamed, and shook his fists, but the boat smashed into him nevertheless. In that final moment he saw that it was an empty boat. The lesson: There are a lot of empty boats out there. Instead of screaming and shaking your fists at them, let them open your mind.

CONCLUSION

When people no longer believe they have influence over their own lives, resilience is depleted and health is jeopardized. We must remember, however, that context influences views about mastery and that situations of loss and trauma call for different levels of it. What this means is that therapists must pay attention to research findings about the average and at the same time see the phenomenology of the individual or single case differences.

With ambiguous loss, mastering a problem is not possible. This requires a new look at mastery and strategies to temper its value and use. When we witness the pain and suffering caused by loved ones who are missing in mind or body, we must be aware that the same event often means different things to different people, depending on gender, generation, culture, and experience. The classic grief and PTSD therapies are not sufficient. When clients no longer have a sense of mastery or manageability in their lives, our task is to help them reconstruct helplessness to avoid hopelessness. People have the power to shape how they respond to the trauma of ambiguous loss. This is tempering mastery.

Chapter 6

Reconstructing Identity

When loved ones are absent in body or mind, people understandably become confused about identity. One's former status and roles no longer fit; confusion abounds. A woman whose husband has physically vanished wonders if she is a wife or a widow. A man whose mother has Alzheimer's disease wonders if he is now her parent instead of her son. Such situations can traumatize unless people are able to reconstruct who they are.

Knowing who we are in relation to partially absent or present family members requires cognitive and emotional reconstructions of roles, status, boundaries, and rituals. It is this ability to revise one's identity in relation to the physical and psychological family that fosters resiliency. To help reconstruct identity after ambiguous loss, clients can ask themselves the following questions: Who am I now? Who is really my family now? What roles am I expected to perform now? To what community do I now belong? Where is home? Although such identity questions must be grappled with individually, the process is essentially relational. Couple and family members struggle together to renegotiate and reconstruct identities and roles to accommodate for the missing person.

IDENTITY AND AMBIGUOUS LOSS

Ambiguous loss can cause the loss of identity for both patient and family member, for the imprisoned and those left behind. The trauma from the ambiguity disrupts everyone's ability to think clearly about who they are and what they are expected to do. This relational dynamic leads to identity

115

confusion. Symptoms may include uncertainty, indecision, inattention, and lack of concentration—symptoms that are often interpreted as signs of depression. In the case of ambiguous loss, these symptoms reflect a form of mental blocking that is externally caused. The confusion about who one is or what role to play is not the fault of the client but rather stems from the ambiguous context.

Reconstructed labels for people often reflect the reconstruction of identity after ambiguous loss. After divorce, for example, people take on such identities (and roles) as ex-spouse, coparent, single parent, or noncustodial parent. After leaving a religious order, people become ex-nuns or ex-priests as their identity shifts. If a woman gives up her baby upon birth, her identity officially shifts to birth mother, implying that there will be another kind of mother involved through adoption or foster care. In all these cases, the adjective before the noun revamps the person's identity, roles, and relationship to others. Even though psychological ties may persist, when people leave their relationships, they must revise who they perceive themselves to be. This is essential for resiliency and health.

Definitions

Identity is defined here as knowing who one is and what roles one will play in relation to others in the family and community. People also define themselves in relation to how others define them. The process is interactional. A clear identity represents a stage of psychosocial development in which adolescents seek a coherent sense of self, including the role they will play in society (Erikson, 1950; Papalia, Olds, Feldman, 2004). But when ambiguous losses occur, identity confusion becomes a normal response to an abnormal situation. People of all ages find they need to reconstruct who they are in order to function.

Normally, as people mature, they are able to revise their identities to bring into alignment their perceptions of who they are with their standards of who they should be (Burke, 1991; Burke & Reitzes, 1991). With ambiguous loss, people can't do this. Not being able to clarify their loss, they can't bring their perceptions of who they are into line with personal, familial, and community expectations. Not knowing who they are or what they are expected to do in relation to a physically or psychologically missing family member, their identity remains in limbo and they feel increasingly confused and ambivalent.

The good news is that although symptoms of ambiguous loss are externally caused and outside of personal control, people can be helped to internally reconstruct their sense of themselves in relation to others. Although the task is more traumatic when there is ambiguous loss, the maintenance of health depends on the resiliency to be able to tolerate an identity that is not quite clear—and may never be.

Erikson wrote about patients saying "I don't know who I am" (Piers & Landau, 1979, p. 176) and their search for identity. He defined this lifelong search as having confidence in one's inner continuity amid change (1950). What he denied, however, was the impossibility of continuity. How can people maintain continuity when they don't know for sure if a loved one is in or out of their lives? I often hear people say: "How do I continue to live with a ghost?" "How long am I expected to wait for a reunion?" Or, "Dead or alive, I just want them back." When the loss is psychological from dementia or brain injury, I hear: "There is no one home inside of him anymore; I no longer have a father." "My wife is still here, but I am no longer married."

A single person can have multiple forms of identity that are distinguishable and yet interrelated. One can be a parent, child, spouse, breadwinner, and caregiver all at the same time. The roles are distinguishable but interrelated in that they compete for time and energy. For example, caring for an elder with Alzheimer's disease or a brain-injured child competes with the identities of wife, mother, and breadwinner for time and energy. Indeed, people who take on such multiple identities must examine how to do this without eroding their resources for resilience. As an ambiguous loss demands identity shifts, the stress can threaten identity development in other relationships. We see this, for example, when a marriage falters due to the pressures of caregiving. The challenge for people who increasingly must carry multiple identities is to reconstruct their identities to fit the needs of the situation and the complexity of their lives and other relationships.

Individual Identity

Psychoanalyst Erik Erikson defined individual identity as confidence and clarity in one's inner continuity amidst change (1968). So defined, identity is a theory of self (Elkind, 1998). From the ambiguous loss perspective, however, identity is a relational concept. It is one's understanding of who one is, what roles to play, and what status and agency one holds.

Erik Erikson's own life, more than his theory, illustrates the impact of ambiguous losses on the search for identity in complex life situations. His biological father, a Dane, abandoned his mother before he was born. She, Karla Abrahamsen, was a young Jewish woman who later married Dr. Theodor Homberger, Erik's German pediatrician. Erik was given the name Homberger and his biological paternity was kept secret. Looking Nordic but being Jewish, he was rebuffed in school by his Nordic classmates *and* in his father's synagogue where he was called "the goy." "Erikson's exploration of the effects on the individual of ambiguous background and the resulting uncertainty about one's identity—which originated in his personal conflict—and which is an acute problem in contemporary Western civilization—is one of his main contributions to the understanding of individual psychology" (Piers & Landau, 1979, p. 174). In 1932, with the rise of Nazism, Erikson left Germany and came to the U.S., thus experiencing another ambiguous loss—that of an immigrant who loses his homeland. When he applied for American citizenship, he changed his name from his stepfather's to a Nordic name. Why he chose the name Erikson is not clear, but it does suggest his own search for identity amidst the ambiguity of unknown paternity and conflicting cultural and religious heritage in times of Nazi terror.[1]

I recount this story about Erikson only to illustrate the challenging process of reconstructing identity in a world made more complex by multiple ambiguous losses. The disappearance of a biological father, the politics of race and religion, and a lost homeland and family through immigration— these are all examples of ambiguous losses in a career built on the search for identity. The challenge of constructing and reconstructing one's identity, not according to linear stages but rather within a shifting context of family and society, indeed reflects the real-life experiences of many people today.

If the search for identity is successful despite the ambiguity, there will be relatively low levels of stress and no trauma. Immobilization is minimized; resilience is maximized. Rather than reaching a final identity, we accept an ongoing process of both continuity and change. It is the comfortable acceptance of the dialectic that is the essential core of resiliency.

Couple Identity

Couple identity is the subjective sense that two people in an intimate relationship have about themselves as a unit and about their place in the world together. The couple's interactions, not only between each other in the therapy room and at home, but also with others at home and with neighbors and friends, become their identity. Some couples, identified as "Bickersons," bicker over every issue. An example would be George and Martha, the lead couple in *Who's Afraid of Virginia Woolf?* The bickering couple's dance gains momentum and no one stops. When such a couple experiences ambiguous loss, they do not have the resilience to reconstruct who they are and how they are with each other. Although they appear to have great resilience for continuing this dysfunctional interaction, in fact, they are brittle. They cannot shift gears to stop the dance and change to more positive couple interaction. In a circular motion, the negative couple identity influences self-identities and the interaction becomes deeply distressing or traumatic. The wife becomes who her husband thinks she is. The husband becomes who his wife thinks he is.

According to Blumstein, the very nature of intimacy "implies that two people have developed a profound awareness of who the other is" (2001, p. 298). The danger in this is that the couple's identity can harden, as in the dance just described. There is no resilience for changes that occur over the lifespan. In a couple that identifies themselves as hard-working and productive, there is no resilience for aging and retirement. In a couple that prides themselves on never having conflict, the husband is hesitant to confront a wayward wife. In a duo known as the "party couple," neither dares to refuse invitations, despite their exhaustion, lest they lose who they are in the community. None of these couples wants to risk change—and the reconstruction of their identity.

Just as family members may merge a person's behavior and identity (good girl; bad boy), individuals also observe their behavior and make attributions to themselves. This illustrates the dramaturgical view of individuals acting out the parts assigned to them by their families. As Blumstein (2001) asserted, if identities are projected frequently enough, they eventually produce modifications in the self. He called this ossification, a process of rigidification that is so slow and gradual that we only suddenly notice that we have ossified into a particular identity. For example, when one's parent has a stroke, brain injury, or dementia, the family often implicitly assigns the role of caregiver to one family member, usually a female. That person is often expected to give up all other identities. If she complies, she will ossify into the exclusive identity of caregiver. Better than this slide into ossification, which is often detrimental to the caregiver's health, is learning to hold on to multiple identities—wife, mother, friend, and employee— along with caregiving daughter. To continue being a marital partner, for example, while also being a caregiver is not without stress, but is possible if there is flexibility and resilience in both partners.

Family Identity

Psychiatrist and researcher Lyman Wynne, who worked with families of schizophrenic patients, defines family identity as the family's subjective sense of its own continuity over time, its present situation, and its character (Falicov, 1988). This definition is congruent with earlier works on shared belief systems and family themes by Handel (1967), Jackson (1965), Riskin (1963); on family rules by Ford and Herrick (1974); on family myths by Ferreira (1966); and on family paradigms by Reiss (1981) and Reiss, Neiderhiser, Hetherington, and Plomin (2000). Reiss and colleagues (2000) researched the effects of heredity and environment on adolescent development and found that each family creates its own identity or paradigm based on shared assumptions about the world and ways to interact that emerge from heritable as well as environmental influences. This means that each family struggles with the reconstruction of its identity when the external environment involves an ambiguous loss.

To alter family identity, there must be intentional reconstruction of rules, roles, and boundaries. I recall two adult sisters who came in for therapy to change their family identities from that of their family of origin—which they described as an alcoholic family. They explicitly wanted to avoid replicating the way their mother had become a martyr with a husband who drank too much all the time. I invited the mother to come with her daughters to the next session. She did not, but sent word that she would talk with her priest instead. Importantly, she gave her blessing to "her girls working on changing things." With this message, the martyr mother clearly indicated that "her girls" could be different than she was, and that they had her blessing to reconstruct who they were as women and in relation to their own husbands and children. With dyadic and family therapy, her daughters did indeed reconstruct personal and marital identities. To change their family's identity, they learned they also had to change the family culture. Instead of allowing holidays and birthday celebrations to be centered on drinking, they now planned these events without liquor and with the rule of sobriety. They invited their parents to come to their celebrations, but only if they were sober. The mother had always been sober, so her choice was whether to hold the status quo and stay with her husband on the day of the celebration or reconstruct who she was and on some occasions leave him behind. She eventually learned, with the help of her daughters, that she could do that (Boss & Weiner, 1988) and still be a good wife. As time went on, her husband also wanted to attend, and he quelled his drinking and followed the rules set by the daughters. Clearly, individual, couple, and family identity are intertwined in systemic interaction.

Steinglass, Bennett, Wolin, and Reiss (1987), who wrote about the "alcoholic family," defined family identity as the group's shared sense of itself. One wonders how a whole family can be alcoholic, but Steinglass and his colleagues found in their research a dynamic that creates a collective identity. Only one person may be addicted, but other family members adapt in dysfunctional ways by accommodating the drinking behaviors. Diversion from this family pattern is discouraged and the family becomes brittle. When the identity as "alcoholic family" has solidified over time, family members adapt daily routines of mealtime to the drinking, while the drinker adapts to no one. Social activities in the home, housekeeping, and meals are arranged to minimize interference with drinking or hangovers.

Special rituals and celebrations are cancelled or bent to fit the addiction. Such adaptations further reinforce the "alcoholic family identity" (p. 73).

With addiction and other ambiguous losses, therapists can stimulate change and help families make healthier and more functional adaptations—one of which may be to no longer tolerate the behavior and seek treatment. The process toward family health and resiliency begins with the reconstruction of who they are individually and relationally. Through their patterns of interacting, they define identity. If they do not like the identity of "alcoholic family," they must not stop family meals and celebrations to accommodate drinking behavior; the family must not allow alcohol or drugs to be the center of special events and parties (Imber-Black & Roberts, 1992; Steinglass et al., 1987). Through healthier family rituals and celebrations, the family can define who they are and what they stand for—over and above any illness or condition of ambiguous loss.

Community and Tribal Identity
Community and cultural identity refers to a collective view of the world and the group's place in it. The tension and trauma emerge when a person's diverse community identities clash. Take, for example, the Indian families of North America. In the push to assimilate and make them "more European," Indian children were taken from their families as early as age 6 and forced into the federal government boarding schools, often hundreds of miles away from their parents. These children were forbidden to speak their native language or dress and eat "Indian." This inhumane process nearly succeeded in eradicating the identity of the American Indian tribes. Today, there are intentional efforts to relearn what was lost—the language, the ritual dances, the way of dressing, the food, the life in the bush, and the old spirituality. As tribal members reclaim their traditional roles, rules, and values, they are demonstrating how to hold two opposing ideas. While they are reclaiming their tribal family, they are at the same time being patriotic Americans whose young people serve in the U.S. military at a higher rate than any other minority. Their traditionally valued role of warrior was long ago reconstructed for the benefit of country and larger society (Bixler, 1992; Meadows, 2002).

Indeed, there are multiple truths about who we are over time and place. Many American Indians are actively teaching their children to reclaim their elders' tribal identity. They do this to find a personal identity that reflects self-worth and esteem. To become aware of one's cultural identity, I recommend the family of origin work outlined by McGoldrick, Gerson, & Shellenberger (1999) and the cultural mapping outlined by Hardy and Laszloffy (1995) and Keiley and colleagues (2002). Identities are not static, however, so I recommend repeated efforts in doing this work. Whether we are from a particular cultural or racial group, whether we are single, coupled, married, divorced, or widowed, our own identities change as life moves on and brings losses and developmental changes. Ideally, we become more resilient and willing to expand who we are in relation to others.

SOCIAL CONSTRUCTION AS A THEORY BASE

The theory of social construction holds that people's perceptions of who they are (their identity) are shaped by their social relationships. That is, who we are reflects back to us through interactions with significant others. Each person, however, has differing social relationships and experiences, so each person's "truth" about who he or she is in the world differs. Furthermore, based on diverse couple, family, and community contexts, each person's identity requires reconstruction over time as social relationships shift and mature. Interventions for reconstructing identity after ambiguous loss require a theoretical framework that is inclusive of multiple views and multiple truths, not only about the situation but also about the diversity of people whose identities are challenged by ambiguous loss.

Social construction historically has roots in the symbolic interaction of George Herbert Mead (Mead & Strauss, 1956), but most notable to therapists are the classic works of Berger and Luckmann's *The Social Construction of Reality* (1966), Reiss's *The Family's Construction of Reality* (1981), and Kenneth Gergen's *Realties and Relationships* (1994). Family therapy researchers used this perspective to broaden the meaning of family identity and family worldview (Olson & DeFrain, 2003; Patterson & Garwick, 1994). The framework of social construction allows for change over time, as truth is never absolute. As one's relationships and communities are revised, so too must one's identity change.

It is from the perspectives of these authors that I use the framework of social construction to reconstruct relational identity after ambiguous loss. When absence and presence remain a mystery, personal and family identities are uniquely confused. With no facts available and no solution in sight, social construction, with its multiple truths, becomes the theory of choice for deciding who one is and what roles to play.

According to Gergen (1994), there are multiple views of the same situation, but this does not mean that "anything goes." In previous writings, I have agreed with this assumption and said, "Perception matters, but of course it is not all that matters" (Boss, 1992, p. 118). Indeed, facts are also part of reconstructed truth, but it is precisely the lack of facts and scientific evidence that makes identity reconstruction after ambiguous loss so difficult and traumatizing. The situation of ambiguous loss makes us more dependent on perceptions than we would like to be.

Based on Schutz (1962), Gergen (1994) also assumed that people find meaning from interactions influenced by history and culture. Languages and rituals, for example, are products of community. Repetitive patterns are eventually taken for granted and become traditions. To be sure, cultural and historical traditions can be positive influences on shaping human identity, but I have also observed times when cultural traditions are too tightly held and block resiliency. In Kosovo, for example, holding on too tightly to ethnic and religious identity and historical scorekeeping ossified identity to the point where hate was being passed on from generation to generation. If family identity is to have a positive meaning with fewer traumas and more health, someone has to change the destructive patterns of interaction. Although a community's traditional rituals, languages, and ways of interacting are often useful, they may at times have to be reconstructed before families and family members can know who they are in a more positive way despite missing family members. Professionals, who work with increasingly diverse individuals, couples, and families, need to keep an open mind about history and culture. With social construction as a framework for reconstructing identity previously unheard voices can be heard, and their stories can be used for building resiliency.

The social construction perspective is also ideal for work with ambiguous loss because it requires self-reflection by therapists, professionals, and researchers—not just by patients and clients. Guided by the assumptions of social construction, we must constantly be alert to the multiple truths in our singular professional interpretations and diagnoses as we treat people from cultures and histories unlike our own.

With children, the process of reconstructing identity often includes weathering the pressures of parental change. There may be divorce, remarriage, or migration to a new community, so the young need to be able to redefine who they are in relation to their place in the family. Whether a parent is missing from divorce, incarceration, war, or illness, children and adolescents must be helped to resist the premature assignment of identities that are meant to replace the missing parent. For example, well-meaning extended family and community may tell a young boy whose father is missing that he is now "the man of the family"; they may expect a young girl to be the "mother" of her younger siblings when her mother becomes disabled. Such misassigned adult roles lead to further loss and trauma for the overburdened children. They lose their identity as a child and become little adults. Remaining parents must instead lean on other adults and relatives (not children) to socially reconstruct the family's identity, as well as their own.

WHAT HELPS RECONSTRUCT IDENTITY?

This list follows the three developmental tasks suggested by Steinglass and colleagues (1987) for developing relational identity. More will be said about these tasks under "Guidelines for Intervention" on page 131. For now the tasks as I adapt them more generally for revising one's identity after ambiguous loss are: defining family boundaries, selecting major developmental themes, and developing shared values and views. This is what helps to:

Define family boundaries
- Establishing who the family is. Who is in and who is out?
- Reconstructing roles
- Being flexible about gender and generational roles
- Recognizing ex-identities
- Becoming more aware of cultural identities and diversity in individuals and families
- Broadening family rules for problem solving
- Revising family roles and tasks for rituals and celebrations
- Using symbols to indicate reconstructed identity
- Learning a new language for additional identity
- Discouraging intergenerational transmission of hatred of other religious identities
- Uncovering secrets about family identity

Select major developmental themes
- Identifying positive family themes about resilience through genograms (family maps)
- Co-constructing rituals without the lost person
- Exploring themes about gender
- Knowing that sometimes people hide their identities for safety

Develop shared values and views
- Developing a spiritual identity under harsh and uncertain conditions
- Finding choices about family values and identity
- Assuming that the world is not always just and fair
- Modeling dialectical rather than absolute thinking

WHAT HINDERS?

The following factors and conditions hinder the reconstruction of identity after the trauma of ambiguous loss.

Discrimination and Stigma

Among the most deleterious contexts in which to reconstruct identity after the trauma of ambiguous loss are those that stigmatize and discriminate against race, color, class, sexual orientation, disability, gender, age, religion, and culture. At fairly young ages we know where we are on this list and how the community around us views the list. Whether in school, on the job, in the clinic, or at our place of worship, we know early on whether or not a person's identity fits family and community expectations. Schoolmates may yell stigmatizing epithets or ossify identities by labeling—the retard, the jock, the bimbo, the druggie, the nerd. Too often others in the community don't look beyond the prejudiced identities. The problem worsens as the stigmatized persons shape their own identities by how others see and treat them. In this instance, seeing one's self in the eyes of others has a negative influence on identity construction and reconstruction.

According to O'Brien and Kollock, examples of stigmatized identities are the homeless, mental patients, the poor, and people with unpopular religious beliefs, with the most stigmatized identities being "handicapped, homeless, ex-convict, hooker, drug addict, mental patient, [and] welfare recipient" (2001, p. 500). In many communities, stigma still follows the identities of gay, lesbian, bisexual, and transgendered people. Many people of color still face discrimination and the stigma of racial slurs. It is important for professionals to understand that some identities, because they are stigmatized, cause ambiguous losses. Culturally and personally, prejudice can bring shame and the impulse to hide one's authentic identity from others. Interaction is stifled and trust is rare. In this way, stigma and discrimination hinder resilience.

In some cases people who have suffered stigma, prejudice, discrimination, and genocide change their identities to pass as someone other than who they are. Passing as straight, as white, as a man or a woman—all may be related to safety and reconstructing an identity to escape a stigmatized identity (Crawford, 1993; Kroeger, 2003). Whatever the reason, trying to maintain an inauthentic identity strains resiliency and health.

Forced Uprooting

Identity is also challenged when people are forced to uproot and leave their homeland and relatives behind. Due to the dangers or impossibility of returning, refugees and those seeking asylum are cut off from their cultural identity. Hardy and Laszloffy (1995) wrote about loss of cultural identity and the confusion of knowing where home was or who one's family was after the subjugation of slavery. With any kind of forced uprooting from one's homeland, identity needs to be reconstructed. Who are we in this new place? If we become attached to this new land, will we feel guilty? Clinicians must contextualize and normalize the ambivalence and identity confusion and see it as cultural ambiguous loss.

Winona LaDuke, a Mississippi Band Anishinabe, wrote about the legacy of identity confusion due to racial discrimination: "The colonialism in North America, as well as in Central and South America, has been particularly brutal. Historically, it should be characterized as genocide, but we never talk about a North American holocaust. What we talk about are isolated massacres that occurred and Indian people who generally dissipated during the period of Manifest Destiny. It is very sad because, from the standpoint of knowing your history and knowing what the implications of a history are, it is very difficult, as Native or Non-native people, to piece back together what was truth" (Farley, 1993, p. 107).

Isabel Allende, who had to flee from Chile and now lives in California, also wrote about the effects of forced uprooting: "I am not obligated to make a decision: I can have one foot in Chile and another here" (2003, p. 197). "In California I'm a misfit; I wear silk while the rest of the population wears sneakers, and I order beef when everyone else is on a kick for tofu and green tea" (p. 190).

The good news is that many people can and do reconstruct their identities after the trauma of cultural ambiguous loss. Some, like Allende, eventually learn to like the sense of freedom that comes with an identity blurred by forced migration. "I have constructed an idea of my country the way you fit together a jigsaw puzzle, by selecting pieces that fit my design and ignoring the others. . . . I have also created a version of myself that has no nationality, or, more accurately, many nationalities. I don't belong to one land, but to several . . ." (Allende, 2003, p. 178).

Like LaDuke, Allende saw the reconstruction of identity from cultural ambiguous loss as a puzzle in pieces that needs to be put back together. When there is ambiguous loss from forced diasporas and emigration, the reconstruction lies not in one absolute identity but rather in a dialectic of the old and the new. Their words remind us that resilience comes from holding two opposing ideas. Allende saw herself as both Chilean and Californian. LaDuke saw herself as Anishinabe and American. Other descriptors such as Irish-American, Chinese-American, and Mexican-American reflect cultural mergers. Indeed, the dialectic may be all that is possible for people who have left behind loved ones in other countries or islands, or have been left behind themselves. The lesson is that we must take on multiple identities if there is to be resiliency in a new place. The uprooted will hold on to some of the old ways while taking on some of the new. Continuity and change are pieced together.

Isolation and Disconnection

Relational connections are the means to shape a resilient identity. Human connections provide the forum to work through the contradictory ideas and tensions over who we are (and are no longer) in the context of those we love. Staying in isolation hinders this process. Ideally, human connections have histories and futures and thus support the self in the continuing process of constructing and reconstructing identities from youth to old age. Relationships should supply an individual with a position of strength and thus interpersonal motivation to change one's self-presentation as time goes on and circumstances alter. Gaining confidence in who we are as a result of positive interactions with others, we grow more confident that we can cope with the pressures of new environments, new people, and novel situations. When there is ambiguous loss and few facts, being able to reconstruct who one is requires trust in self and others.

Abraham Maslow (1961) suggested that people require adventures and peak experiences as identity markers, and that satisfactory life stories shape identity. But I believe some peak experiences exceed what Maslow called adventure. They are traumatizing and forever painful, even though they may have been satisfying (in that one survived them). When loved ones disappear, the remaining family members must reconstruct who they are, individually and relationally. This process is far more traumatic than Maslow's adventure or peak experience. Remaining isolated hinders the process as missing loved ones disturb relational connections and thus identity.

Hanging on to One Absolute Identity

The process of reconstructing identity after loss requires embracing change while maintaining some historical continuity. This means giving up the idea of one absolute identity. Like puzzle pieces coming together to form a whole, holding multiple views of oneself in relation to past and present strengthens resiliency. The Hmong refugee who was a military leader in his old land becomes a civic leader in his new community to organize vegetable farmers to supply urban markets. The wife of a man with Alzheimer's disease still sees herself as the wife of the competent man she married but also as the head of the family and his caregiver. With both physical and psychological ambiguous losses, rebuilding one's identity requires the tolerance of multiple truths. If one holds on too strongly to an absolute identity of self or family, the inflexibility blocks resiliency. People tend to deny the ailment or situation that causes a mind to be missing, or they prematurely extrude a missing person, acting as if the person is already dead. Without tolerance for ambiguity, the reconstructing of identity in relation to loved ones absent or present is impossible.

Resisting Change

Hanging on to the often-impossible dream of reversing ambiguous losses prevents change and thus weakens resiliency. But changing identities too quickly or saying "anything goes" is also dangerous. The goal instead is to enter into a process of searching for new options about who to be and what to do now but still leave the door open for possibilities that may emerge down the line—including, in some cases, the return of the missing persons (as with adoption or illness in remission).

Rebuilding one's identity after ambiguous loss requires trusting that the stress of change will be less painful than maintaining the status quo. Although many people have experience in risking loss and change in sports arenas or financial markets, fewer know how to shift roles and identities in the midst of unclear loss. After such trauma, the goal is to avoid foreclosure on revising identity. Saying things like, "This is what I was before I lost my kids in the divorce, and this is what I always will be!" is resisting change and a barrier to resiliency.

THERAPY METHODS AND GUIDELINES
FOR RECONSTRUCTING IDENTITY

"Personal stories are not merely a way of telling someone (or oneself) about one's life; they are the means by which identities may be fashioned" (Rosenwald & Ochberg, 1992, p. 1). Clinical methods using personal narratives are based on social construction that emerged from the work of social psychologists George Herbert Mead (Mead & Strauss, 1956), Berger and Luckmann (1966), Reiss (1981), and Gergen (1994). From this perspective, narrative intervention is one of the methods consistently recommended throughout this book. In this chapter, the narrative approach is specifically applied to reconstruct personal and family identity.

The Narrative Tradition

The founders of the narrative tradition in the family therapy field are White and Epston (1990) and Anderson and Goolishian (1992). White and Epston equate resilience with the family's ability to have room for an alternative story or narrative—one that is less pathologizing and externalizes the problem rather than letting it be center stage. When clients refer to their families as "winners" or "losers," and to themselves as "bad" or "good," they frequently have accepted that identity from their larger community. To find a more positive identity or story about oneself or family, a more positive community of listeners who do not blame or shame is essential—another justification for broader systemic therapy.

Today, relational scholars apply the narrative tradition by merging the classic methods of telling one's story to heal with social constructionism (Dickerson, 2004; Fishbane, 2001; Lipchik, 2002; Weingarten, 1994). Compatible are the ideas from Imber-Black and Roberts (1992) concerning family rituals, as well as ideas concerning development (Carter & McGoldrick, 1999; Gilligan, 1982). Yet, whereas maturation and aging make the reconstruction of identity and family rituals a predictable necessity, having an ambiguous loss elevates the need for identity reconstruction to the unexpected and often traumatic.

How do narrative methods help? Because identity is socially constructed, it follows that it must also be socially reconstructed. Telling and listening to stories in interaction with others who suffer the same ambiguous loss sets the stage for one's identity to be relationally expressed through the symbolic interaction of language, rituals, and cultural, gendered, and generational patterns of coping and adaptation. For example, a couple with the ambiguous loss of infertility comes to therapy to understand their distress at not being parents as others in their age group are. Healing comes from the interaction between the spouses as well with other spouses, and through this, they receive relational validation of their ambiguous loss as well as trust that they can move forward with some kind of identity shift even if they remain infertile. Someone raises the idea that they could be generative and nurturing in numerous ways; they have options beyond their own fertility. As with varied types of ambiguous loss, perceptions of physical and psychological relationships—absent or present—are critical in influencing identity and the resiliency to reconstruct it when someone is missing in one's life.

When the narrative method is used in a trusted and familiar family or community setting, traumatized adults, teenagers, and children are more likely to come to therapy. Telling and listening to stories together, voluntarily, and in a safe and familiar setting begins the process of reconstruction

(Boss et al., 2003). Listening to clients tell about a favorite holiday ritual and how there is now an empty chair, and then brainstorming together about how to reconstruct the event, is useful. With a focus on strengths, resilience, and competence, people begin to help each other revise roles, rules, rituals, and boundaries. In so doing, they then discover their own options.

Importantly, clients reconstruct their psychological family. Who is in and who is out now? How is the missing person's presence or absence influencing the roles they now play? Gradually, in interaction with others through the narrative process, identities shift toward resiliency and health.

The Therapeutic Relationship

With ambiguous loss, shifting one's identity to maintain resilience requires multiple truths about absence and presence. This affects the therapeutic relationship because with more than one means to the same end, the process is necessarily collaborative. Neither therapist nor client has the answer. There is no best solution. Closure is impossible. The reconstruction of new identities ideally becomes an integration of who people were before the ambiguous loss and who they must now be in order to overcome the trauma and remain resilient and healthy.

To do this work, therapists and professionals must first reflect on their own identities. When there are no answers and ambiguity dominates our personal relationships, we may feel helpless. In that context, we may have trouble knowing who we are as a competent professional while doing this work with ambiguous loss. For example, therapists who grew up in families where loved ones were lost from the Holocaust or genocide may need to seek supervision or therapy to minimize countertransference. Recognizing the ambiguous losses that confuse our own identities is essential in the process of helping clients to rebuild their identities.

Second, it is important that we not assume that client and therapist hold the same knowledge base. For example, the parenting roles we identify as appropriate for women and men may not be the same in the client's culture. Regardless of our training and method, we as therapists must empathize more with families unlike our own and assume we have some bias in the assessment of their identities. What looks like identity confusion now may have been lifesaving resiliency in the past. Taking on unusual roles may once have been a functional adaptation. To help people shift out of an identity that has become maladaptive, professionals need to be open-minded about diversity. This does not mean that anything goes but rather that there are multiple ways to reach the same end—survival and health.

Finally, compulsory participation in storytelling after the trauma of ambiguous loss is not therapeutic and is unethical. It is our responsibility to set up a structure for therapy that is welcoming to people who are accustomed to telling their stories of pain and trauma in differing ways. Not everyone chooses the couch; many prefer a familiar community and family setting for healing.

Guidelines for Intervention

With methods of narrative and collaborative therapies grounded in social construction, the following therapeutic guidelines amplify what helps the process while mitigating or eliminating what hinders. The goal of therapy for reconstructing identity after ambiguous loss is to make more flexible the relational processes of resiliency so that change is possible. With this unique kind of loss and trauma, the balance between who people were and who they must now become to cope with the ambiguity is anxiety-producing, but clearly less so than not changing.

As stated in the "What Helps" section, I borrow the three developmental tasks suggested by Steinglass and colleagues (1987) to organize my guidelines for reconstructing identity after ambiguous loss. I believe that these three tasks apply to individuals and families adjusting to *all* types of ambiguous loss, not just addiction. The therapeutic questions are: What helps define family boundaries, what helps select major developmental themes, and what helps develop shared values and views?

Clients must first be aware of their perceptions of family membership and boundaries. Who is in and who is out? Is family viewed as the extended family, the community, the tribe, the clan, the nuclear family, or the couple? Are any nonrelatives considered family?

Second, developmental qualities related to enmeshment and differentiation are considered. Is change in family members over the life course tolerated? Does everyone have to be or do the same thing they always did? Can the intensity of family life vary between intimacy and detachment? Can differing identities be tolerated without anyone being ostracized or thrown out of the family circle?

Third, can people trust the world outside their home? Can mates and family members reflect on these matters and evaluate their own experience without feeling defensive? Does each member or partner have the resiliency to determine right and wrong in relational interactions? People must become more aware of their families of origin and any traumatizing history from contextual events (such as war, terrorism, epidemics, natural

and economic disasters, murder, and suicide) that influence present expectations and patterns of interaction. Without intervention to shift to more
functional ways of being together, couples and families who have experienced such catastrophic assaults to identity tend to develop maladaptive
patterns and beliefs that may continue in subsequent generations.

Finally, for all three categories, therapists must urge people to give fuller
stories about who they really are. The individual's or family's description of
their identity with regard to ambiguous loss may be thin or thick. If thin, the
family has decided absolutely what the problem is (Mary is a bad girl; if
only she would straighten up, the family would be fine). Such certainty
closes off other options for change. By asking questions about strengths
rather than pathology, a therapist can thicken client's descriptions and create opportunities for more positive identities to develop. As competence
(rather than badness) becomes central to the reconstructed story, new possibilities and new identities begin to emerge. For example, Michael White
(1989) was questioning a family who had labeled their son as a fire-setter.
In the course of the discussion, they discovered the boy was also a competent young man. In just a 2-hour session, his identity shifted from "bad" to
"responsible," and the family's identity shifted from "shame" to "hope." The
family did not destroy their photo of the shed the boy had burned, but they
no longer considered it proof that their son was bad. Deep descriptions
tend to privilege strength over pathology and thus hope over futility and
shame (White, 1989).

Rather than asking about facts and data, the social constructionist therapist asks clients about their patterns of relating with significant others—
spouses, parents, partners, siblings, friends, coworkers, and so on. Gergen
believes the important questions to ask people are "how do they function,
in which rituals are they essential, what activities are facilitated and what
impeded, who is harmed and who gains by such claims" (1994, p. 53). With
more family and community focus, I provide the following guidelines to set
the stage for narrative interventions with the specific objective of rebuilding
relational identity after the trauma of ambiguous loss.

What Helps Define Family Boundaries?
As said earlier, people must become more aware of their perceptions of family membership. While flexibilty remains important for resiliency, external
and internal boundaries need to be maintained. Are different rules tolerated
between spouses and among family members? Must mates and family members fill the same assigned roles all the time? Can a spouse or child disagree
without being discounted or thrown out? What are some guidelines to
deepen the answers to these questions and find options for change?

Establishing Who the Family Is. Who Is In and Who Is Out?   To reconstruct a new identity, one must first know who the family is. This means
identifying one's psychological family and one's physically present family
to clarify roles, rules, and boundaries for both. For any system to function,
it must be able to maintain its boundaries. Regardless of contextual differences, we must know who is inside our family psychologically and physically as well as who is outside. We must know the people who transverse
our relational boundaries, entering and exiting over time. Spouses may differ in their perceptions; siblings may differ with parents or each other.
There is no absolute answer. Certainly in divorced and stepfamilies, there
are multiple truths. Perceptions change over the years as the cast of charac-
ters and roles in the family change. Who one is changes and takes on multiple and often paradoxical identities. Couples can be divorced and still be
cooperative parents. A child can be a son and stepson at the same family
dinner; remarried newlyweds can be lovers, parents, and stepparents at the
same time.

Reconstructing Roles   Reconstructing identity after trauma and loss
means reviewing and probably reconstructing the meaning of who the
client is, as well as the client's values and beliefs about his or her control of
the situation. Alternatives can be explored in a collaborative search for
what to keep in one's identity and what needs revising. Alternatives are explored relationally. In multiple family groups and in family therapy with
children present, new options emerge more quickly. Role confusion is inherent in remarried families. From the perspective of the children, their parent's new spouse is not their parent but the absent parent is. The new
spouse's identity is challenged. She asks, "Am I a mother of his children or
not?" The children often have similar identity confusion. It affects loyalty.
Conflicts arise. Talking about the normalcy of overlapping boundaries—
even drawing them out—is useful for the reconstruction of role identities in
couples and families experiencing ambiguity in membership.

Being Flexible About Gender and Generational Roles   People need to
see options and choices, not ossification in their identity. This calls for flexibility in roles, rules, and patterns of interacting. For example, flexible gender roles (as opposed to rigidly prescribed roles) are more conducive to
resilience for families under pressure. But often we hear, "In our family we
don't do this; in our town, we don't do this; or we do it this way." When
couples and families are already destabilized by the trauma of ambiguous
loss, such rigidity in roles and expectations only block the identity shifts
that support relational and personal health. When a family has a member
with chronic mental or physical illness, healthy members must find identities

beyond the illness so that they do not become the alcoholic family or the schizophrenic family. Most families see themselves as normal and are surprised and offended by illness identities. I agree with their chagrin. They are trying to manage despite having a family member with an illness that causes relational loss and identity confusion.

When people have resiliency, they do not require rigid gender or generational roles in order to know who they are. They can be the parent of a chronically ill child and still live life with them to the fullest. The balancing act is possible as the blurring of roles and identity continues, often for years. A frail elderly mother may one day treat you like a daughter and the next ask like a child for your help. Both therapist and client, each in their own lives, must reconstruct their own identities as the process of integrating who we were with who we must now be is a reality for everyone.

Recognizing Ex-identities   The reconstruction of who one is requires discussion of one's ex-identities—ex-spouse, ex-mate, ex-priest, ex-nun, ex-military, ex-employee, ex-convict—or any role or status left behind. Ex-identities often result from ambiguous losses—immigration, incarceration, divorce—but even more traumatically, from having a spouse disappear. Survivors suddenly are given the identity of "widow" but without the legal validation of a death certificate. Therapists must ask if the ex-people are perceived as in or out of the family or one's life now. What is their role now? What are the rules about their participation in the family's activities now? Because losing an identity can be as stressful as finding one, the therapeutic emphasis is on integration of the old and new, not absolute change. Because ex-identities all imply transition, the need for integrating who one was with who one is essential. Ebaugh pointed out, "In a very real sense, the process of becoming an ex involves tension between one's past, present, and future" (2001, p. 330). One's previous identity—like a hangover identity—has to be revised into a new role and patterns of relating to others.

After 9/11, our therapeutic goal was to help the families of the missing reconstruct their identities beyond *victim* to that of *competence* and *resiliency*. Since 2001, family meetings as interventions have been held in the labor union hall. Now, nearly 4 years later, the family meetings continue but without the therapists and with more focus on recreation and information than on loss. Adults and children see themselves now beyond the single identity connected to the horror of 9/11. They can talk about how they are families of restaurant workers who belong to a community of strong people who have always bounced back from hard times. Taking on the identities of resilience and competence reflected in stories about their elders and ancestors, they have moved forward despite having had loved ones vanish on that terrible September morning.

Becoming More Aware of Cultural Identities and Diversity in Individuals and Families   The maintenance of family identity depends on the transmission of family culture from one generation to the next through established themes and patterns of interaction that clarify roles, rules, and boundaries. I encourage family members to go outside of their own family boundaries to experience people with identities unlike their own. In therapy we talk about the adventure of getting to know people with different identities. I encourage experiences that extend the client's boundaries—and perceptions—of what individuals, marriages, and families are like in other cultures and regions. Traveling helps, of course, but it does not have to be far—perhaps just down the street. There is diversity in every community, and especially in communities where former competitors or even enemies live side by side.

Oppression and genocide erase family identity. People who have undergone such traumas may feel shameful about having lost the battle. Reclaiming one's cultural identity is the only way to regain pride. Examples of such uprooted people include African-Americans and refugees, who are now reclaiming their identities by melding old ways and rituals with contemporary ones. Healing from loss and trauma in the context of oppression often comes through a spiritual reconnection with the past and the old ways of ancestors. This does not mean rejecting contemporary society but rather including old ways with the new in the reconstruction of lost identity.

Broadening Family Rules for Problem Solving   Stereotypically, families stuck in an outdated identity repeatedly problem solve in the same way. Usually their ways cluster in blaming, shaming, and finding a scapegoat. If anyone disagrees with the established way of thinking, that person is extruded or shunned. Our therapeutic goal is to interrupt rigid types of family rules and problem-solving behaviors by increasing affective expressiveness, self-responsibility, and flexible decision making. Anger management may be required if tempers flare. Psychoeducation is useful for finding more information to make decisions and for negotiating disagreements To bring about shifts in dysfunctional family identity, the family may first have to recognize their dysfunctional interactional patterns. What is the dance? When there is a problem, does each play a predictable role—for example, Dad drinks, Mom reads, and kids go over to a friend's house?

Revising Family Roles and Tasks for Rituals and Celebrations   Developing some spiritual identity deepens personal identity. This is ideally done in family or community settings. Family rituals are the observable behaviors that provide a window for assessing a family's identity. Imber-Black and Roberts (1992) defined rituals as highly structured, repetitive, symbolically rich sequences of behaviors associated with holidays, major family transitions, mealtimes, birthdays, graduations, homecomings, and reunions, as well as with daily problem-solving behaviors.

After ambiguous loss, a major way to reconstruct identity is through the revision and continuation of family rituals. Because interacting in such meaningful ways with others stimulates the reconstruction of personal and family identities after ambiguous loss, early intervention to revise family rituals and relational symbols is essential for regaining resilience. For example, dining out, family meals at home, and birthday and holiday celebrations need reconstructing to accommodate the psychological or physical absences of a family member. This is not an easy task; many people prefer canceling such events. This is maladaptive. The glue of family life, rituals and celebrations must be continued.

Therapists need to ask clients: What helps? What is assumed with this ritual or symbol (e.g., a wedding ring, a birth certificate, a law degree)? What are the symbols of identity and rituals that mark transition to new identities—graduation, baptism, bar mitzvahs, weddings, retirement dinners, funerals? Not knowing if an absent person is returning or not requires talking about who one is, what one is expected to do, and what hopes for the future are realistic given the ambiguous loss. Our clinical task is to help the family reconstruct the rituals and celebrations so they can know what roles to play in order to manage the ambiguity, loss, and trauma. For example, with a soldier deployed to a far off land, the remaining parent plays both father and mother to the children on holidays and birthdays. Regardless of the parent's usual way of dividing up tasks, the remaining parent now takes on the identity of both as head of the family, instrumentally *and* expressively, taking up the role of the other until he or she returns.

There are times, however, when rituals do not take into account the identity confusion and havoc that ambiguous loss plays on marital and family life. When the Trade Towers were burning after 9/11 in New York City, some orthodox Jewish and Islamic men, who knew they were in danger of dying and their bodies never being found, telephoned religious officials to say that they were offering their wives a release from the marriage so that, should the worst happen, the women would not be restricted by tradition as "abandoned" but rather, have the identity of "divorced" and thus free to remarry. They took it upon themselves to prevent identity confusion for their wives. To be sure, although one's identity is influenced by the mirror reflections from relational interactions, the ability to reconstruct identity in the interest of resiliency is often more strongly influenced by the community in which that relationship occurs. Sometimes, this too needs revision.

Using Symbols to Indicate Reconstructed Identity   Our story of ourselves is reflected in the symbols we choose to wear and how we dress. Wedding rings, for example, help the couple and the community to understand their identity as married and unavailable. Hair length and dress are also symbols of identity. Military personnel, rock stars, and clergy often distinguish their identity from others by dressing with symbols of who they are. To help clients change their identities to manage the traumatic stress of ambiguous loss, we may have to ask questions about how they dress now and what will be expected of them as they change roles. If they are preparing for a job, for example, it may be therapeutic to discuss collaboratively how to dress and what symbols are needed to do the work and stay resilient on the job.

Learning a New Language for Additional Identity   Loss of language is a part of losing one's original identity. With the ambiguous loss of immigration and migration, one's mother tongue, the symbol of one's national identity and homeland, is lost. In these cases we help clients use, once again, the both/and approach. That is, we encourage clients to hold on to both languages. When the language of one's childhood is kept alive, identity is enriched, but it must be balanced with learning the language demanded by contemporary society. I tell clients they should be proud of their mother tongue because it is a part of their identity, but also that it is pragmatic and an indication of resiliency to learn the language of the culture in which they now live.

Discouraging Intergenerational Transmission of Hatred of Other Religious Identities   Appealing to the parents' concern for the health of their children may help in this process. Often they seem surprised by the fact that it is not healthy for children to grow up in an atmosphere of vengeance. New options for regaining a prideful identity can be explored. In Kosovo, with Serbian Catholics and Albanian Muslims, we saw such hatred when some of the parents said they had to continue the hate or their children would forget their ethnic identities. What I have learned is that family members in peace and in wartime use extreme measures to maintain identities. To remain the person they are used to being, they may kill, shun, or simply ignore anyone who challenges their status quo. They act as if "the other" is demonized. You are either on their side or an enemy, with no in-between.

Such brittleness indicates a fragile identity without resilience, and it often leads to more violence and killing.

Uncovering Secrets About Family Identity   Family secrets can rigidify identities (Imber-Black, 1993). A family may begin therapy thinking there were never any problems—no drinking, no divorce, no suicide, no incest, no abuse. They have only told the good stories and glamorized the family identity. As storying and restorying proceeds in therapy, family members hear that grandmother was sent to an asylum, that great-grandfather was in jail, that there might have been a suicide or some drinking and abuse. The reality is that all families have both good and bad in them, and that most of us stand somewhere between those two extremes. Recognizing that most people are both saints and sinners enriches individual and family identity and expands their reservoir of resilience.

What Helps Select Major Developmental Themes?

Identifying family themes and patterns of interaction over the life course as well as across the generations will help reveal positive examples of identity reconstruction for resiliency and health. This means that the therapist and clients collaborate to find the family's dominant story and then reconstruct it to find a more positive and strength-based identity.

Identifying Positive Family Themes About Resilience Through Genograms (family maps)   Family activities become the major organizers of family themes across the lifespan. Examples are sports, music, and religion, but whatever theme is chosen tends to determine roles, rules, rituals, and the community with whom the family interacts. Themes such as sports or music often continue across generations. In clinical work, we want to reinforce the positive and life-enhancing themes—the themes of resilience and strength in activities over the generations—and change those that are life-threatening—addiction, violence, abuse, and crime. We begin clinically by asking questions to determine the privileged plot in a story. As an individual, couple, or family, who are they now and who were they historically? Who are they as individuals? Resiliency may be hidden by a dominant story of being victimized or enhanced by a dominant story of strength and optimism with themes like "we shall overcome."

Identity is challenged throughout the lifespan, so I recommend repeated efforts in both family and cultural identity work. Again, I recommend the family of origin work outlined by McGoldrick and colleagues (1999) plus the cultural genogram work of Hardy and Laszloffy (1995).

Co-constructing Rituals Without the Lost Person   Family rituals are a way to express personal and family identity across the life course. While reconstructions often take place during such transitions as one matures, they are especially problematic when relationships are frozen by ambiguous loss. In such cases, helping clients to reconstruct their family rituals experientially helps them reconstruct their identity. Because the focus is on their own family material, there is little reluctance. It may seem trivial to encourage stories about menus and recipes and who will carve the turkey now that father is missing, but these are essential components of identity and an ideal forum for revisions and adaptations.

Exploring Themes About Gender   Historically, the identity of females has involved compliance and silence (Boss, 1996; Elkind, 1998; Gilligan, 1982). Women speak of having no voice for anger or for complaining. Girls, for example, were to be quiet, nice, and compliant. Boys, on the other hand, had permission to disagree or even act out their anger (Taylor, Gilligan, & Sullivan, 1995). Of course, gender inequities that impede female identity development still exist, but today we take the position that the dominant culture may impede a mature identity formation for both boys and girls. For the exploration of new roles and identities after an ambiguous loss, therapists must support the discussion of feelings about taking on new roles and tasks, and what all this means to both genders, old and young. Hopefully, for all family members, the therapeutic process encourages the tolerance of flexible roles for more healthy development despite ambiguous loss.

Knowing That Sometimes People Hide Their Identities for Safety   Professionals must pay special attention to the traumatic aspects of identity when people are stigmatized. For example, gay, lesbian, bisexual, and transsexual individuals—and their families—are often forced to hide their identities. The children of the homeless also often hide their identities in school to avoid teasing. Jewish families in Nazi Germany lived under cover, and some even sent their children to live with Christian families to ensure their safety. But when the danger is past, most families prefer to pass on to their offspring their own cultural identities.

What Helps Develop Shared Values and Views?

To reconstruct one's identity when a loved one is missing, the goal is to become more at ease with the paradox of who they were, who they are now, and who they will become. To lower stress, the therapeutic goal is to develop a spiritual tolerance for not knowing, to discover options for reconstructing identities, and to accept the world's unfairness and see that others also suffer from it. The goal is to become more comfortable with paradox than with dogma.

Developing a Spiritual Identity Under Harsh and Uncertain Conditions Based on cultural and religious identities, people worship in different ways. Spirituality goes beyond religious affiliation, however, and involves a kinship with the world and the others in it. I know farmers who feel spiritual about working the land and being its steward. I once talked with a whaler in Alaska, a small man weighing no more than 120 pounds, who went to sea in an open canoe to kill the whale that now sustains his family in the harsh Barrow winter. He talked of the spiritual process of reading the sea, the ice, the whales, and the boat's movements. It all came together in a spiritual process that he called the circle of life that helps feed his people. Although these examples are from people who live off the land or sea and may seem foreign to people in urban settings, I tell the stories in therapy sessions precisely for their uniqueness. Because they lie outside of client and therapist experience and carry no judgment or proselytizing, the stories are more likely to stimulate thinking about one's own spirituality and how it is or can be integrated into daily roles and identities.

For me, spirituality lies in being able to be comfortable with uncertainty and having trust in ambiguity. Much in life delivers this challenge. With my mastery-oriented socialization and training, I have had to incorporate into my identity a spiritual trust that things will work out even under harsh and uncertain conditions.

Finding Choices About Family Values and Identity   Sometimes a member of a family has values that differ from the others. Just ask the child of an alcoholic whose parents, grandparents, and siblings suffer from addictions. At an early age, this individual learned that getting drunk or high is part of every family holiday and celebration, that being drunk is what the family does, that fun is defined as drinking a lot. The family identity is centered on partying, drinking, being hung over, and then repeating the cycle. When one family member grows uncomfortable with this and finds an identity not centered on drinking, he or she often rebels against the family identity, leaves home, gets thrown out or joins with another group with values more like his or her own—through athletics, religion, scouting, music, theater, the military, college, job, or career. (Unfortunately, some rebel by joining groups that are just as harmful as their families.) Therapists must be aware that rebellion against an unhealthy and dangerous family identity is a good thing. It helps people find new options and choices for more positive identity.

Assuming That the World Is Not Always Just and Fair   Rooted in American psychology, the "just world" theory leaves us with the assumption that if people are good (and moral) they will receive just outcomes. This simply is not so. (Boss, 1999, 2002c; Gergen, 1994; Kushner, 1981). As noted earlier, I talk in therapy about the imperfect relation between one's effort and outcome. Working hard and doing the right thing do not always guarantee a good outcome or solution. Good people can have bad experiences. Good people can have loved ones disappear physically or psychologically. Many have elders whose minds are gone from dementia, or they may have children whom they rarely see due to divorce or estrangement. They may experience the loss of identity and status when their jobs disappear. To avoid blaming the people to whom bad things happen, therapists must collaborate with clients to dispel this myth of effort always matching outcome.

Modeling Dialectical Rather than Absolute Thinking   Identities that require absolute thinking create brittleness rather than resiliency in contexts of ambiguity and uncertainty. Allende (2003) illustrated the envy for certainty but recognized the need for dialectical thinking. She wrote about her husband and then about her own integration of opposing identities: "I envy his certainty. . . . There's a certain freshness and innocence in people who have always lived in one place and can count on witnesses to their passage through the world. In contrast, those of us who have moved on many times develop tough skin out of necessity. Since we lack roots or corroboration of who we are, we must put our trust in memory to give continuity to our lives . . . but memory is always cloudy, we can't trust it. . . . I have absolutely no sense of certainty" (pp. 78–79).

Allende could no longer picture her homeland, Chile, as a precise locale; the landscape was now imagined more like a dream. In order to see her homeland, she had to look into her heart or read the poetry of Pablo Neruda. Artists know well about paradox, and professionals model both/and thinking as they collaborate with clients. New possibilities as well as conflicting truths emerge in the interaction. Narratives that are relational (not individually oriented) open the possibility for conflicting views and thus new possibilities for rebuilding identity after trauma and loss. Family therapy and community groups are therefore highly recommended. Traumatized children are treated with their parents so that we can interrupt the parentification of children's identities and roles; first responders are seen with their spouses and mates to interrupt relational isolation and conflict. First responders may have conflicting identities—firefighter as well as husband and father—and must not be cut off from spouse and family. Both are part of his identity. Tolerance for paradox is the clinical goal for reconstructing individual, couple, and family identities after the trauma of ambiguous loss.

CONCLUSION

The focus in this chapter has been on identity confusion caused by ambiguous loss. Maintaining confidence about one's identity is difficult after
any loss, but it is extraordinarily difficult when that loss is never clear. People understandably want to maintain hope for returning to the status quo,
but at the same time, they must change in order to stay healthy. Not knowing if a loved one is dead or alive, they must reconstruct their relational
identity under the most difficult of circumstances. Therapists can help people revise how they see themselves, what roles they play, and who they see
as their family and community.

Determing who one is, who the family is, and who the community is can
be difficult in the face of ambiguous loss, but it is not impossible if there is
resilience. The continuity that is needed for resiliency comes from being
able to live with both the absence and presence of the people close to us
and in whose reflection we come to know and reknow ourselves.

Chapter 7

Normalizing Ambivalence

Ambiguous loss inevitably leads to ambivalent feelings, emotions, and behaviors toward the missing person and others in the family. With a deficit of information about the whereabouts or status of the absent person, people don't know how to respond and feel torn about what course of action to take. If the ambivalence remains unconscious, overwhelming anxiety and somatic symptoms may result. If the ambivalence is recognized, guilt may follow, especially if one acts out the negative side of ambivalent feelings—for example, anger, hate, or picking a fight with a parent who is terminally ill. The poet, Sharon Olds, illustrates conflicted feelings when she writes, "I wanted to watch my father die because I hated him. Oh, I loved him" (1992, p. 71). Linda Gray Sexton, daughter of poet Anne Sexton, writes of her surprise when she sees her often psychologically absent mother on stage in full presence for the audience. She wrote, "In that moment I hated her and her power absolutely. In that moment I loved her and her power absolutely" (1994, p. 161). Regarding physical absence, Francine du Plessix Gray, described similar mixed emotions after her pilot-father disappeared during World War II. Living with the effects since childhood, she called her ambivalence about finding her missing father as "the astonishing struggle that lasts forever" (personal communication, June 16, 2005). The writings about ambivalence are vast, and span the centuries, but it is our task now to understand the role of ambivalence in the painful human struggle with ambiguous loss (Boss & Kaplan, 2004).

Primarily, normalizing ambivalence means acknowledging its existence. Once recognized, people can and do cope with the tension so that it does not overwhelm. Resiliency depends on knowing that the ambivalence from ambiguous loss is normal and can be managed.

AMBIGUITY AND AMBIVALENCE

In order to see the clinical connection between ambiguity and ambivalence, we first clarify the difference between the two terms (Boss, 1999, 2002c, Boss & Kaplan, 2004).

Ambiguity means a lack of clarity. When the adjective *ambiguous* is used to describe a loss, it means there is no validation or clarification of the loss, and thus a lack of knowing whether the lost person is irretrievably lost or coming back again. Whether the ambiguous loss is physical or psychological, people are painfully aware of the lack of information.

Ambivalence, a term originated by Eugen Blueler (1911), refers to conflicted feelings and emotions. With ambiguous loss, ambivalent emotions can manifest as simultaneous or fluctuating, but in both cases, the emotions are contradictory (e.g., love and hate for a person, attraction and repulsion and wanting a person dead and alive). Torn between two extremes, people experience anxiety, and if the anxiety is not managed, they suffer from traumatizing stress.

Ambiguity feeds ambivalence; ambivalence feeds the uncertainty about which action to follow, which decision to make, which role to play, or which task to perform. Immobilization follows. In this way, ambivalence decreases personal agency and paralyzes relational processes. People may be aware of their ambivalent feelings, but often they are not, especially if the feelings are negative and guilt-producing. If emotions are too horrific to accept (e.g., wishing someone dead), the destructive side of the ambivalence equation often is repressed and goes unrecognized by the client.

Although the focus here is on how ambiguous loss leads to ambivalence, the reverse may also be true. That is, ambivalence can also lead to ambiguous loss. For example, a fiancé's ambivalence about marriage or parenting can lead to ambiguous loss if the female partner is reaching the end of her reproductive years. If a partner is ambivalent about getting married or having a child, his presence in the relationship becomes distressingly unclear. Another example of ambivalence leading to ambiguous loss is when members of a feuding family are so immobilized by conflicted feelings of love and hate that they cannot move forward and reconnect in some way. The ambivalence freezes the healing process, and family members are ambiguously lost to one another forever.

Our focus here, however, is on the external situations of ambiguity that create a psychological ambivalence in individuals. If not recognized, the conflicted feelings erode resilience for people individually and relationally (i.e., for mates, friends, and families). The resulting guilt and indecision freezes grief, coping processes, and relational dynamics.

Professionals can view the problem from various perspectives.[1] From a sociological perspective, the couple or family boundary is no longer maintainable—roles are confused and daily tasks remain undone. Conflict is high. From a psychological perspective, anxiety is high, cognitive and emotional coping are blocked, decisions are delayed, rituals are canceled, and isolation replaces intimate attachments (Boss & Kaplan, 2004). The ambivalence from ambiguous loss is only a problem, however, when it leads to paralyzing guilt, indecisiveness, immobilizing depression, paralyzing anxiety, somatic symptoms, abuse, and life-threatening behaviors.

HOW DOES NORMALIZING AMBIVALENCE RELATE TO RESILIENCE?

Being able to bend and adapt to situations of ambiguity rather than struggle endlessly for answers can minimize the harmful immobilizing effects of ambivalence. But minimizing requires resilience. Guilt can be assuaged by letting people know that wanting a suffering loved one to live and also wishing the person dead is not an unusual response.

Being resilient means recognizing such ambivalent feelings in order to manage them and thereby avoid harmful behaviors that will be regretted later. If the negative side of ambivalence is not recognized and managed, the anxiety becomes overwhelming and leads to trouble, such as generalized anxiety disorder, panic disorders, obsessive-compulsive disorder, PTSD and phobias. Knowing ambivalence can be managed will help normalize the anxiety and guilt that can traumatize after ambiguous loss.

Therapeutic Action

Giving the problem a name—ambiguous loss—and externalizing the cause begins the process of normalizing ambivalence. Both cognitive and psychodynamic therapies (e.g., relational) are needed to continue the process. The voluntary use of narrative methods with trusted others is especially suited to bring unconscious material and the symbolic into awareness. Ambivalence can be assessed directly by asking, "Do you feel torn about this or that?" (Pillemer & Suitor, 2002). Or it can be assessed indirectly through qualitative or psychodynamic interviews. My preference, however, is to assess ambivalence by listening to the stories people tell to each other in family sessions (Boss et al., 2003). After 9/11, the wife of a worker lost in the World Trade Center felt especially guilty about her rage toward her missing husband: "How can I be so mad at my husband; he was a hero who rescued thousands of people. But why did he have to go back into the building to rescue even more? I am so mad at him for not thinking of his kids—and me. I hate him for that. No, I'm sorry I said that. I love him. I'm proud of what he did."

Responses like this are typical from family members of loved ones gone missing physically, but I also hear similar responses when loved ones are brain-injured or ill with dementia. Through telling their story and our witnessing, survivors come to see that they can live with the conflicting feelings and emotions. Their guilt for having the angry feelings lessens. With more understanding and comprehension, coping begins. Although there is never a solution to the puzzle of ambiguous loss, people can and do learn to live with its ambivalence. Seeing it as normal lessens anxiety.

Our therapeutic goal is to help people with ambiguous losses attain what Parker (1995) referred to as *manageable ambivalence* and discover that dealing with ambivalence can be "a source of social creativity" (Lüscher, 2004, p. 28). After ambiguous loss, the problem is not ambivalence but rather being unable to manage the guilt and anxiety it provokes. To prevent pathology and build resilience, then, our task is to help people deal with and manage their anxiety and guilt from the ambivalence that understandably follows ambiguous loss. While tempering is needed, the ability to manage one's ambivalence emerges from agency (Waters, 1994) and what Pearlin and Schooler (1978) called a *sense of mastery*.

THEORY BASE

Not surprisingly, as a therapist concerned about the client's external context, I gained insight into how to normalize the ambivalence from ambiguous loss from sociological theory. The theory of Andrew Weigert (1991) was especially helpful. He, too, distinguished ambiguity from ambivalence, noting that ambiguity is something one knows (cognition), whereas ambivalence is something one feels (emotion). He wrote: "Although both contradictory ideas and contradictory feelings may be experienced together, it is important to distinguish between knowing ambiguity and feeling ambivalence" (1991, p. 42). He emphasized the difference in a way that can guide clinicians attending to a client's knowing (cognition) and feeling (emotion).

From the psychological perspective, we see individuals whose cognitive and emotional coping strategies are blocked by ambivalence. Grief is unresolved; coping processes are blocked; decisions are put on hold; identity is confused; and attachment becomes complicated.

From the sociological perspective, we see the context and social environment in which the individual and his or her family experience trauma from ambiguous loss. We see boundaries, roles, and tasks blocked by the contextual ambiguity. People no longer know whether a member is in or out of their relational circle, and the boundary of the couple or family can no longer be maintained. Roles become confused and daily tasks remain undone.

What psychologists call ambivalence is often a normal reaction to an ambiguous social situation, not an individual pathology. In the case of Alzheimer's disease, adult children may be filled with mutually conflicting thoughts and feelings about their roles and identity. Anticipating even more confusion in how to proceed, they both cling and push away. They often feel guilty because they fluctuate between wanting their parent to both live and die. They both accept and resent the caregiving role, and they may be unclear about the best care for an elderly parent, which now takes time away from their own marital and parenting roles (Boss & Kaplan, 2004).

Whether one is working with individuals, couples, families, or even communities, situations of ambiguous loss provide fertile ground for increased ambivalence at multiple levels, and may or may not be problematic, depending on cognitive awareness, emotional expression, and the resilience to deal with it. Ambivalence does not have to be problematic, but when people do not know who is in or out of their lives, anxiety, guilt, and trauma immobilize relationships and interactions at various levels. For resilience and health, the status, roles, and identities of the people we interact with must be relatively clear and the boundaries of the system must be maintained, albeit with flexibility. In this way, the ambivalence that understandably follows ambiguous loss can be kept at manageable levels and continually reassessed for the duration of the ambiguity.

Methodological Suppositions

Strengthening individuals, couples, and families who are immobilized by ambivalence[2] calls for using both cognitive- and emotion-based coping.[2] I use cognitive and psychoeducational approaches to reduce stress and to strengthen cognitive and problem-focused coping. To find meaning and new hope, I use psychodynamic and relational therapies—what is called emotion-focused coping. Using object relations and other relational approaches aids personal and familial processes to reconstruct identity and attachment. Both emotional and cognitive coping are necessary for strengthening resiliency when there is ambiguous loss.

More is said about the emotion-focused and psychodynamic interventions in Chapters 8, 9, and the Epilogue. What follows here is information of a more didactic nature that is necessary for professionals to understand the link between ambiguous loss and ambivalence. I use this information to guide my own clinical work, as well as in workshops to train therapists, medical professionals, chaplains, and trauma specialists to work with families of people who lost loved ones physically or psychologically.

WHAT HELPS NORMALIZE AMBIVALENCE?

Following is a list of what helps in normalizing ambivalence. Each item is discussed in depth in the section "Guidelines for Intervention" on p. 154.

- Normalizing guilt and negative feelings, but not harmful actions
- Using the arts to increase understanding of ambivalence
- Regaining personal agency
- Reassessing and reconstructing the psychological family
- Seeing the community as family
- Reassigning everyday roles and tasks
- Asking questions about context and situation
- Bringing ambivalent feelings into the open
- Uncovering latent or unconscious ambivalence
- Managing the ambivalence, once aware of it
- Seeing conflict as positive
- Valuing diverse ways of managing ambivalence
- Knowing that closure does not lower ambivalence
- Developing tolerance for tension
- Using cognitive coping strategies

WHAT HINDERS?

It is important to know what hinders the process of normalizing ambivalence that inevitably follows ambiguous loss. The process is blocked if clinicians use only a symptom focus and expect only typical coping strategies and adaptations from couples and families.

Using Only a Symptom Focus

Symptoms of the stress and anxiety of ambivalence are depression and anxiety, and they must, of course, be treated. But the root cause of ambivalence must also be addressed in treatment. A symptom-only focus hinders because noticing the pathology without acknowledging the context of ambiguity negates the opportunity for clients to cognitively recognize their conflicted feelings. After ambiguous loss, the context, not just personal pathology, must be validated as the source of symptoms.

Expecting Typical Coping and Adaptations

If professionals look only for typical and so-called normative ways of coping and adapting, they may add to clients' guilt and shame about unique ways of coping with ambiguity and loss. Seeing only the typical hinders the normalizing of ambivalence in that it misses the possibility of diversity in how people manage ambiguous loss and the conflicted feelings that follow. Professionals need to expand their views of how people manage the nuances of absence and presence.

THERAPY METHODS AND GUIDELINES FOR NORMALIZING AMBIVALENCE

As noted, both cognitive and emotion-based interventions are needed in the process of normalizing the ambivalence that follows ambiguous loss. The therapist must also work on both psychodynamic and cognitive levels. This means the therapist must be fully present to do the work, as well as be aware of the professional debate on conscious and unconscious processes for stress reduction and self-protection when feelings are conflicted.

Being Fully Present

In her clinical work with survivors of trauma, Graziano referred to "bearing witness" (1997, p. 400). Bearing witness validates the experience and begins the healing process. To bear witness, however, it is important for therapists to be fully present. By not pressuring ourselves to achieve what textbooks define as closure and by being more tolerant of unanswered questions, we can become more fully present for the people we serve and less prone to blaming ourselves—or them—for the continued manifestations of ambivalence. With a fuller presence, we become better listeners to their stories and more authentic witnesses to their pain. In this way, we help open people up to the emotion-based collaboration for normalizing ambivalence in long-term ambiguous loss.

Being Aware of the Professional Debate

When struggling with the mix of ambiguity and ambivalence, there is a complicated interplay between conscious and unconscious processes of stress reduction and self-protection. Figuring out which represents intentional or cognitive coping and which represents unconscious defenses may be necessary for research, but I do not think it is in clinical work. Regardless of their source, we need to bring conflicted feelings into awareness so they can be managed and lived with. I agree with Newman (2001) that efforts to categorize a psychological process as a conscious coping process or as an unconscious defense mechanism are more likely to hamper the therapy process than facilitate it.

I have seen in my research and clinical work what Erdelyi (2001) called the "unfolding of consciousness," with no one identifiable instant when the ambivalence surfaces and becomes conscious or deliberate (intentional). To be sure, clinicians see "lightbulb" moments in people who suddenly understand how it all fits and begin to do something different in their interactions with the ambiguously lost person and with others. But usually, the process is slow, and changes emerge gradually. What matters most is that healing and change can occur either way—from a gradual unfolding of consciousness as well as from a sudden epiphany. Both can serve to lower ambivalence and somatic outcomes (Boss & Kaplan, 2004).[3]

Although the debate continues in psychology about conscious coping versus unconscious defenses, it is my view as a therapist that bringing any unrecognized guilt-producing feelings into awareness helps to lower the ambivalence to manageable levels. Toward this end, I discuss cultural rituals and symbols, community values, and religious beliefs, all of which may play a large part in determining whether or not a person's conflicted emotions are consciously recognized. What we feel guilty about doing or not doing, feeling or not feeling, is, after all, largely determined by the community around us. (For immigrants, it may be the community they left behind.) Hearing the voice of a missing person is normal in many cultures whereas the same behavior is declared pathological in Western psychology. Clearly, the guilt and shame for negative feelings about one's spouse or parent will be greater in the community that declares such feelings abnormal. People will repress to defend themselves and to survive the trauma of ambiguous loss. For now, clinicians and researchers must view cultural differences with less judgment and certainty. What is typical is not always useful data for treating the trauma of ambiguous loss.

The Therapeutic Relationship

The goal for therapy is not to get rid of ambivalence but rather to bring it into recognition and thus make it understandable and manageable. We do this through applying both emotion-based and cognitive approaches, working individually and conjointly, seeing the ambiguity as the stress-producing culprit, and, above all, working with a flatter hierarchy. The client's responses are normalized, but at the same time maladaptive responses and interactions are pointed out as needing change. A healthy resiliency is the goal.

In my case, clinical referrals often come from psychiatrists who want me to work with partners or families of loved ones with chronic mental illness (e.g., bipolar disorder, schizophrenia, depression, and Alzheimer's disease). I think of Jake. He and Helen were married happily for 30 years. They had long conversations together each day, good sex often, and enjoyed many sports and social events together. Suddenly it all stopped. Jake called and told me a physician had recommended therapy for him. He had heard I did something with Alzheimer's disease, so he thought he'd call me. I told him I was not a specialist in Alzheimer's disease, but that I saw people who were struggling with the stress of living with it. "Do you want to bring your wife, too?" I asked. "No," he said almost too quickly. "Fine, come alone," I replied. I trusted his judgment.

In the 1970s, trained in bilateral systems theory, I might have insisted that Jake bring his wife along. I no longer do that. I have learned that there is often a valid reason why the caller may want to come alone. I do not assume I know more than they do about their situation or who should come. The call, in fact, is where therapeutic collaboration begins.

So I saw Jake alone. He began slowly: "I love my wife dearly, but lately, I am always mad at her." "Why?" I asked. "She's slipping away," he said. "The doctor thinks it's Alzheimer's. We always talked together about things, and went out with friends, but now, there's nothing. She's off on a cloud somewhere. We mostly stay home now, and I say nothing—but then I blow up. I never did that before. She gets scared, and then I feel awful."

At the second session, Jake voluntarily brought Helen. She, too, knew something was wrong. She was able to say that she also missed Jake and their talks. She admitted to forgetting things more and more. "It feels like I'm losing my mind," she said, "and I guess I am." Because I thought she might not return due to her condition, this was the time to help them talk to each other about their fears, their sadness, and, importantly, their enjoyment of what they still had together. Helen was able to ask Jake to continue talking to her even when she couldn't answer. "And touch me," she whispered. "I want that." He was shaken by her unexpected clear request but seemed assured. "This gives me a way to help," he said tenderly, "so I won't feel as helpless."

Knowing this did help Jake manage his anger better, but the stress didn't go away. His outbursts diminished, however, with the exertion of racquetball and the social contact of singing in a choir. Jake continued to care for Helen (with the help of others he arranged to have come in), but his social life increasingly shifted to others.

I continued for some months with Jake, and sometimes Helen, depending on how she felt. The immediate issues had been his rage and feelings of helplessness about his wife's condition. Now we also talked about roles that needed to shift and how their former pattern of depending on each other would need to change as the dementia claimed more and more of his wife's ability to help. And we talked about ambivalence—how her being psychologically gone could lead to his conflicted feelings of love and hate. Talking about the dark side of what he was feeling and doing and having a name for it helped him to face his utter despair about his wife's memory loss and his abusive response to it. He loved her, but came to know that he also hated her for leaving him behind. As he became more aware that he was angry with the woman he loved, Jake was better able to understand his situation. His wife was not the problem; the illness was. He was not the culprit; the ambiguity was. But the ambiguous loss from the illness was now an integral part of their marriage. He understood that as the healthier partner, he would have to do the adapting, as Helen no longer had that capacity.

With a heavy caregiving workload at home, Jake's free time had to be divided between therapy or racquetball, and I encouraged the latter. He did, however, return again for a few sessions, especially when Helen's condition dropped to a new low—not being able to walk, not knowing him any more, and, finally, not being able to eat, which required him to make the agonizing decision about whether the doctors at the nursing home should insert a feeding tube or let her go. He chose the tube, and continued faithfully to visit Helen long after she no longer knew him. When I next saw him, he was distressed with anxiety and guilt. He wondered if he had made the right decision. "I have a wife, but I don't have a wife," he concluded. I agreed. His resiliency was wearing out.

Jake continued to spend time with Helen, talking to her and holding her, as he had promised years earlier, but he also developed a social life with other people, and eventually with a woman with whom he dined regularly.

He talked about conflicting feelings about this, but he knew he needed to have human connection in order to stay healthy and resilient himself. I reminded him that feelings of guilt and mixed emotions were to be expected in his situation, and I supported him for being able to verbalize them. He came to accept his reality of ambiguous loss—and the ambivalence of joy and sadness. When Helen was in a nursing home and no longer knew him, he was more able to handle his wanting it to end and wanting it to go on without being overwhelmed.

As therapists, we can't make ambiguous losses such as Jake's go away, but we can minimize the ambivalence and symptoms of anxiety, guilt, and relational conflict. As with Jake and other clients, I work to bring conflicted feelings into awareness through telling and listening to narratives and normalizing negative feelings (but not actions) as well as the swing of ambivalent feelings. As we worked together, I asked Jake a lot of questions about his context, what the situation meant to him, how he felt about the ambiguity, and whether there were any indicators of trouble. I asked about which people he felt were still close to him. I saw early on that he missed his wife, even when she was sitting next to him in my office.

Countertransference

Knowing more about the link between ambiguous loss and ambivalence reduces the chance for the therapist's countertransference—getting emotionally hooked by something the client says, does, or represents. For example, when Jake talked about his sadness at his wife's decline, I reacted personally with my own sadness—not about his wife, but about my mother's decline at that time. I knew I needed to talk with a peer consultant about this. It is not unusual for a client's story to remind us of an ambiguous loss of our own—a divorce, a baby given up, a mate who left mysteriously, or an elderly parent who is declining.

In addition, clients who come from cultures or communities different from our own may react to therapy—and us—in unexpected ways. They may appear, according to textbook definitions, resistant, and that can make us impatient or angry. Their stuckness may consciously or unconsciously irritate us or remind us of some other therapeutic or personal experience of being rejected. Normalizing ambivalence allows for a more inclusive framework that acknowledges diversity and avoids judgment about normalcy. It gives the therapist permission to see resilience in unexpected places without adhering to one normative baseline.

Although countertransference is an understandable experience, therapists must be aware when it occurs in the therapeutic relationship and deal with it. Peer consultation is what I use most often, but on a few occasions, I have had to refer the couple or family to another therapist who could serve them better.[4]

Expanding the Repertoire of Therapeutic Models to Include Teamwork

Since working with so many different kinds of ambiguous loss, I am more convinced than ever that we must expand our treatment for traumatizing ambivalence beyond individual therapy, individual approaches, and one favorite therapeutic approach. As noted earlier, both emotion-focused and cognitive therapies are useful. In addition, while mixing psychoeducation, cognitive, psychodynamic, and trauma therapies, we need to include family-and community-based interventions. One person cannot be expected to do all this; thus, I recommend collaborative work among social workers, physicians, psychologists, psychiatrists, and, importantly, community leaders such as clergy, first responders, and local educators. Paraprofessionals from the community are also essential, but should be trained to work with families of the missing in quieter times so they know what to do when a disaster occurs.

Guidelines for Intervention

The therapeutic goal is to normalize ambivalence so as to lessen guilt and increase resiliency after the trauma of ambiguous loss. To strengthen resilience to live with ambiguous loss, the following considerations have been useful for normalizing ambivalence—personally and professionally.

Normalizing Guilt and Negative Feelings, But Not Harmful Actions

Although some believe that guilt is given to us to help us move and change, my view is that guilt prevents movement and change. After a traumatic event, it is one of the most common reactions, and there is where we must begin our intervention. It is not your fault that the tsunami happened; it is not your fault that your loved one has disappeared. Blaming, shaming, and guilt stop movement in the process of healing. The story must be told and heard and retold until there is more positive attribution. Traumatized clients fear our negative assessments, and they will stay away to avoid them. They do not want to be told that their agony is pathology. Squelching any side of a client's feelings and emotions is not helpful unless, of course, they are life threatening or violent. Rather, we help them to tell their story, no matter how strange, and we listen. They need our full attention—and our patience. The process of normalizing negative feelings paradoxically helps to minimize them.

Using the Arts to Increase Understanding of Ambivalence

In situations where hard data are unavailable, I frequently use the arts (whichever form is favored by the clients) to bring their mixed emotions to the surface. Whether it is through film, dance, music, creative writing, literature, painting, or theater, artists often reflect the ambivalences of real-life experience. Through these artistic means, client and therapist together can see that ambivalence is common and not necessarily negative. Rather it implies a need to live with the manageable stress of life's paradox heightened by ambiguous loss. The arts can help us to lower ambivalence to a level where it is no longer immobilizing and traumatizing. Clients may even begin to see humor in what was previously frightful.

Regaining Personal Agency

The idea of managing ambivalence is compatible with the idea of mastery or agency. Ambiguous loss, with its lack of information, skews personal agency and one's ability to solve a problem. For example, when an adult child must care for their now brain-injured or demented parent, the skewed power differential heightens their ambivalence more than when a parent cares for an ill or brain-injured child. Situations of ambiguous loss from brain injury, illness, or addiction interfere with expectations about personal agency and sense of mastery.

My own value of mastery has been tempered most often by having to live with unsolvable ambiguous losses—among family members and dear friends—but out of this pain has come the knowledge that I can survive and move forward despite ambivalence and sometimes confusion about my role and personal agency. My need for mastery is slowly replaced, not with resignation but with a spiritual acceptance that gives me resilience far beyond where, in my younger years, I thought I could stretch.

Reassessing and Reconstructing the Psychological Family

Theologians deal with the reality of death, and psychologists and sociologists study ambiguity and ambivalence: We should come together.

Understanding both helps to shape one's psychological family. For example, the identity of a couple or family lies in more than physical presence and physical interaction. Distance and even time separates, but loved ones can be held present in one's mind long after they are physically gone. With ambiguous loss, this is often how people find their resiliency. The wife of a soldier still missing in action from the Vietnam War tells me that her second marriage did not work because she "was married to two men." She writes, "Once I accepted that I could not be married to two men and stopped trying to do what I thought society expected of me (forget and move on), I regained a peace and power in my life that I have not enjoyed since before losing my husband" (D. Campbell, personal communication, June 27, 2005).

Seeing the Community as Family

Finding resilience from ambivalence is a slow process, and it occurs more easily in the presence of others who have had similar losses. Meeting together as a family is ideal for most cases, but one's "family" may also be the people one works with or attends school with, people from the same religious or ethnic community, or simply friends. In treating PTSD or stress from disaster, trauma groups are almost always composed of individuals or limited to peer groups (e.g., coworkers such as police, firefighters, clergy, war veterans, and trauma nurses). All need to go home eventually and live with their families and friends. Treating traumatized individuals only in peer groups ultimately distances them from their mates and families. It changes the psychological family to one of work partners. After loved ones go missing, we need to help survivors strengthen resilience on the home front. Regardless of the work group, one's family and community are major resources for support and healing, and they need to be included in postdisaster and traumatic loss work. Our therapeutic task is to make sure that the traumatized person's partner and family are resilient enough to provide him or her with an everyday place for healing to occur. Thus far, only a few intervention programs for trauma are family- and community-based (Boss et al., 2003; Landau & Saul, 2004).

When working with immigrants and migrants, one must ask which community they feel they belong to. The older generation may clearly say their homeland is somewhere else; the younger generation may see their new land as homeland. Those in the middle may be torn between two lands, with an immobilizing love-hate relationship with the old land and the new. Neither feels just right. These twin tensions may be the normal state of being for many new Americans today—for example, the Hmong woman who remembers the forest life in Cambodia and now is graduating from college in urban and wintry Minnesota; the boy soldier whose family was killed and who is now living on a farm in North Dakota; the Liberian teenagers who were ripped from their homes and families and are now living in Staten Island; the Russian physician who is not allowed to practice in the United States. Love and hate for a new community are to be expected, for ambiguous losses are inherent in the move. If there are clinical symptoms, we must see them contextually as results of the ambivalence that is inherent in ambiguous loss.

Reassigning Everyday Roles and Tasks

Reassigning tasks, roles, and boundaries helps individuals and the family as a whole manage the ambivalence that follows ambiguous loss. By naming the problem and placing it outside of the client's own volition, we normalize their plight and their understandable anxiety. When therapists externalize the cause (White & Epston, 1990), clients can more easily understand and unravel for themselves the connection between the ambiguous loss and their personal ambivalence about what to do about it, how to act, how to think, how to be, and who to be. Said another way, *sociological* ambiguity about tasks, roles, and boundaries prompts *psychological* ambivalence, resulting in clinical symptoms such as depression, anxiety, relational conflict, and identity confusion. But from a resilience perspective, it can be managed and does not have to immobilize if we present it as a stress-management challenge as opposed to a pathology (Boss, 2002c).

Asking Questions about Context and Situation

To enhance the collaborative process, I also ask questions about the person's situational context. What is distressing that is not obvious? If there are symptoms of unresolved grief but no death has occurred, I ask if there is or has been a loved one who is missing physically or emotionally. For example:

- Who is your family? Biological? Psychological?
- Who is not?
- Whom do you see as somewhere in between?
- Have you had any ambiguous losses (e.g., divorce, adoption, a breakup, a baby you gave up, a child who ran away, a missing parent, a person you care about who is no longer as he or she used to be)?
- Are you in any relationships where the other person seems to be missing emotionally or physically?
- Do you have mixed emotions or feelings about this? Do you feel torn about what you should do?

As with Jake and Helen, such questions probe the responses that can guide the therapeutic narrative. Rarely are all needed, but they are all useful for the therapist to have on hand. The information a therapist needs mostly comes up naturally in personal and family stories with trusted loved ones as they continue talking together in a safe holding environment. Such relational questions are not typical for most PTSD or grief therapies, but they begin the process for finding a more positive meaning in the ambivalence and thus less trauma from ambiguous loss.

Bringing Ambivalent Feelings into the Open

The unconscious is made more conscious by supporting clients in talking about the dark side of their feelings about the lost person or themselves; we encourage them also to talk about their feelings of guilt. The key is to bring the ambivalent feelings into the open, embarrassing as they might be, and to talk about them. As therapists, we must be open to dealing with our own ambivalence about seeing certain clients. We also must be open to hearing about feelings that may be viewed (from our experience and culture) as abnormal: "I spoke with my missing husband last night." "I saw him coming up the sidewalk." "He touched me last night." "I dreamed I killed him again last night." I heard all of these statements from different women with missing husbands during the Vietnam War and after 9/11. I believed them. I respected their perception of their reality. Labeling what they so cautiously shared as abnormal would only have engendered resistance. Worse, it would have been dishonest, as I did not perceive their words as reflecting pathology, despite my earlier training. Perhaps this is how trust develops.

Uncovering Latent or Unconscious Ambivalence

Normalizing ambivalence depends on lowering it to a level that allows for coping with it. The first step in the coping process is to recognize what the problem is. I have already discussed labeling ambiguous loss as the problem; now the goal is to help clients uncover their conflicted feelings and emotions about the situation. Through the use of storytelling and artistic expression, they can become more aware of contradictory feelings—hoping a parent will live or die or wanting to help but leaving town. Ambivalence confuses who is included in one's perception of family (the psychological family) as well as confusing who performs what roles and tasks. To bring a person's ambivalent feelings into awareness, it is necessary to lower the guilt and blame and normalize conflicting impulses that result from the painful ambiguity of absence and presence in close relationships (Boss, 1999).

Managing the Ambivalence, Once Aware of It

Because we cannot eliminate the ambiguity or even all of the ambivalence, we must help clients develop a tolerance for both. We try to lower the ambivalence by bringing it into cognition and thus allowing the coping process to begin. However, clinicians must first distinguish between ambivalence that is the normal outcome of an abnormal context and ambivalence that is pathological and requires medical or psychiatric treatment. Knowing the difference between sociological and psychiatric definitions helps us triage and know how to proceed. People can cope once they are aware of their conflicted feelings.

Seeing Conflict as Positive

The couple or family's level of conflict is often heightened by unrecognized ambivalence. Without awareness of mixed emotions, normal conflict and disagreement may escalate into violence or abuse. Identifying the couple or family's situation as one of ambiguous loss (and not their fault) and their ambivalent feelings as normal (and manageable) offers clients a way to view their situation with less guilt and anxiety. Meeting together, with a therapist who can moderate the levels of conflict, they can tell stories and listen, agree and disagree, laugh and cry, and, over time, slowly begin to find they can live with conflicted feelings and roles. It can be painful to tell or listen to the darkest feelings and thoughts about a missing person, and it helps to have someone listen fully and patiently. Our job is to moderate disagreements that may arise in the process in order to prevent escalation into serious conflict and estrangement.

Valuing Diverse Ways of Managing Ambivalence

As we work with people from increasingly different cultures and religious beliefs, differing perceptions about ambiguity, ambivalence, guilt, shame, and blame continue to abound. Because we cannot possibly know each family's beliefs and values before we see them, I begin therapy by asking people what the situation means to them—for example, how they see the status of the missing person and what it means for them right now. I ask them how they have been coping and what is working despite the ambiguous loss. From their stories (admittedly subjective data), culturally influenced perceptions and feelings illustrating ambivalence emerge. We have begun the collaborative process without a normative baseline and thus with more openness to culturally diverse ways of being resilient. Many people we see today come from cultures or religions that intentionally "keep the dead present." Ancestors, as well as the recently lost, remain part of many psychological families. Closure is viewed as a barrier to healing. Using the lens of ambiguous loss then allows more culturally sensitive assessment and interpretation to help our increasingly diverse clients.

Knowing That Closure Does Not Lower Ambivalence

The ideas of absolute absence (closure) or absolute presence are not meaningful for those who have a loved one who is demented, in a coma, brain-injured, autistic, mentally ill, or missing physically. The assumption that there is such a thing as absolute presence or absence makes people feel inept and guilty even with more ordinary ambiguous losses such as divorce and adoption. This feeling of failure hampers the discovery of hidden feelings and emotions that cause anxiety and relationship problems. Boundaries are blurred; people are confused about who they are and what roles they should play.

Developing Tolerance for Tension

The only way to ease the trauma and avoid immobilization is for therapists to help people live with the tensions of contradictory feelings and emotions. We must also help ourselves to do this. It is wise for therapists to have regular supervision or a peer consultation group where they can talk honestly with other professionals (not necessarily from one's own work group) about conflicted feelings and emotions stirred by a particular case. Sometimes we also need therapy ourselves if a client's ambivalence triggers an overwhelming emotion in us. Participating in continuing education can also help calm professional tensions.

As clinicians, we therefore are less concerned about whether ambiguity and ambivalence are intentional or unconscious phenomena. Instead, we intervene to bring both constructs into awareness through labeling each, linking them, normalizing them and the subsequent stress they cause, and then encouraging people to start talking together to find new meaning in who their family is, what the relationships are, what is lost, and what is still here. When ambiguity and ambivalence are intentionally recognized, people are able to cope with them, manage the stress, and reconstruct their perceptions of who is there for them, perceptually and physically. Without such awareness, cognitively and emotionally, the guilt and anxiety from ambivalence can become overwhelming and immobilizing.

Using Cognitive Coping Strategies

Our task then is "to give structure and meaning to a family's predicament" (DiNicola, 1997, pp. 3–4.) From the perspective of social construction, we merge Lazarus's (1966) cognitive appraisal model with the ambiguous loss model to help families reconstruct their view of what the problem really is. By telling their story and listening to others, they begin to see that their mixed emotions and conflicted feelings are not the problem. Rather, the challenge is to keep the ambivalence at a manageable level.

CONCLUSION

When someone we love disappears psychologically or physically, the subsequent ambivalence can be overwhelming and can lead to short tempers and maladaptive behaviors (like Jake's abusive outbursts). With catastrophic illnesses like Alzheimer's disease, natural or man-made disasters, and even divorce, the old assumption about the necessity of "getting over it" is not useful. Ambivalence is a normal part of human relationships, especially when loved ones are missing in mind or body. Resiliency does not lie in its eradication but rather in being able to acknowledge and manage the tensions from ambivalence at a level that prevents traumatization.

The normalizing of ambivalence essentially depends on helping people therapeutically to acknowledge their conflicting feelings. By itself, ambivalence is not pathological, but the inability to cope with it can erode resiliency and lead to pathology. Feeling love and hate simultaneously or fluctuating from grief to rage can traumatize people if they cannot acknowledge and manage the tension.

Chapter 8

Revising Attachment

Closely attached people who become separated through ambiguous loss suffer a trauma even greater than death. To regain resiliency, revising one's attachment is essential. This is a gradual process of learning to live with the prospect of recovering the lost person while simultaneously recognizing that the loss may become permanent. It means living with the ambiguity of a close attachment while simultaneously finding new human connections. Neither ceremonies nor rituals exist to help clarify and honor such threatened attachments. The agony of those left behind in ambiguous loss is akin to that expressed in Auden's poem "Funeral Blues." It begins:

> Stop all the clocks, cut off the telephone,
> Prevent the dog from barking with a juicy bone,
> Silence the pianos and with muffled drum
> Bring out the coffin, let the mourners come.

And ends with:

> The stars are not wanted now: put out every one;
> Pack up the moon and dismantle the sun;
> Pour away the ocean and sweep up the wood;
> For nothing now can ever come to any good.
> *(Auden, "Funeral Blues," stanzas 1.4)*

Whereas Auden's words soar to support those who have loved deeply and are now separated by a validated death, the parents, children, and partners of the missing are on their own. Whether the loss is physical or psychological, there is no body to bury, no coffin to carry, no mourners to give eulogies. Metaphorically, the pianos keep playing because the loss goes unrecognized. It is this lack of witnessing and validation that creates extraordinary pain for those who love a missing person. Life is put on hold, and other relationships are avoided. New attachments are blocked because with ambiguous loss, the old attachment still has possibilities.

In the midst of ongoing ambiguity, people must nevertheless find some resilience to stay healthy. This means they must begin to revise their attachment to the lost person. How can we help in this process? If it is true that without clarification of loss, people tend to hold on to hope for reunification, even to the detriment of health, what can we do to unfreeze their grief and help them move forward again despite the ambiguous loss (Boss, 1999)?

Understandably, the ambiguity blocks the inclination to let go of a beloved person. I think of Nancy Reagan who so devotedly stood by her ailing husband for 17 years as he fell deeper into Alzheimer's disease. As the dementia deepened, she became "alone" in the relationship but did not detach. Mrs. Reagan's example is like many others, much less public, where a beloved family member is gone but still present. Letting go is impossible. A caregiver in our dementia study summarized the feeling: "I'm a widow waiting to happen."

We also saw enduring attachments in the aftermath of the 2004 tsunami. Without proof of life or death, traumatized survivors held out. Early on, they hoped for a happy reunion. Later they shifted to hoping for a body to bury, and much later, they hopefully found ways to accept the ambiguity.

Even when clarification of the ambiguity occurs finally through verification of death, the attachment to a loved one still continues. We saw this with Mrs. Reagan when she reached out to touch the coffin of her husband and then rested her head on it. We hear it in stories from South Asia. Human attachments are deep and not easily severed. But at least with the clarity of a funeral to honor the beloved person, the process of reconstructing and revising deep relational connections can begin. It is, after all, not attachment that ends when a person we love dies but rather the relationship as it was. The connection has to be revised. When, however, loved ones are missing rather than clearly dead, this revision is blocked, thus elongating the trauma.

ATTACHMENT AND AMBIGUITY

I use the term *attachment* here in a more general sense than in the specifics of recent attachment theory. With ambiguous loss, the attachment one has for another may stay the same, but there is now a categorical difference in the relationship. Connection as it used to be is impossible. Closure is also impossible, so letting go is not the goal. Instead, the therapeutic goal is for a perceptual shift in the relationship—one that accepts the ambiguity and uncertainty of absence *and* presence.

Attachment is traditionally defined as the relational and reciprocal connection to a constant other.[1] It reflects the human need for a close relationship with a single and constant object. Here, I define attachment more generally, as the deep connection between individuals in couples, families, or other close relationships. Clearly, a person to whom you feel attached would be viewed as part of your psychological family.

Revising attachment (as opposed to detaching) means not needing to have closure with a lost person but also not denying the loss. Furthermore, with ambiguous loss there is no linear process of letting go (e.g., protest, despair, and acceptance): Rarely is there acceptance, and there is never closure. Rather, the revision of attachment means shifting the relationship to take into account the ambiguity surrounding the loss. From this perspective, a disappeared loved one could still be perceived as an attachment figure and serve the function of being a safe haven and secure base even if he or she is physically unavailable. For example, after 9/11, women frequently told me that thinking of their mothers in faraway countries gave them comfort and courage to cope with their trauma of having a missing husband. Not only did they keep their absent mothers present by phone, but many said they also kept these loved ones close in their hearts and minds daily, thinking about what they would advise. Many said the psychological presence of a physically absent parent or sibling was immensely comforting. It was as if they had internalized a still-living figure that was physically out of reach so as to receive comfort and advice for their present trauma.

As a therapist, I now acknowledge connections to the psychological family even more, and I often ask traumatized clients, "How do you think a family member you care deeply for would advise you now?" Although answers vary, children and adults always have an answer to that question, and it appears to give them comfort when other family members become unavailable or missing. Sometimes the psychological family is all survivors have for support and comfort.

When treating people traumatized by ambiguous loss, we begin to revise attachments by rebuilding both psychological and physical connections. People may seek comfort from parents or loved ones who are physically faraway or deceased but who nevertheless provide the essence of support. Our professional task is to welcome and build on the presence of the client's psychological family.

How Revising Attachment Relates to Ambiguous Loss

Paradoxically, having a loved one's body and personally participating in the funeral begins the process of letting go and revising attachment. Not having a loved one's remains impedes that process. Six months after the 9/11 attack, the wife of a man still missing in the World Trade Center said, "I would be happy just to have a part of him to bury—even if it's just a finger nail." She believed he was dead, but she was frozen in place. She was full of rage because he was still missing, and even more so because she felt she had no part in his burial. The terrorists had taken that from her by burying him under the collapsed building. When a loved one disappears, it may be impossible to shift perceptions about absence or presence until one can actively participate in the rituals of honor and farewell that begin the process of revising the attachment. For this woman, it was impossible to see her husband as dead without actively participating and having some control in his ceremony of honor and farewell.

After the South Asian tsunami of 2004, an ambiguous loss of epic proportions, nearly 300,000 were dead or missing. Thousands were buried in mass graves with no identification. Children had missing parents; parents had missing children. Couples were separated. This ambiguous loss emanated from nature's catastrophe, but there still were feelings of guilt in not being able to hold on tight enough or run fast enough. There still were feelings of anger and betrayal about not being able to say good-bye or actually see the dead body of a loved one. In every culture and religion, this makes the loss harder to deal with.

Not having remains is often viewed as betrayal. Numerous surviving 9/11 spouses told me they felt cheated out of a chance to bury their husbands *their* way. Besides feeling they had no mastery in this very personal rite of passage, they yearned for verification—of life or death. Until verification occurs, reconstructing attachment is, for most people, confusing and understandably met with extreme reactions.

When a person to whom one is attached disappears, a survivor often turns away from the world and withdraws into apathy. Our therapeutic task is to moderate this tendency and to encourage renewed and revised human connections to relatives, friends, and community. It is through these new connections that people can gradually revise perceptions of their relationship to the missing person. Clearly, this means helping people revise their psychological families as well.

How Revising Attachment Relates to Resiliency

To lower stress and anxiety in the face of ambiguous loss, the abandoned person may freeze or protest, but in either case, he or she feels pain. Unsuccessful in finding the lost person, survivors may have absolute reactions—for example, prematurely closing out the missing person by acting as if the person is already dead, or by denying the person's absence and acting as if nothing has changed. Other absolute reactions may be refusing to think about the missing person at all or thinking about the person all the time (Boss, 1977, 1980c, 1999, 2004b). Such categorical and extreme reactions are maladaptive and prevent relational revisions that are needed for resiliency. A healthier adaptation to a missing attachment is to gradually disconnect while at the same time reconnecting to available and caring persons. Through this process of synthesis, one's attachment to a missing person thins. This change marks the beginning of the revision process that helps regain resiliency.

To clarify, although the anxiety from ambiguous loss is not the same as classically defined anxious attachment (Barry, Barry, & Lindemann, 1965; Bowlby, 1973), there is with ambiguous loss a negative anxiety that is produced by not being able to find the person to whom one is attached. Negative anxiety (in a generic sense) can also result from the threat of loss while a loved one is still physically present, for example with dementia, brain injury, addiction, or chronic mental illness (Boss, 1999). All too often, I see people detach or close the door on a living person as if the person were already dead. But I understand their motives. To protect themselves from the pain and anxiety of a painful on-again off-again relationship, people become hardened and psychologically disconnect from the ambiguously absent/present person. Other people choose the opposite absolute of holding on too tightly. For example, after 9/11, some of the surviving parents hung on too tightly to their children, forbidding them from even leaving the house. Many of the traumatized families huddled together in one bed in order to feel safe enough to sleep. Early on, the family bed may be a useful coping mechanism, but sleeping together can last too long. As time went on and boys and girls matured, therapists were direct in saying it was no longer appropriate. Interventions focused on more flexibility in letting teenagers come and go. With intervention, the children and youth expressed relief. With ambiguous loss, our task is to interrupt the maladaptations that are making families fragile and brittle.

The relationship between revising attachment and resiliency is based on the assumption that the anxiety and trauma produced by ambiguous loss must be eased. Family therapists Whitaker and Malone (1981) described sources of negative anxiety as feelings of personal failure, excessive frustration, rejection, hurt, and separation or loss. These elements are all produced by ambiguous loss because of its inherent insolvability. The abandoned person continues to hope because there is no evidence of an ending. In the early stages, continued hope and searching for information are useful, of course. Resilience early on is indicated by protest and seeking the lost person. The need to resist disconnecting is uniquely strong. Illusions and behaviors to preserve the status quo may also arise: for example, seeing a missing husband come up the sidewalk at the time he always came home from work each day; seeing a missing mate in the middle of the night; keeping a kidnapped child's room ready for his or her return. With more common ambiguous loss, the resistance could mean hoping that the baby you gave up will come back to you one day or waiting for a philandering mate to see the light and come back to you. Ultimately, with both catastrophic and common ambiguous losses, people's health and resiliency depend on discovering when and how to modify and revise attachments to those who are physically or psychologically missing from their lives. This is no easy task, but clinicians can help.

THEORETICAL CONSIDERATIONS
OF ENVIRONMENTAL PROBLEMS AND CONTEXT

In the 1980s, using a psychodynamic perspective, Bowlby (1980) wrote that the loss of a loved person is one of the most intensely painful experiences any human can suffer.[2] He addressed the complexities of ambivalence in lost attachments and the stress that motivates despair and letting go in order to lower stress and anxiety. He did not refer, however, to losses that were ambiguous. Nor did Sigmund Freud in his *Mourning and Melancholia* (1917/ 1957), where he suggested that the goal of recovery after loss is to relinquish one's ties to the absent person and eventually invest in a new relationship. Kohut (1972) also ignored the external context of ambiguity and uncertainty and proposed that trauma could be related to a narcissistic personality and that rage was the response to a narcissistic wound. Could it be that instead of narcissism, the rage associated with trauma might be seeded by loss of mastery and control due to an external power such as ambiguous loss? Instead of narcissism, might trauma and rage be outcomes of an environmental problem with no resolution—like a loved one being swept away by a tsunami? Christopher Lasch (1978) wrote that the characteristic of the U.S. culture was narcissism—loneliness, needing attention, and easy to anger. But are not loneliness, neediness, and rage also outcomes of a time filled with ambiguous losses that even our intelligence technology cannot prevent? It is odd that theorists have not written more about so common a phenomenon as ambiguous loss. Theories that focus too narrowly on the individual psyche miss the ubiquity of ambiguous loss and its frequent effects on human attachments.

After a loved one goes missing, the result is indeed insecurity and anxiety, but these reactions result from the stress of environmental ambiguity, not from psychic weakness. From this perspective, the clinical interventions are not pathology-oriented but rather stress-based with the goal of regaining resilience despite the negative context. The goal of revising attachment (as opposed to closure) flows from this perspective.

WHAT HELPS REVISE ATTACHMENT?

Traditional methods of grief therapy and PTSD intervention are insufficient to revise attachment after a loved one goes missing. New connections must be constructed or old ones strengthened between survivors, families, and their communities. At the same time, the attachment to the lost person is never really severed but gradually modified, softened, and revised to reflect the context of long-term ambiguity.

Following is a list of what can help in revising attachment. Each of these items is fully discussed under "Guidelines for Intervention" (page 173).

- Thinking dialectically
- Moving from despair to protest
- Thinking systematically, but not seeing maladaptations as bilateral pathology
- Developing memorial ceremonies and farewell rituals
- Knowing that fantasies of a missing person are common
- Watching out for no-talk rules
- Paying attention to developmental stages that exacerbate anxiety
- Including children and adolescents in therapy when parents or siblings disappear
- Using multiple-family and couple groups to build new connections
- Encouraging the use of the arts

WHAT HINDERS?

With traumatic and ambiguous losses, revising attachment is hindered by an overemphasis on individuation, closure, and focus on the past. I will explain why.

An Overemphasis on Individuation[3]

Differentiating oneself (individuating) from a parent, child, or mate who is missing in mind or body is difficult. Adult children caring for elderly parents with dementia or chronic illnesses are too often pathologized for being too involved, bringing meals to elders, or dropping everything to care for them when there is an emergency. In marital therapy, for example, professionals must be cautious not to pathologize the real need for elder care (or child care) as part of a couple's reality. Overfunctioning and underfunctioning, viewed in the context of ambiguous loss, are not valid measures of psychological health. To begin individuation is antithetical to the worldview of community, tribe, and connection. Women in particular are viewed negatively if they fail to individuate but at the same time are expected to "stick it out" with caring for ailing family members. Also, the idea of individuation as an indicator of health only further burdens the wife whose husband has lasting trauma from war or illness. Theories of individuation are, therefore, not helpful for assessing those who must live with a loved one who is gone but needing constant care. Stress theory is less pathologizing in such situations (see Chapters 2 and 3). Rather than classic individuation, the goal for clients with ambiguous loss is to grieve and revise earlier hopes and dreams about the person and the relationship, and to do this without the extreme reactions of absolute enmeshment or absolute detachment.

Expecting Closure

As I have already stressed, we should not expect people with ambiguous attachments to reach closure. The results of the relational limbo make closure impossible. Unresolved grief reactions to ambiguous loss are not pathological. For a person, couple, or family to remain strong and resilient in such situations, they must accept the paradox of absence and presence.

THERAPY METHODS AND GUIDELINES FOR REVISING ATTACHMENT

Developing the resilience to balance the opposing ideas of absence and presence and the ability to both stay connected and let go takes time. The overall goal is to reduce the stress and trauma in this paradoxical situation by adapting dialectically rather than settling in at either extreme. We want clients to be able to reach a point where they can say, "I am still attached to this missing person, but I now need to modify that attachment given the circumstances of ambiguity and lack of resolution."

Toward this end, we intervene to move people toward a synthesis between holding out rigidly for return to the status quo and wanting absolute closure to loss. The synthesis manifests in what I have earlier called "being comfortable with unanswered questions" (Boss, 1999). Such a synthesis emanates from a recursive rather than linear process. That is, we do not focus on developmental stages but instead stimulate a circular, dialectical process of moving forward slowly to attend to other attachments (or discover new ones) while still thinking of the lost person. Gradually, as people see that complete letting go is not the goal and that they can hold on to the lost person even while they move forward, the desire to put life on hold diminishes.

The Therapeutic Relationship

Although many people can revise on their own or with the help of psychoeducation and social support, when the anxiety and trauma from ambiguous loss continues to immobilize, revising attachment requires professional help. When external conditions complicate attachment and loss, I recommend shifting to psychodynamic and relational approaches. Importantly, we must do so in terms of contextual and environmental perspectives. The narrative tradition, based in social construction and phenomenology, was previously described as compatible with these perspectives and approaches.

To clarify, although relational approaches and in-depth psychology are useful for disconnecting from ambiguous loss, a broader systemic perspective that includes relationships and external context is essential. For example, with couples and families, energy is directed at understanding and improving the emotional relationships within the larger systems in their lives—extended families, neighborhoods, schools, clinics, workplaces, and spiritual communities. With a broader systemic approach, family and community rules may be discovered to be inadequate (Imber-Black & Roberts, 1992; Luepnitz, 2002b). People facing ambiguous loss must be able to adapt these rules to fit their unique situation. In the company of others, memorial rituals can be reconstructed and some measure of meaning found. During this process, the therapist must also challenge cultural attitudes and illusions—the client's and their own—that may immobilize or block the revision of attachment.

Overall, with psychodynamic approaches, the primary tool for therapy, individual or conjoint, is the relationship between the therapist and clients. Who you are may be more important than what you do as a therapist. It is therefore essential that positive transference and trust occur between clients and their therapist. Knowing ourselves so that we can be fully present is an important part of this kind of therapy. Because of this centrality of the client-therapist relationship, the following list of implications for the therapeutic relationship is lengthy.

Because the goal in therapy is revising one's attachment to an unavailable object, it is critical that positive connections or transference develop between client and therapist. For an individual, therapy rests on the development of positive transference. For conjoint therapy with couples and families, it is another matter. Instead of transference, the goal here is to develop trust in the therapist and each other, as well as an active connection to the systemic relational process.

Connections and trust will develop more easily when the therapist is comfortable with diversity and culturally competent. Therapists of all races, religions, genders, ages, and sexual orientations must stretch their own resilience to include a wider diversity of ideas and people in their work. Veteran therapists as well as trainees need continuing education or periodic research updates and travel experiences to build cultural competence.

Family of origin work and cultural genograms are critical preparations for helping clients to adapt to having lost loved ones. Early trauma and loss may lead to resistance in disconnecting from even the most painful relationships (Firestone, Firestone, & Catlett, 2003). Complicated attachments freeze the process of letting go (Boss, 1999). Psychodynamic approaches for therapy—and training—are necessary to access emotions associated with early trauma and future relationships (Firestone et al., 2003; Hardy & Laszloffy, 1995). When such issues are unresolved for therapist as well as patient, the therapy is stymied.

A safe holding environment and trust between therapist and client is essential for the expression of frightening feelings, especially guilt, shame, rage, and helplessness. Once people feel safe and respected, they are more likely to begin expressing the feelings that have immobilized them. In a safe holding environment, they begin to tell stories, raise questions, and reach out to each other. Through the psychodynamic and narrative process, meanings are found, mastery is tempered, identity is reconstructed, and ambivalence is brought into consciousness where it can be normalized and managed. With this complicated revision process, change usually begins. No one should push the process of synthesizing relational absence and presence, but we can motivate it by fostering people's connections to others. Letting go is never complete, nor should it be, but the survivors can move forward with their lives despite the ambiguity.

More time is needed to work with people traumatized by ambiguous loss. Because of confusing attachment it takes more time for a therapist to access emotions associated with a missing loved one. In this chapter I focus on in-depth psychotherapy and experiential methods, but cognitive-behavioral methods of intervention are also needed over the course of treatment. The complexity requires time and multiple methods.

Individual, couple, or family group work is useful in forging new connections. Especially with trauma and loss, groups are useful for reconnecting people (Boss et al., 2003; Herman, 1992). The group should include familiar people who have had similar traumatic experiences. I agree with Herman (1992) that no one should have to face traumatic loss alone.

Multiple family groups in a community setting are useful for revising attachments after large-scale ambiguous loss and trauma. Conjoint therapy with multiple couples and families can be an effective way to work with large numbers of people who may be traumatized by the same natural disaster or terrorist attack. This time however, the safe holding environment may be a place in the community—a school, church basement, firehouse, or community center. The concern for safety remains. People need to feel they are in a safe and familiar place. Rather than seeking transference, professionals working with large numbers of couples and families must build trust, feelings of safety, and connections among multiple adults and their children. To do this, we must genuinely care about them and not mind working with multiple generations in a community setting.

Therapists may have to be more resilient about leaving their offices to treat families traumatized by ambiguous loss. Whether we are leading support groups for spouses and children of Alzheimer's disease patients or working in the aftermath of disasters where people are physically lost, we can become more resilient about where we do our work. After 9/11, clinical offices in high office buildings were often frightening to the traumatized, so we moved our work to the familiar labor union hall, where people felt more comfortable. In Oklahoma church basements were used. For other disasters, it could be a school. To treat the trauma from a large-scale disaster, we must go to the people rather than waiting for people to come to us. The growing prevalence of in-home family therapy is a testimony to the need for such decentralization. It is also a tribute to the resilience of the therapists who can do this challenging work.

Therapists and medical professionals trained to find solutions should not transfer their frustration with ambiguous loss onto their clients or patients. Although there are differences between treatment and palliative care, all professionals, for our own humanity, must resist absolute detachment. Dropping out of a patient's life when he or she is no longer curable, for example, is hurtful to the patient. Turning a patient over to hospice care without further word is a cutoff—an absolute termination that constitutes an abrupt loss for both patient and professional. We need to give more training to professionals who are expected to cure and heal but who at times cannot.

If there is threat to life or persisting immobilization from trauma, professionals should seek psychiatric or psychopharmacological consultation to determine if medication is needed. From my perspective as a family therapist specializing in loss, medication can be useful to ameliorate immobilizing depression or anxiety. However, medications should not inhibit the expression of emotions and feelings including anger, guilt, and shame about attachment to the lost person. Finding the balance requires ongoing collaboration with medical professionals.

When working with ambiguous loss, we need to be more patient. The goal is not closure but rather finding a way to live healthy lives despite ambiguous loss. The work therefore takes longer, and the end result is understandably imperfect. Professionals need to understand that the complications inherent in ambiguous losses require more clinical time (Becvar, 2001). Costs can be allayed by working conjointly and in multiple family groups.

For ethical reasons, collaboration must sometimes be replaced with directness. Even with a commitment to relative truths and collaborative revisions, a therapist working with families of the missing may at times need to be direct. If there is abuse, addiction, illegal activity, or threat to life, one's professional codes of ethics and legal procedures must be followed. We must know and follow the laws to report child abuse, sexual abuse, and battery. We must update ourselves regularly on the professional codes of ethics for our specific profession and the laws of the state in which we practice. If we believe the codes and laws are not right or do not meet the criteria of fairness and equality, we must work to change them.

Guidelines for Intervention

Before attachment can be revised, we must help clients lower and manage their stress and anxiety about threatened attachment. As a relational disorder, ambiguous loss responds to relational treatment. The following six tasks apply to each set of therapeutic guidelines presented throughout this book, but they are especially helpful in implementing the guidelines for revising attachment. It should be noted that these steps assume that the therapeutic setting includes other people familiar to the clients—couples, families, or multiple groups of either.

First, provide empathy and understanding of the fact that the situation is a stressful one. Second, allow family members to express and hear each other's perceptions of the situation. Third, encourage clients to seek as much information as possible about the loss. Fourth, put family members in touch with support groups and others who have had similar experiences of trauma and loss. Fifth, facilitate a process of revising attachment through the search for meaning, tempering mastery, and reconstructing identity. Finally, help individuals, couples, and families identify with peers to regain relational strength. Community connections that give support will ease individual, couple, or family trauma.

Thinking Dialectically

Regaining resilience by revising attachment after loss and trauma requires balancing opposing ideas: clinging to hope and considering the possibility of change. It marks the beginning of the difficult process of softening the attachment to the lost person. As we watched the televised pictures of agonized parents at the shores of the Indian Ocean waiting for the missing bodies of their children to wash up, after the tsunami of 2004, we saw vividly the immobilizing effects of ambiguous loss. Synthesizing conflicting views about absence and presence is the only way to move forward. This requires a both/and approach to therapy rather than one standard intervention or answer. This may require shifts in the thinking of both clinician and client. Paradoxically, clients will maintain some attachment to the lost person and at the same time begin to shift. For example, a wife who still hopes for her husband's recovery or return may replace the bread-winning role he played in order for the family to function. I encourage clients to discover what they still have of the missing person while recognizing what is lost. What must pragmatically be replaced as soon as possible for them to survive? What can take more time? For health, ongoing revisions will help individuals and families through the ordeal of long-term ambiguous loss.

Moving From Despair to Protest

Although despair is an expected reaction to the loss of a loved one, I am always glad when I see clients protest an ambiguous loss. Their protest means they are beginning to move out of the immobilizing trauma. Some months after 9/11, I was reading *USA Today* and was surprised to see a photo of one of the mothers we worked with. When I first met her, she was frozen with anger and despair. She would not talk. Now, here she was pictured and quoted in *USA Today*. Even though she spoke no English, she gave an interview about her anger that noncitizens were being discounted as victims of 9/11. I was delighted to see evidence that she was moving again. Protest is, after all, action, and this is better than remaining immobilized in despair.

Thinking Systemically but not Seeing Maladaptations as Bilateral Pathology

The idea of systemic bilateral balance was critiqued in the late 1980s by Goldner (1985) who warned that systems theory was "an inadequate explanatory matrix from which to build a theory of the family" (p. 31). I agree. Saying that a husband drinks because his wife nags is unfair. Rather, the systemic interaction is that one person maladapts to the other's illness. This is different from saying both are ill, or both are at fault, or that the whole family, for example, is alcoholic. Helping people to see the systemic dynamic as adaptation (or maladaptation) to the stressor of ambiguous loss (rather than as bilateral pathology) is less blaming and thus more conducive for revising attachment as opposed to absolute cut-off.

Developing Memorial Ceremonies and Farewell Rituals

As mentioned earlier, because there are no rituals for ambiguous losses, therapists may have to help clients create them. Shapiro wrote that rituals create "avenues for the public articulation of deeply felt emotions" (1994, p. 228). Motivating the expression of anger and despair, and providing community comfort for the anxiety, rituals help restore the social order disrupted by death (Shapiro, 1994). But what happens when there is ambiguous loss? The very reasons Shapiro gave to explain why death disrupts a community— needing to accommodate for the lost member, alter social roles, and confront the existential reality of death—are also the reasons communities ignore ambiguous losses. Not knowing the outcome, everything is put on hold.

In Oklahoma City after the terrorist bombing, the community rituals and memorial ceremonies brought people closer together than before the attack (J. Martin, personal communication, June 18, 2004; Sprang, 1999). In New York, a city of eight million people, neighbors helped neighbors during the 2003 blackout. Perhaps the resiliency learned from surviving 9/11 stimulated the neighborliness and cooperation.

Knowing That Fantasies of a Missing Person Are Common

Hallucination may be viewed as pathology by many therapists, but with ambiguous loss, I view such experiences as normal. They indicate that the loss is not yet recognized. Hearing the missing person's voice or feeling the person's presence is commonly reported by those who are attached to the missing person.

Watching Out for No-talk Rules

It is difficult to detach when the fact of a missing person is kept secret or simply ignored by one's community. Until recently, officials did not want to hear about the missing. This added to the distress of those who were attached to them. Therapists can help such family members by informing communities that it is just as important to support families of the missing as it is to support families of the deceased. An example might be people from faith communities making it possible for caregivers to go to services weekly, with various people taking turns to provide respite care and transportation. In this way, the community helps support those who are having difficulty revising their attachment to an ambiguously lost person.

Paying Attention to Developmental Stages That Exacerbate Anxiety

Whether it is a mother leaving a baby to go to work, a couple sending their child off to college, or adult children authorizing hospice care for an elderly parent, it is human nature to be upset and become anxious when close relationships shift. Yet, across the life cycle, they do. Maturation and death occur even without disasters or illness. Letting our children go is normal but nevertheless anxiety-producing. Burying our parents and grandparents is normal but often traumatic. What is not normal is having loved ones simply vanish. Such losses block normal developmental transitions and may freeze people in the stage they were in when the ambiguous loss took place.

Including Children and Adolescents in Therapy When Parents or Siblings Disappear

When children and youth are abandoned—volitionally or non volitionally—and become victims of broken attachments, they need immediate interventions to prevent attachment problems and posttraumatic stress disorder later on. Family and community based interventions, because they are relational, can help rebuild parent-like or sibling-like connections to compensate for a child's missing family members.

Children traumatized by a missing parent or sibling should not be disconnected from the people they know and trust just at the time they most need them. Multiple-family groups including parents and children of all ages are ideal to therapeutically rebuild security and new connections after a loved one disappears. A successful example of children healing in a family and community context is the New York Theater project in lower Manhattan for the children in Public School 234 who were traumatized by the losses of 9/11 (Saul, 2003).

Using Multiple-Family and Couple Groups to Build New Connections

Groups for therapy, support, and psychoeducation are helpful for individuals, couples, and families who suffer trauma from lost attachments. The prevention of premature extrusion and closure or denial that anything has changed happens more effectively in a group format, as such maladaptive coping strategies will be challenged by peers in the group. The synergy of the system helps shift perceptions and erode defenses. Peer groups also help normalize ambivalence, guilt, and shame, and thus minimize the complicated emotions that hinder the revising of attachments after ambiguous loss. Whenever stress is beyond normal human experience, revising attachment and connecting to others is more possible in a safe holding environment with trusted others who are in a similar predicament.

Encouraging the Use of the Arts

Because revising attachment is primarily an experiential process, the arts are especially helpful. Clients have their own way of doing this, but the therapist can encourage their sharing of art, poetry, music, literature, photographs, or film. John Lennon's "Mother" musically encapsulates the poignant example of a child whose mother disappeared from his life, came back, and later died. Psychotherapy can be enriched by such artistic expression, and one can find a song, story, or film that addresses almost any conceivable broken or ambiguous attachment. The point is that when people are experientially moved by emotions evoked through the arts, they are in a place where change is less frightening, and relational revisions become more possible.

CONCLUSION

When human beings are deeply attached to one another, and when the pain of separation is shrouded in ambiguity, there is understandably resistance to let go. The therapeutic goal, therefore, is not closure, as there is no possibility for it. Rather, we work therapeutically to help people accept the paradox—the person they love is gone, but may not be. They can, despite the ambiguity, make new attachments and at the same time hang on to the one that is missing. With this permission to avoid closure, people's resistance is lessened and change becomes more possible.

Unfortunately, I see more judgment than empathy about the persistent resistance to let go of a loved one who is physically or psychologically missing. Professionals from all disciplines need more patience and understanding about this unique kind of loss that can remain ambiguous for decades or a lifetime. Without proof of death, detachment is impossible. Instead of focusing on closure, we must help people build new connections with others. With revised attachments, new hope can be discovered.

Chapter 9

Discovering Hope

We have now come full circle. The work of finding meaning, tempering mastery, reconstructing identity, normalizing ambivalence, and revising attachment ideally culminates in discovering hope, a circular process that links back to meaning. Without meaning, there is no hope. Without hope, there is no meaning.

As people struggle with the trauma of ambiguous loss, they and their loved ones must sort out what to continue hoping for and what hopes to relinquish. These relational processes can move them toward discovering new hopes. In a collaborative process, which at times seems chaotic due to its circularity, couples and families gradually see that hope lies in change rather than a dearly held status quo. Despite the difficulties with uncertainty, many people can and do discover hope—but it is a reconstructed hope for a future altered by ambiguous loss.

Hope is defined as belief in a future good. It is a positive belief with the expectation of fulfillment. It is believing that suffering can stop and that comfort is possible in the future. Hope is a "desire with expectation of obtainment" (*Merriam-Webster's Collegiate Dictionary,* 2003, p. 598). Such definitions of hope reflect a more mastery-oriented view of the world (Chapter 5). That is, hope involves the assumption that things will turn out as we want them to be. We assume favor or goodwill from a higher authority. In theology this is called *grace.* In psychology some say this is the ego wanting its own way.

While it is not useful to generalize about Eastern and Western views due to global mobility and the fact that there are countries (e.g., Russia) where

177

currents from both sides are found in the culture, I nevertheless see variation in people about how hope is viewed. Often, in people who accept Western philosophies, hope is desired, while those who accept more Eastern philosophies view hope as unnecessary, even detrimental.

Tibetan monks, for example, believe that suffering is an inevitable part of human life and that hoping for something better is not a worthy goal. However, like Victor Frankl, most Westerners reject the idea that suffering is inevitable and accept instead the hope that there are positive outcomes to problems.

The dilemma arises in cases of ambiguous loss when the problem cannot be solved. Indeed, in cultures that value hope, we often resist the reality of loss (a suffering) and ambiguity, both of which defy mastery. We wait too long to discover a new hope. Unaccustomed to being held captive by losses we did not seek—a mate with traumatic brain injury, a missing child—we hold out for the outcome we wanted. A more existentialist view, however, is that if hope for the status quo goes on too long without revision, it stops one from doing what needs to be done—paying attention to those still present in one's life, going back to work, taking care of the children. In therapy, I often refer to Sisyphus, the character from ancient Greek mythology who continued to push the rock up the mountain even though he knew that he had no hope of succeeding. As part of discovering hope, we must ponder the question: Is this resilience or just plain egocentricity and stubbornness?

In defining hope, I must also clarify what it is not. Hope is not the same as faith, but the two are linked. With faith we are willing to take whatever comes. With hope, we expect a *good* outcome. The actions of Dietrich Bonhoeffer, a Protestant pastor imprisoned by the Nazis and later stripped naked and shot, illustrate the link. Before he knew his fate, he wrote from his cell about ambiguity and faith: "We throw ourselves at the mercy of God without knowing where it will end. That is Faith" (Till, 2000). What Bonhoeffer's words mean to me is that having faith in God's benevolence is evidence of humility and meekness rather than of a hope for a positive outcome. With faith, people trust in a higher authority, and as most believers view God as benevolent, the assumption of a good outcome may still be there. Without faith as the link, however—or fatalistic beliefs in destiny over which one has no control—hope may depend totally on one's own powers of mastery and control. But hope must be broader than the personal. When it becomes relational and considers the greater good for family and community, hoping is not egocentric whether or not it is linked to faith. More will be said about this later.

Hope is also not optimism. As Vaclav Havel said, hope "is not the conviction that something will turn out well [for me], but the certainty that something makes sense, regardless of how it turns out" (1990, p. 181). Havel brings us back, then, to the central idea of meaning, to which hope is inherently linked. How we see the world will determine how and what we hope for. In the Jewish death camps of the Holocaust, Frankl discovered that meaning had to contain some hope for a better life, not just escape. For if all this suffering and dying had no meaning, ". . . then ultimately there is no meaning to survival; for a life whose meaning depends upon such a happenstance—whether one escapes or not—ultimately would not be worth living at all" (Frankl, 1963, p. 183). Without a meaningfully positive outcome—an outcome that goes beyond ourselves—there is hopelessness and despair.

HOPE AND AMBIGUOUS LOSS

Hope is ideally based on a reasonable appraisal of the situation. But what if a reasonable appraisal is not possible? When losses remain unclear, extraordinary means are needed to find hope. During the first days after a disaster where loved ones disappear, the hope is for finding the lost person and a happy reunion. But when ambiguous loss goes on for years or even decades, having hope requires periodic reevaluations and discovery of more realistic things to hope for. A woman whose two sons disappeared during Argentina's 1976–1983 military dictatorship said her hopes were originally to find them alive. Now they have shifted to discovering where they are buried. Her ultimate hope is that before she dies, she can honor them with flowers on their graves. As she grows older, she may have to revise these hopes once again. Clearly, when losses remain ambiguous, what one hopes for changes over time. The process of discovery never ends.

What has to be grasped is the absurdity of finding hope in ambiguous loss. A therapist in one of my workshops asked, "Isn't the capability to live with ambiguous losses like Keats's 'negative capability'?" Indeed, Keats had written about ceasing to reach after facts and reason and simply being comfortable with the uncertainty, mystery, and doubt—"remaining content with half-knowledge" (Forman, 1935, p. 72).[1] This is an apt description of what people must do to maintain resiliency after ambiguous loss. Keats's description of "negative capability," then, is precisely the skill needed to discover new hope when the ambiguity will not alter.

How Does Discovering Hope Relate to Resiliency?

Is the maintenance of hope the same as resilience? Not really. In the short term, hoping for a return to the status quo helps maintain resilience (Boss, 2002c; Walsh, 1998) but over time, it does not. Hoping too long for what used to be erodes resilience. A New York grandmother told me a story about her 10-year-old grandson, whose father was missing in the rubble of the towers. When the mayor invited families down to Ground Zero for a ceremony, the little boy was elated. He was certain that once there, he would be able to find his father. His grandmother could see his hopes were too high because he was so happy on the ferry going over to Ground Zero. Once there, the boy was stunned to see the acres of rubble, and he grew quiet. He realized then that finding his father was hopeless. He cried for the first time. On the positive side, the visit to the disaster site allowed him to move forward in the process of grieving and to begin to find new hope, a necessary requirement for resiliency.

Unrelenting hope that is static and rigid erodes resilience and health. Whether loved ones are missing in mind or body, our hopes and dreams for staying connected to them must eventually be transformed into something attainable. This is also true for more common experiences of ambiguous loss such as divorce, adoption, and immigration. To complicate matters, reconstructions of hope are needed across the life cycle due to normal maturation as well as relational changes—births, marriages, and deaths (Boss, 1980b). One could say, as Steven Cooper did, that "the ability to create, resurrect, challenge, modify, and even renounce our hopes is as good as any other definition of health as I have come across" (2000, p. 73). Like the grandmother who took her grandson to Ground Zero to see the reality of his father's fate, the discovery and rediscovery of hope needs to be a lifetime capability if one is to have resiliency over the life span. The grandmother had that capability, and hopefully she passed it on to her grandson.

THEORY BASE

Without finding some new hope in the trauma of ambiguous loss, there is no meaning to life, but without meaning, there is no possibility of discovering that new hope. Because hope is so closely allied to meaning, the social construction theory described in Chapter 4 is useful also in this chapter. Emotion-based therapy and cognitive and psychoeducational interventions are also appropriate. Emotion-based therapy is, however, especially important in finding hope in that it makes central the human connections people need to feel secure enough to let go of old hopes with the missing person. (For books on how talking and emotion-based therapy help heal when things have gone wrong, see Luepnitz's *The Family Interpreted,* 2002b, and *Schopenhauer's Porcupines: Intimacy and Its Dilemmas,* 2002a[2]).

Because individual and relational resilience are so interconnected, therapeutic work is both relational and intrapsychic. We attend to latent and manifest ambivalence, guilt, shame, and denial—all common outcomes in the inherently confusing ambiguous loss. Unlike traditional psychoanalysis, people's stories, dreams, fears, and hopes can be expressed in the presence of others—friends, family, and peers. The relational connection is not just with a therapist. Rather, after a traumatic ambiguous loss, the therapeutic goal is to help people rediscover hope in human connections in a community *outside* the therapy room.

Despite managed-care restrictions, there is a renaissance of emotion-based talk therapy. Johnson's (1996, 2002) emotion-focused therapy (EFT) is becoming more prominent, and Leupnitz (2002a, 2002b) has proclaimed, "Talk therapy works!" But we must make sure that talk therapists encourage more than therapeutic discussion *about* parents; rather, parents and children should be included in some of the therapy sessions—if not physically, then psychologically through family of origin work. The psychological family can be included even in therapy with individuals.

Hope is embedded in the search for human connection. According to Sroufe (2002), hope for marital as well as child-parent relationships involves an individual intrapsychic development of possibilities and limits. When attachment is anxious, and hopelessness develops, hope has to be reclaimed. The question with ambiguous loss, however, is this: When the attachment figure disappears—for example, a mother is swept away by a tsunami or psychologically disappears into depression—how does a child know when to let go and hope for something different? In laboratory experiments, a toddler relaxes when its mother returns to the room. But what happens if she goes missing for years or forever? And what if the child's remaining parent becomes so depressed or addicted that he or she is once again denied attachment? Similarly, what about parents bereft of their children? What if one's child is ripped away by a kidnapper or illness? These questions, all too real across cultures, require a broader, more contextual theory—the theory of ambiguous loss, which is based in stress and resiliency theory (see the Introduction and Chapters 2 and 3).

Children are immensely resilient, and if professionals build on resiliency rather than deficits, we will learn that new hope is discovered in vastly diverse ways. For the time being, to alleviate hopelessness, I recommend for children and adults the interventions using ambiguous loss, stress, and resiliency theories.

Methodological Suppositions

From a contextual and competence-based perspective, both adults and children will eventually make the best adaptations they can to the hopelessness of reunification with lost loved ones. In these interventions, there must be a communal opportunity for emotional expression through storytelling, the arts, and physical movement, ideally in the presence of peers who have experienced the same kind of loss. There needs to be opportunity for new and trusted human connections—again preferably to peers, not just therapists—to provide the community interaction that helps mobilize the process of finding new hope, individually and collectively. Our professional task is to mobilize and collaborate within the community to guide and stimulate the discovery of hope.

WHEN HOPE HELPS

When impossible hopes are turned into newly discovered opportunities, growth occurs. We finally lose hope for saving a loved one with a terminal illness, but our hopes shift instead for a good death, one with less pain. Instead of hoping for a mate to quit drinking we shift our hopes to strengthening our own health and well-being. Losing hope for a marriage due to addiction means profound despair, but such crises can be opportunities for growth and change.

Hope builds resilience if it is realistic. With narrative techniques, psychodynamic therapy, and a safe environment, unconscious material emerges even in couple and family therapy. Stories, dreams, poems, and symbols are shared. Sadness is normalized in recognizing lost hopes and dreams. Once we let go of hoping for an impossible past and shift to hoping for a future that has some realistic possibility, a more mature hope develops. Hope also helps with the following, which are discussed later in this chapter under "Guidelines for Intervention."

- Finding spirituality
- Imagining options
- Laughing at absurdity
- Developing more patience
- Redefining justice
- Finding forgiveness
- Creating rituals for ambiguous loss
- Rethinking termination
- Revising the psychological family

WHEN HOPE HINDERS

There are times, however, when hope can hinder the healing process. Hope hinders in the development of resilience when people suffering from ambiguous loss persist in hoping for closure and finding definitive answers. Hope is a hindrance when people look too long for lost loved ones or continue to long for life as it used to be. The therapeutic task instead is to build tolerance for paradox. Schopenhauer and Freud both warned us about searching for the perfect cure (Luepnitz, 2002a).

So is it pathological to hope? From the stress perspective, health and resiliency depend on some element of hope. In the case of ambiguous loss that means leaving the door open for what was (because there is no verification of death) but also being open to the discovery of new hopes and dreams. The hope for a return of the missing person is held concurrently with moving forward and envisioning a hopeful future without the lost person. Without this dialectical movement, hope is dysfunctional. Hope is a hindrance then when the desire is for an unrealistic outcome that denies the ambiguous loss. It is also a hindrance when the sufferer, to alleviate the trauma and pain, seeks closure when there is none. For example:

- An abused wife takes no action and continues to suffer the pain, hoping that her abuser will see the light and stop beating her.
- A husband passively continues to hope that his alcoholic wife will stop drinking without taking some action or seeking help himself.
- The partner of a terminally ill man continues frenetically to search for a cure instead of being there for him and living life to the fullest in the time that is left.

In such cases, continuing to hope, simply preserves the status quo. Change is often needed in what one hopes for, but this is a difficult shift to make even for professionals. We too despair when hopes of making things better fade. Some call this a lust for cure and caution us to be careful about what we hope for because our wishes may come true. Hoping for an ill person's return from the brink of death may bring greater suffering. The denial of death that parallels unrelenting hope may bring greater suffering to loved ones kept alive but brain-dead for years—and to those who love them. Clinicians as well as family members know all too well the ambivalence that comes from hoping too long and the agonizing decisions that have to be made about whether to use technology to extend people's lives or let them go. The Terri Schiavo case was an agonizing example.

Hope can also be toxic when it feeds revenge and hate. It hinders resilience when we have hoped for one thing so long (e.g., freedom from abuse, from illness, from oppression) that we are disillusioned when we are finally free. Ironically, the moment a hope is fulfilled is also the moment that requires new hope. Without the resilience to discover new hopes, the disillusionment predominates until we find another meaning for our lives. I see this difficult transformation in soldiers who return to their families and hometowns from the trauma of war. I see it in abuse victims who, now free of the abuse, struggle to find new identities and hopes for themselves beyond the victim role. I see it also in devoted caregivers of the terminally ill or demented who, once released from their vigil by the death of their loved one, struggle desperately to find new hope for a future that is more life-affirming. Disillusionment is not inevitable, but it may be greatest for those whose meaning during the period of ambiguity was based on the hope for the outcome they wanted for themselves.

It is because happy endings are rare with ambiguous loss that new hope has to be discovered. When we realize that a person we love is fading further and further away, or that he or she will never again be the person we knew, we must face the fact that what we originally hoped for is no longer possible. For the sake of health and resiliency, we need to find something new and positive to look forward to—some other human connection and a cause beyond ourselves that has meaning. Like a Möbius strip, hope leads to meaning, and meaning leads to hope.

THERAPY METHODS AND GUIDELINES
FOR DISCOVERING NEW HOPE

The goal of therapy is to discover new hope via a curiosity and imagination that transcends the relational life that used to be and is now partially gone. The transformation often comes as an epiphany, a sudden realization that life can go on despite a missing loved one. I have seen transformation in the parents of missing children who after many years still hope for their return. In a previous book I wrote about Betty and Kenny Klein in Monticello, Minnesota, who still 45 years later advertise annually for their missing boys while also tending to their subsequent children and grandchildren (Boss, 1999). Patty Wetterling in Minnesota also has never given up hoping for reunion with her kidnapped son, Jacob, missing now since 1989. Through a foundation that led to faster reporting of missing children and public service, she hopes for the prevention of other kidnappings and, at the same time, honors her son and her private hopes.

I have also seen this transcendence in a woman whose longtime mate was hit by a car running a red light. He was in a coma for a month and still today suffers from traumatic brain injury. Eventually, she had to make painful decisions about moving him to assisted living. Psychologically, he was still in her life, but it became impossible for him to be at home. He now lives in a facility near her home and has the professional help he needs. Her transcendence in this dilemma came when she realized her hope to have him live at home was no longer possible, but that having separate living quarters made their life together possible again. They could visit, dine together, joke, and go to movies or play piano. She had discovered the paradox.

Needless to say, revised hope is forever a compromise and less than what one desired (which is usually a return to the ways things were before the ambiguous loss). The paradoxical outcome is therefore inherently unfair. Justice is compromised. The good news is that although the solution is imperfect, it is better than the alternative of hanging on to unrealistic hopes. People come to see that risking change is less painful than the status quo.

How Does Hope Link to Therapeutic Action?

Hope cannot be willed. It emerges from a growing excitement about the possibility of attaining one's desires, of being happy again, and of reaching some larger desired goal. Our therapeutic task is to help people without hope to discover it. With those whose hopes are shattered or too rigid to allow for change, our task is to help them reappraise the reasonableness of their hope and to prevent permanent family splits or couple breakups over conflicts about what is hopeless and what can become new hopes and dreams. Together, we reconstruct an excitement for alternative hopes and what might be possible despite not getting the outcome originally wanted. Creativity and spirituality help in this process, but discovering new hope can also be aided by nature, the arts, and interactions with trusted family, friends, and colleagues.

Finding hope is based on inner feelings, so the therapeutic process at this stage primarily includes psychodynamic approaches along with the cognitive and psychoeducational. The goal is to nurture belief in self and personal power (e.g., tempered mastery). A support system of trusted others back up a sense that "I can do it!" Through narratives, hope is reviewed and reconstructed. We encourage creativity and exploration in this process and have used, among other activities, painting, music, dancing, imaging, and improvisational theater techniques. Movement is essential. Once can't just talk about discovery. We have to seek hope actively. New experiences in both familiar and diverse contexts help this process.

This consideration of change versus status quo is born out of motivation for self-preservation. That is, people go to great lengths to preserve the relationships they need in order to survive. The therapeutic goal to maintain hope after ambiguous loss builds on that single-minded desire to preserve a lost relationship but then shifts that desire gradually to a more attainable hope. Therapeutically, the goal is to discover hope for something good, not retribution, though this often comes up when loved ones are lost through man-made destruction. Developing trust in the therapist is essential in moving from negative to positive hopes. Working with New York City families after 9/11, we saw that lost hopes were eventually balanced with new hopes and connections, including the therapeutic connection. But most helpful for positive hope was the collaborative discovery of the possibility of something better down the road.

After 9/11, our assumptions of resiliency gave families the respect they needed to discover new hope about their missing persons and their future lives without them. It also gave us as therapists new hope about being helpful and effective with these families. Amidst the chaos and ambiguity, families persevered, helping each other at the family meetings, as well as back in their neighborhoods between meetings. Human connections increased resilience, and resiliency increased the discovery of new hope. The adults in these families, mostly uprooted immigrants who had lived through hard times and even terrorism in their homelands, said that knowing they had bounced back before gave them hope now. Using the resiliency model, therapists became more patient and looked for strengths. People told us they felt relieved when we did not push for closure. We did not make them feel guilty for hanging on to hope. With an emphasis on building family and community connections, therapists, too, benefited from this process of discovery. We were delighted to witness the unique—and functional—strengths that people used to regain hope. The discovery of hope is a process that requires both clients and therapists to recognize the possibility of positive outcomes.

Guidelines for Intervention

What is the therapeutic process? Two premises guide our work. First, to discover hope, active coping is needed (Boss 2002c). Although we cannot know with a particular client whether this action to discover hope emanates from psychological, biological, social, religious, or artistic processes, we can assume that finding new hope requires action, not passivity. Second, although we value and use both cognitive and psychoeducational interventions, the goal of discovering hope especially benefits from emotion-based talk therapy in interaction with others, especially peers who have experienced the same kind of ambiguous loss. Merging these two points, we strengthen resiliency by setting the stage for interaction with extended family, friends, and community. This allows for various sources of hope and varied healing stories from diverse cultures and religions. The following guidelines build on these premises.

Finding Spirituality

To find hope after ambiguous loss, trusting in God, Allah, or an entity larger than oneself gives comfort to many. Research evidence indicates that spiritual support with meaning and a sense of hope helps people cope better with their situation (Pargament, 1997; Walsh, 2004). Research evidence is growing on the benefits of religion and spirituality to one's health (see Chapter 4). But more than other situations of loss, ambiguous loss requires spiritual acceptance.

Jung said his patients had fallen ill because they lacked a religious outlook and were not healed until they got it back. He believed this had nothing to do with church or dogma but with the human psyche. From my perspective, I leave it up to clients to tell me the specifics of what the ambiguity means to them, how they perceive control and mastery, and how they see themselves in relation to hope. I do not judge their belief system, but I do nurture discovery options that are spiritual if they are healthy and life-enhancing. That is, I do not condone life-threatening options such as homicide, suicide, abuse, and retribution, even if they are within the client's religious beliefs.

Ambiguous loss often brings anger and disillusionment with others or with God. When this happens, our clinical task is not to discuss theology or proselytize but rather to raise more general ideas about hope and suggest that we cannot always control what happens. At the same time, we nurture individual tolerance for ambiguity and unanswered questions. As we continue psychotherapy in this vein, I may refer clients to their clergy for further religious exploration. This stance vis-a-vis religion is for me a matter of ethics.

Although psychotherapists can discuss matters of trust and faith in the unknown when there are ambiguous losses, those of us who work in public institutions cannot ethically promote one specific religious belief. We must instead be inclusive and attend less to personal religious values than to universal beliefs and values—for example, kindness, forgiveness, equality, honesty, fairness, and treating others as we wish to be treated. Because I am not trained in theology, when it comes to private religious beliefs or anger at one's God, I refer clients to their own clergy or invite them to bring their clergy member in for a session. Overall, although religion and spirituality are clearly important, I focus therapy on the more general levels of resiliency—finding meaning, tempering mastery, reconstructing identity, normalizing ambivalence, revising attachment, and discovering hope—rather than prescribing a particular religious dogma or belief. This more general approach to finding hope allows me to work with vastly diverse clients and families without disrespecting their personal values and beliefs.

Ultimately, the therapeutic goal is to gain acceptance about the fact that we can't control everything that happens to our loved ones—or to us. Knowing that there are more unanswered questions than certainty in life, people are more able to temper their desires for mastery and control. If clients are religious, they put more faith in God while hoping for something better; if they are not religious, they trust in a greater entity or cause that will make their lives more manageable despite uncertainty. Many people combine both. In a myriad of ways, people find new hope, but whatever road they take to get there, hope is linked with meaning

What clients tell me after their traumatic ambiguous loss is rarely within my own experience. A woman hopes to talk at night with her missing husband—and for a while after he went missing, she tells me she did. A man hopes for a return to health and intimacy with his brain-injured wife. I have never experienced this kind of hoping, but I am not going to say that the people who do are unrealistic. Realistically, what can be hoped for after one loses a mate to brain injury, dementia, terrorism, or kidnapping? Our therapeutic task is help people with losses beyond our own experience find hope and meaning. To do this, they need to draw on something larger than themselves. Some call this transcendence. I call it the resiliency manifested by discovering new hope for a positive future despite unanswered questions.

Imagining Options

With the trauma, there is often outrage. Analysts might call this "narcissistic outrage." But with the trauma of ambiguous loss, it is an irrational external force that vetoes one's options and rational choices. Meaning and thus hope must be imagined. Albert Einstein said that imagination was more important than knowledge because "knowledge is limited, whereas imagination embraces the entire world, stimulating progress, giving birth to evolution" (Calaprice, 2000, p. 10).

Our task is to present what may be the individual's or family's only remaining option—to imagine how to move forward in the fog. With no solution in sight, the creative arts can provide new ideas for hope. Playwright John Guare said at the Guthrie Theater in Minneapolis that "especially when situations are weird and crazy, it takes an artist to figure them out" (personal communications, April 5, 2003, & December 4, 2004). Writers and painters have always given us insight about the meaning of ambiguous loss. Many plays have been written about it—Guare's and almost all of Arthur Miller's, for example. The novel *Winesburg, Ohio,* by Sherwood Anderson (1921), is in my opinion also about ambiguous loss—the ambiguity and ambivalence about leaving one's hometown for the city with loved ones left behind. Artists have long struggled with the meaning of ambiguity and uncertainty in human relationships, and we can learn from their creative insights. From Shakespeare to contemporary films like *Finding Nemo* (Stanton & Unkrich, 2003), emotions can be touched and loosened. Seeing new options, hope becomes more possible. The poet imagines a couplet, the playwright a scene, and the musician a score. As for clients, hopefully they imagine a new way of relating to loved ones both absent and present.

Literature, poetry, film, art, and music often spur individual and collective unconscious processes toward creating a new way of being together—symbolically and functionally. What motivates this process, however, must emerge from people's own culture. They may not love movies or music, but it is important to discover what does move them. The discovery of hope lies within their family and its community, and therapists need to employ that systemic perspective when seeking options for hope. After 9/11, we included painting, dancing, and singing in family memorial ceremonies because family members, young and old, requested them. Other projects focused on improvisational theater and narrative collections (Landau & Saul, 2004; Saul, 2003). Such emotion-based activities help adults and children face their hopelessness, a necessary step before moving toward the future with reconstructed hopes. The arts show us that there are multiple truths but also some common desires. Artists, therapists, researchers, and survivors—each group has its own perspective on truth, and each discovers it in their own way.

Laughing at Absurdity
Humor is an acknowledgement of things being the crazy way that they are. If we remain humorless, we are without hope. If we can begin to laugh, we have the capacity to find hope.

In 1949, George Orwell wrote, "It was a bright cold day in April, and the clocks were striking thirteen" (p. 5). If only for a moment, lines like Orwell's can grab our attention even in the midst of despair. As humor is used to reach for hope, the absurdity of ambiguous losses can often be relieved by a laugh. A wife whose husband was never found after 9/11 says at a meeting after someone makes a proposal she dislikes, "My husband would roll over in his grave—if he was in one!"

When people traumatized by ambiguous loss begin to laugh, they are beginning to transcend suffering by mocking it. Dark humor reflects the absurdity in their situation and provides momentary relief from hopelessness. Pressure is released by laughing.

People have always laughed at the proverbial man slipping on a banana peel because it gives them hope. They feel superior because they are not the one falling. If this jerk who is the butt of the joke survives a fall, we can, too. Suffering can be overcome. Hope is alive. Laughing at the other guy's fall releases our fears of loss and shame. Said another way: Laughing at the absurdity in ambiguous loss helps people rediscover hope.

Whether it is laughing at oneself or another person, we like to see the powerful fall and the vulnerable recover and stand up again. From Charlie Chaplin to Lucille Ball and Carol Burnett, the more irrational a situation, the more potential there is for hope. The clown becomes the mayor; the mayor becomes the clown. Barump! If the clown falls, it's comedy; if he doesn't get up again, it's tragedy. Both comedy and tragedy can stimulate the discovery of hope.

But what if there are jokes in the therapy room? If a client tells a joke in a therapy session, is it all right to laugh? Ellenhorn says it is, as long as you laugh with the patient, not at them (T. Ellenhorn, personal communication, April 4, 2003). (I add that it is all right to cry with them as many therapists found themselves doing after 9/11.) A safe holding environment for therapy may indeed include laughing or crying *with* clients. If, however, a therapist's laughing or crying is counter transference that goes beyond empathy, consultation is in order. Clearly, letting one's own unresolved losses override the therapy session is not ethical, so we need to be acutely aware of our personal needs to laugh or cry. Is humor used as a defense mechanism to hide underlying hostility and shame? Does telling jokes hide our own anxiety or lack of a sense of humor? Do we use humor to control or hurt others? Finally, is the humor aiding connection to others? The therapeutic value of a joke about absurdity is greater when humor becomes a means for new connection and hope.

Developing More Patience

Patience is a therapeutic hallmark for discovering hope. Rather than holding out for a perfect solution or cure, we help people become more patient with unanswered questions. This takes time. Professionals, too, must overcome impatience with their own feelings of helplessness when treating ambiguous loss. We, too, must learn to be comfortable with ambiguity. Hope can only be discovered by embracing the ambiguity—and knowing we aren't there, yet. We may never be. We may have to help clients find another "there"—that is, another place to aim for that is more within their reach. To revise one's hopes is not failure but rather resilience in the face of a world that is at times unfair.

Redefining Justice

The nature of ambiguous loss is inherently unjust. Kidnappings and rape, as strategies for war and genocide, require our outrage. (Sluzki & Agani, 2003). Whether in a hospital, nursing home, courtroom, or refugee camp, people deserve and expect justice. It is not always forthcoming. Danieli's (1985) words remain helpful:

> Having been helpless does not mean that one is a helpless person; having witnessed or experienced evil does not mean that the world as a whole is evil; having been betrayed does not mean that betrayal is an overriding human behavior; having been victimized does not necessarily mean that one has to live one's life in constant readiness for its reenactment; having been treated as dispensable does not mean that one is worthless; and, taking the painful risk of bearing witness does not mean that the world will listen, learn, change, or become better a place. (p. 308)

Effort and outcome do not always match expectations. Bad things can happen to good people. When the perpetrators of kidnappings go free, or the causes of illness are not found, we must find justice—and hope—in new ways. Working to prevent other abductions or illnesses are examples of other routes to justice. With long-standing conflicts and ethnic cleansing, justice hopefully comes through the human rights courts and, perhaps later, some meaningful work together as neighbors in a common cause—for example, raising children in peace.

Justice is desired but not always possible in the way we originally hoped for. There are surprise outcomes in murder trials and in human rights trials. Perpetrators may go free after serving short sentences. Victim's families must live forever with their pain. Instead of seeking vengeance, hope is found by devoting oneself to working against the injustice. Such activity is movement toward new hope.

Finding Forgiveness

Robert Kennedy said that "each time a man stands up for an ideal or acts to improve the lot of others, or strikes out against injustice, he sends forth a tiny ripple of hope." Retribution is not therapeutic. Most families of those killed in Oklahoma City say Timothy McVey's execution failed to make them feel better (J. Martin, personal communication, June 18, 2004). In Oklahoma City, I asked a group of surviving family members what did make them feel better; they said it was sharing stories with other survivors and with the many people who come to see their memorial (Boss, 2004c). The caring exhibited by others who listened to their stories of loved ones lost in the bombing on April 19, 1995, brought feelings of connection and justice that eventually helped them let go of the hate.

A less catastrophic example of the need to let go of the hate is the refusal to forgive a spouse after divorce. One mate continues to harass the other over who gets the children, when, and for how long. Anxiety from warring parents may hurt the children more than the divorce itself, for persisting in seeking retribution certainly does not help them. The need for retribution and the refusal to let go of the hate in divorced couples denies hope for the future good of the parents and, above all, the children.

Creating Rituals for Ambiguous Loss

George Herbert Mead, a pioneer in symbolic interaction, said that meaning arises in the process of interaction with other people (Mead & Strauss, 1956). For a positive meaning that allows for hope amidst ambiguous loss, family gatherings and celebrations must be revised in order to continue. And continue they must. Social gatherings promote human interaction and thus set the stage for discovery of hope. Rituals and celebrations keep couple and family interactions going despite a partially absent or present family member. Such interactions are also powerful means to avoid secrets and effect change (Boss, 1999; Imber-Black, 1993; Imber-Black, Roberts & Whiting, 1988).

One of the most useful interventions my team and I used with families of Alzheimer's disease was to help the group discuss and reconstruct their traditional rituals and family celebrations rather than cancel them. They needed to adapt the family events for partial presence or absence rather than closing out the missing person. The ill person was included at the celebration, often in an honored place, but others covered his or her traditional tasks. A similar intervention was used after 9/11 for families of the physically missing. Here, through symbols—a photograph, a candle, some favorite food, an empty chair, or a favorite song—missing family members were kept present in family holiday celebrations and rituals. In most cases, after ambiguous loss, the families intend to cancel their usual rituals and celebrations.

Indeed, some families reconstruct the holiday celebration by going to a new place or traveling, but we recommend keeping some part of the event the same, and including symbols of the lost person—wherever the celebration is held.

In family meetings, we encourage questions like: Should the children still participate in trick-or-treating because Halloween is about ghosts and death? What should I do for Thanksgiving without my husband at the head of the table? Why shouldn't I stop celebrating anniversaries and birthdays? How can I get to church now? Although these are practical questions, they all have deeper psychological meanings critical to future hopes and well-being. Our clinical work follows the assumptions of symbolic interactions and social construction—in other words, that the family is a unity of inter-acting personalities (Burgess, 1968). This means that to preserve the family, interactions must continue. In the confusion from ambiguous loss, the best place to start is with familiar rituals and routines.

A word must be said about rituals not being helpful. When there is no body to bury, memorial rituals must rely on symbols alone. Bound by rigid rules of burial, sometimes religious doctrine prevents adaptations of ritual. This is very hard on the survivors, who want to honor the person who vanished. In ancient Greece, cenotaphs were used to mark the graves that were empty. Usually cenotaphs were "used for those who lost their lives far from home or those whose bones were for some reason irrecoverable, as in loss at sea. . . . They received the same offerings and respectful treatment as other graves. In some cenotaphs the body of the dead was supplied by a large stone around which offerings were placed" (Kurtz & Boardman, 1971, pp. 99–100). . . . In other cases, possessions cherished by the lost person—such as jewelry, mirrors, toys or weapons—were often buried in place of a missing body (Kurtz & Boardman, 1971). This is not unlike what New York families did after 9/11 in burying a missing husband's guitar or bowling ball when there was no body to bury. In ancient times, an unidentified poet wrote, "The certainty of death is attended with uncertainties, in time, manner, and places. The variety of Monuments hath often obscured true graves: and Cenotaphs confounded Sepulchres. For beside their real Tombs, many have found honorary and empty Sepulchres" (Kurtz & Boardman, 1971, p. 247). Indeed, they still do.

Rituals are necessary to mark the end of life, but if loved ones vanish, adaptations can be made symbolically. People can in their own way mark empty graves with cenotaphs. The rituals are necessarily adapted to demarcate new boundaries, roles, and rules in the family and thus give hope. For example, the gathering can symbolize to children that they do not have to take up the adult role of a missing parent. Rituals emphasize that there are other adults to support the remaining parent, and that children are free to be children a bit longer. On anniversaries of the loss and on special holidays formerly spent together, rituals and symbolic celebrations bring the unconscious longing into a social context, allowing survivors to honor and remember the lost person in the company of supportive others. The psychological family becomes explicit at such times and serves to help people find hope again.

Rethinking Termination

The termination of therapy is uniquely difficult with ambiguous loss. Shutting the door on the possibility of future visits with a therapist may be perceived as a betrayal and as one more ambiguous loss.

In my practice, I have an open-door policy. We may terminate, but at the same time, I clarify that if there should be new need for therapy in the future, clients can return for new work. To be sure, many people handle future losses and traumas on their own, but some cannot, and they return for more sessions to renew their hope.

Freud never wrote of termination as essential, but it has become a necessary step in modern analysis and many therapies. Without getting into the debate about kinds of termination, I question the value of absolute termination with cases of ambiguous loss. Of course, when the present therapy is completed, the relationship between therapist and client is transformed, but that does not mean future therapy is impossible. Bringing absolute closure to the therapeutic relationship runs counter to the treatment goal—developing resilience for ambiguity. Rather than closure and termination, people learn to live with ambiguity by holding the paradox of absence and presence. We must also.

According to Davies (2003) a termination can be a life-affirming process. There is, indeed, a mutual letting go and the recognition of having enough hope to move forward with one's life, but the door can be left open for future work. Growth and transformation are, after all, processes, not linear steps in one therapeutic period of work. To rediscover hope after ambiguous loss, therapists as well as clients must struggle against the ideas of absolute terminations and endings, for resilience lies in becoming comfortable with ambiguity, not in closing the door.

Any ending is marked by ambiguity. That is the nature of human relationships. With therapeutic and personal relationships, we often feel we need a little more time. This feeling is exaggerated with ambiguous loss. When there are leavings without good-byes, and good-byes without leaving, closure is inevitably incomplete. With ambiguous loss, the goal may be what Davies refers to as a "good-enough ending."

If it is true that therapists/analysts are stand-ins for all the unresolved losses and abandonments that went before (Davies, 2003), what is needed for marking an end to therapy that will maintain hopefulness? The therapeutic process may be, as Davis proposed, a series of many good-byes. In the guidelines listed here, I have suggested various ways that the therapy process can symbolically be a series of multiple endings, each gently grieved, yet none a closure. They are simply good enough to regain one's hope.

Revising the Psychological Family

The psychological family is an essential part of rediscovering hope. After a massive and confusing disaster, a person's psychological family may be the only thing familiar, and no one can take it away. This psychological connection to family, when all else is lost, becomes a resource for discovering hope again. This is true for professionals as well.

At the same time, however, we may miss the lost person and our life with them as it used to be. On special days, they are psychologically with us, not only in heart and mind but also in the symbols we use at dinners and in dress—a recipe, a tablecloth, jewelry, a particular flower or song, a silk scarf bought in a foreign city while shopping together. The people we love who are ambiguously lost are still in some way with us. This is an optimistic and hopeful idea. They are part of our psychological family—and can be as real to us as those fully present in our lives.

CONCLUSION

With ambiguous loss, hope must be discovered despite imperfect endings and unclear terminations. But such endings can be symbolically understood and, through narrative and relational therapies, reconstructed so as to renew hope. To discover hope is to embrace the ambiguity and then find meaning in it. The paradox becomes easier to live with than holding on to what was—an impossible hope.

We have now come full circle in Part II of this book. In the guidelines for resiliency and health after ambiguous loss, we began with finding meaning and ended with discovering hope, but the two are linked like a Möbius strip. Meaning and hope cannot exist without each other. One starts where the other ends. Both meaning and hope are needed for resiliency and health. In between the finding of meaning and the discovery of hope, the process involves tempering mastery, reconstructing identity, normalizing ambivalence, and revising attachment. The therapeutic process is circular, and not in linear stages. It is stress and resiliency focused, but does not ignore symptoms that need medical treatment. The overall goal is for skill collaboration, not just among patient and therapist, but among professionals who treat individuals, couples, or families.

Self-reflection becomes an essential part of this complex dialectical process of finding hope and meaning. Because this is true for therapists as well as clients, an epilogue follows that will focus exclusively on the self of the therapist. Our hope for professional effectiveness when working therapeutically with ambiguous loss depends on our own tolerance for ambiguity and comfort with unanswered questions.

Epilogue

The Self of the Therapist

To strengthen professional resiliency in order to work more effectively with people experiencing ambiguous loss, the goal is first to lower the ambiguity in the therapy process itself and second to increase our own tolerance for and comfort with ambiguity. It is the professional's comfort with ambiguity and the paradox of absence and presence that will ultimately provide the space for the client's acceptance of loss and change.

First, we must reflect on our own absence in the therapy room. We must own the ambiguous loss that can occur in the therapy process when we are preoccupied with other pressures or worries or simply fatigued. Of course, clients often hold back or refuse to participate or talk at all, in which case they are the ones only partially present in the process. But this can also happen with therapists, clergy, and medical professionals who are exhausted or simply burned out.

From the perspective of the people we serve, we are psychologically absent when we open mail during a session, take calls, doze off—or are preoccupied with personal problems and feelings of inadequacy. I have witnessed them all and experienced a few myself. Our psychological absence in a therapeutic session is not acceptable.

Being fully present for the people we work with should always be our priority. And our full presence is especially essential when clients are already suffering from the trauma of ambiguous loss. Minimizing any ambiguity in the therapy process is essential when one is treating people who are already suffering from too much of it. If the ambiguous loss in the client's life merges with ambiguity in the therapist's presence, the additional

197

tension erodes the client's trust in the process and, ultimately, the professional's feelings of effectiveness.

The trauma of ambiguous loss inherently challenges our ways of working. We may see people's failure to reach closure as our own failure. We may see the failure to ease suffering as our own incompetence. We are, after all, trained to make pain go away. But the goal with ambiguous loss is to help people live and live well with the suffering—perhaps for the rest of their lives. This has not been part of clinical training for most of us. It is no wonder that when doing this kind of therapeutic work, we are at times demoralized.[1]

I saw profound demoralization in many therapists and medical professionals after 9/11. Doctors and nurses waited for patients, but many stretchers remained eerily empty. Nearly 3,000 people disappeared on that terrible day. Everyone (professionals included) knew someone who had a loved one who was unaccounted for. The several hundred New York therapists I met with a short time after 9/11 said they were feeling ineffective at a time when they wanted to be helping. These were veteran therapists, highly skilled in classic grief and trauma therapies, but their usual way of doing therapy was not working in this unprecedented situation where so many friends, neighbors, coworkers, and loved ones had simply vanished.[2]

I have seen similar despair, although not so acute, among therapists and professionals who work with the brain-injured and chronically ill and their families. Here, loved ones are missing in mind, not body, but the effects are similarly distressing and traumatizing. Also, doing professional work in the context of patients who are not psychologically able to respond can make clinicians and family members feel isolated and hopeless.

All of us feel ineffective if we ignore the power of ambiguity to confuse and immobilize. If we limit ourselves to traditional ways of working and traditional assessments and interventions, we may miss the source of symptoms, which are situational and located within the client's external relational context. Instead of focusing only on medical symptoms and the traditional linear steps for grieving and identity reformation (with closure being the goal), we must participate in collaborative, dialectical therapeutic processes. We become witnesses who can validate the distress clients are experiencing—especially because no one else may be able to do this. Rather than seeing clients as malingering, we join them in the lack of knowing—for we, too, do not have the answers about this kind of loss.

While accepting the unknowability, therapists and professionals still need some hope that what we do is for the most part helping those who are traumatized by ambiguity. To do this, we focus optimistically on the capacity of human beings to change and remain resilient despite ambiguous loss. This includes us.

THE PLACE TO START

The theory of ambiguous loss theory provides a new modality for professionals to do their therapeutic work, whatever the discipline or training. At the same time, it can provide guidance for understanding one's own ambiguous losses. Whether this is called self-care, or self-of-the-therapist work, it is the essential starting place to strengthen our own resiliency for doing this therapuetic work and for becoming more comfortable with ambiguity ourselves. To begin this process, I recommend that each of us—no matter how senior or well trained—find one or two trusted professional peers to meet with regularly, perhaps monthly, and then listen patiently and nonjudgmentally to each other's stories of traumatic and ambiguous loss. If you prefer, find a therapist to do this with you. As with patients, some of your stories may be horrendous and difficult to hear (as well as tell), but it is a professional's job (even for peers) to listen empathically. Listening to a painful story of ambiguous loss is witnessing, and witnessing is the beginning of establishing human connection that provides the source of new meaning and hope.

Core Questions for Clinicians

When professional resiliency is a goal for training, it becomes apparent that technical proficiency is not enough. Being skilled at assessing others is also insufficient. Rather, we must also be willing to self-reflect and deepen our knowledge about ourselves. To guide professionals in self-work before they actually work with people experiencing ambiguous loss, a set of core questions has proven helpful. I have used these questions for self-study and peer discussion in my workshops around the world with therapists who seek to increase their competency and resiliency in treating the trauma from many different kinds of ambiguous loss.

You may address these questions individually, but the process works even better with one or two peers.

- Who is in your psychological family?
- What ambiguous loss have you experienced?
- What type? Physical? Psychological? Both?
- What did it mean to you then? What does it mean now?

Unless we entertain such core questions periodically, our own resiliency may be under peril, for it is unlikely that we have evaded trauma or ambiguous loss ourselves. To do our work, each of us needs the awareness of our own hopes (dashed and renewed) and meanings (negative and positive). We need the humility to accept the fact that we can't always heal suffering. Sometimes, for professionals, the discomfort regarding the pain we could not ease lies in our own family of origin or original culture. Indeed, early socialization in situations of trauma and loss are often reasons for selecting a career in the helping professions. We may have chosen our profession because we want to help people feel better, and when we cannot, we feel ineffective and helpless.

Traditionally we have been trained to master, fix, manage, and cure, but these goals are out of reach with ambiguous loss. No amount of professional skill, for example, can clarify the loss from Alzheimer's disease or from a loved one vanishing from an explosion or earthquake. When losses persist in being ambiguous, how do we as professionals find comfort despite our inability to bring closure and resolution to the sufferer? The answer lies in our own understanding of the phenomenon of ambiguous loss and our own tolerance for the unknown. It also lies in our resiliency to avoid being traumatized by not being in control.

The Study of Self for Resiliency

Building on a theoretical idea from pioneer family therapist Murray Bowen[3] (1978), therapists who work with traumatic and ambiguous losses cannot bring clients beyond where we ourselves are willing to go. We cannot expect people to understand beyond our own comprehension the links among loss, ambiguity, trauma, stress, and resilience. The people we work with are less likely to tolerate ambiguity if we, the therapists, are primarily oriented toward mastery and control.

Some Personal Reflections

The process of self-reflection can occur in different settings, including supervision, consultation, peer groups, and invited observation (Andersen, 1991; Haber, 1990; Rober, 1999; Rolland, 2004; Sluzki, 2004; Whitaker, 1989). Reflecting on personal experience with ambiguous loss can take place in any of these settings.

My epiphany about my own ambiguous loss came while I was in training for family therapy at the University of Wisconsin-Madison. Learning new information and observing others professionally, I suddenly saw my own case more clearly. In fact, this is the case I referred to earlier in this book. Peg was my nickname.

I was married at 19 to my high school sweetheart, who became addicted to alcohol after a job change into the business world. My way of coping as a good 1950s wife was to smooth the troubled waters so no one would notice. I wanted to stay in the marriage, so I went to Al-Anon for help. "Focus less on his drinking," they said, so I decided to cope by studying. I went back to the university and "coped" my way to a Ph.D.

What I realized was that I was married to someone who was psychologically absent. We had an intact family and lived in the same house, but he was rarely really there. I even wrote my doctoral dissertation on psychological father absence. But I began to know that all the work I was doing to cope was not helping. My health became brittle with numerous psychosomatic symptoms. In class at the university, I was lecturing on first- and second-order change, and I saw myself in the lesson. I was the one who needed a second-order shift. Instead of burying myself in more books or continuing to beg my husband to go for treatment, I took the advice of a therapy colleague and went alone to the weeklong Hazelden Family Program in Center City, Minnesota.

There, for the first time, I learned about addiction, its effect on couple dynamics and family relationships, and how I also was playing a part in maintaining the status quo. I had checked myself in as a patient even though I could have taken the week's work as a professional. I somehow knew that I needed to relinquish my expertise as a trained therapist and professor and submit to the family program simply as a person. It was the beginning of a new kind of coping for me—one less reactive and more about balancing acceptance with mastery. It was about resilience. Sadly, my then-husband did not stop drinking, a humbling reminder that there are things I cannot control.

What I learned was that my years of effort to master the problem of another's addiction only led to hopelessness. With great sadness, I had to accept that even as a trained therapist. I could only change myself. My psychosomatic symptoms had been increasing at an alarming rate. I frequently could not walk from paralyzing back spasms that required hospitalization. Illnesses kept me from work frequently. The children now had two dysfunctional parents. I knew what I had to do, and it was not easy given my beliefs and values. I filed for a legal separation. In reality, I had been alone for a long time before that. Being single and really alone was not as painful as being alone in a marriage.

I decided I needed therapy if I was to change the maladaptations I had learned. I needed to face my part in the dysfunction. I asked Carl Whitaker, my professor, if he would see my husband and me in a last ditch attempt to reconcile, and he said he would. He had, after all, seen the residents and trainees with their spouses. But he called back a day later, saying he could not see us. I was angry, thinking it was discrimination due to my gender. In those days, professors of psychiatry did, indeed, do therapy with the residents, who at that time were mostly male. I challenged Carl, but he held to his decision. "I cannot see you. It would be like doing therapy with my own family." Later on, I realized his refusal for therapy proved a major turning point for me. I knew then that I had to heal myself without a father figure doing it for me. With the help of another therapist, much younger but knowing and skilled, I made progress and knew I had done it without "Dad." I was always proud of finding my own way. Knowing this gave me new strength and the resiliency to make the many difficult decisions in the months and years ahead as a single mother and relatively new professional.

I grew up personally and professionally at the moment this wise mentor sent me out to struggle with my own problems. Carl and I remained colleagues, and he consented to write the preface for my first book on ambiguous loss (Boss, 1999). Sadly, he was stricken with a stroke before I had finished the book. Now he, too, was ambiguously lost. I saw this wonderful teacher and mentor for the last time a few months before he died. In the fall of 1994, I drove alone from St. Paul to Milwaukee on a bittersweet journey to thank Carl Whitaker for all he had taught me.[4]

What happened to my family? My husband and I divorced and later each of us remarried. But we still come together for special occasions. While Whitaker had made me angry when in a lecture he said there was no such thing as divorce, I know now what he meant. There is never closure. Although boundaries, roles, and identities shift after divorce and remarriage, we are all still connected through children and grandchildren and old friends. One never really disconnects from a close relationship, but a change is needed. A personal and relational reconstruction hopefully occurs and makes resiliency and health more possible.

The Professional Culture of Mastery

In professional culture, control is an implicit hallmark of clinical intervention. Discomfort comes when the problem does not lend itself to being mastered. Sadly, this happens quite often: People don't get well; they don't see the situation our way; they don't do what we prescribe; they do not comply. I learned this the hard way in my personal life. Tempering our need to control, then, becomes a major challenge and requires self-study, self-reflection, and self-development. Technique is never enough. We are, after all, sons and daughters of some unresolved loss. Many therapists today have personally experienced divorce, adoption, infertility, stepparenting, foster parenting, single parenting, migration, immigration, or being cut off from family due to difference in sexual orientation. It is the mark of a strong therapist to be curious about his or her own unresolved losses and to seek therapy, consultation, supervision, or peer group work in order to better understand one's self.

INCREASING OUR OWN COMFORT
WITH AMBIGUITY AND LOSS

Professionals can use the theory of ambiguous loss to guide personal as well as professional therapeutic work. We must know ourselves and our ambiguous losses if we are to work without adding more ambiguity to the therapeutic process. We must recognize our own issues so that we can stay fully present and empathic when clients tell their stories of unresolved loss and reveal their issues about meaning, mastery, identity, ambivalence, attachment, and hope.

How do we begin this personal process? In my workshops, each professional begins by privately drawing his or her psychological family on paper. Next, preferably with two or three peers, each struggles with the core set of questions given earlier. Professionals place their own experiences into the typology of physical and psychological losses and then talk about the losses they remember as traumatic. In this process, people almost always share narratives of personal and familial resiliency. This positive evidence energizes and gives hope. For those who want more depth or are stymied or hopeless about their situation, I encourage therapy regardless of whether the losses were recent or generations ago.

Here, as a reader of a book rather than workshop participant, I encourage beginning the process alone, with self-reflection, and after that moving to a small group of two or three trusted peers. You will notice that the following self-study questions expand on the previous core questions and echo the clinical guidelines developed in Chapters 4 through 9. This is because what helps clients suffering from the trauma of ambiguous loss can also help therapists, medical professionals, social workers, clergy, and other professionals.

We all suffer losses, clear and ambiguous, but we may apply the ideas in this book differently to ourselves than we do to our clients. What matters is that we reflect on our own experience. Whether for trainees or experienced therapists, the following questions, exercises, and ideas are meant to stimulate these self-reflective processes. Keep in mind that the process is more important than arriving at an answer, as there is no final answer.

Who Is Your Psychological Family?

To help you know who your psychological family is, I recommend you draw, with dotted lines on a blank sheet of paper, a circle to indicate the boundary of your perceived family. Indicate who is in and who is outside the boundary, as well as who flows back and forth. If you do this with your mate or family, be aware that others may draw their psychological family differently. I suggest sharing the drawings with each other, so that you can see the differing perceptions of who is in and who is out. However, in instances where harm may result from such revelations, keep the information confidential. Differences in perceptions of "who is family" are normal. Knowing these differences gives you insight about how to improve your own dynamics with your own partners and families, as well as with the increasingly complex cases you see today.

Why is this important to do? The therapy process involves the therapist and clients in the room together, plus the people psychologically present in their minds. Written decades ago, the words of Mendelsohn and Ferber (1972) are for me, as therapist and supervisor, still valid:

> Family therapy because of its immediacy and aliveness, much more than individual therapy, elicits therapist responses which relate to the therapist's own family of origin or family of procreation. We do *not* view this as "unanalyzed countertransference phenomena." Rather, we see this as an inevitable and natural process and one which the therapist will be encountering throughout his [or her] professional lifetime. The supervisor's task is not to help the therapist "solve" his [or her] family problems, but to teach him [or her] to be aware of, and to cope with, the secret presence of his [or her] own family in the treatment room. (p. 441)

Indeed, when we are more aware of our own psychological families and the ambiguous losses that have affected us through them, we are more able to help others with their ambiguous losses. In addition, the process minimizes the occurrence of countertransference and what Jordan called blind spots, biases, and "overidentification with the clients" (2003, p. 43). Regardless of what our response to clients is called, it is our responsibility to understand more about ourselves and our reactions when we work with those suffering from ambiguous loss. Knowing who our family is and knowing our own experiences with irresolvable loss helps. In this way, we more clearly own our vulnerability to the pain of ambiguity and thereby discover more empathy for clients. The hierarchy becomes flatter.

Paying attention to the presence of one's personal psychological family is useful for therapists in that it helps us be alert to its existence in professional work. Recently, my husband said, "You said something today that I wish my mother could have heard—because she would have agreed with you." At that moment, his mother, long deceased, and I came together in his mind. I liked his linking us, because I had never had the privilege of meeting her or sitting at her table as her daughter-in-law. What my husband said to me made me feel included in his family—a family I could never meet, due to death, except in his mind's eye.

What Is Your Comfort Level With Ambiguity?

Many therapists become impatient with survivors of ambiguous loss because they are uncomfortable with ambiguity. They need certainty. Yet it is important for sufferers to have someone listen patiently and nonjudgmentally to their stories. Indeed, their accounts are often horrendous and difficult to hear, but it is our job to listen empathically. A person's story of loss, you see, is not real in the social sense until someone is willing to hear it. That someone is often us.

To periodically check my ability to tolerate ambiguity, I borrow an idea from Carl Whitaker: With a child, grandchild, or a willing adult (most often my husband), I get in the car and intentionally get lost—and then enjoy the mystery of not knowing where we are. Of course, eventually we have to find our way back home, and only then do we resort to maps, laughing at our wandering trail. The experience of not knowing becomes associated with fun and is less fearsome when it later appears in real life. One's comfort with ambiguity ebbs and flows over the life course, but it often needs buoying. This is just one playful exercise for increasing that comfort.

How Do You Manage Your Own Stress?

Stress researchers found that the most stressful events involve loss of loved ones through death or circumstances that threaten their loss (e.g., death of a spouse, divorce, kidnapping, imprisonment). The next most powerful stressors are loss of one's health, loss of income, and loss of home (Hobfoll & Spielberger, 1992).

As you work professionally with people suffering from these kinds of loss—or when you experience them yourself—what helps? The answer is different for each of us. In general, we need to find an activity that recharges our spirit and energy. In our private life, we need to associate with people who restore rather than sap our energy. We need to be active and visit places that renew our soul. For some of us, that means going to social settings where people gather; for others it means retreating to a quiet place. Wherever it is, it should involve a passion greater than our work. (Trainees are always surprised by this idea, but in my experience, having a passion outside of one's work is essential to sustain professional resilience.)

I personally am passionate about my family and the arts. For the most part, I cope with the stress of working with ambiguous loss by connecting with loved ones and looking into the beautiful faces of my grandchildren. But when I am exhausted from a long stretch of work with this kind of trauma, I go on retreat to the Rocky Mountains, where I can simply listen to the silence. Unlike the serious hikers who do difficult treks, I meander through the high country on easy paths in the valleys around Estes Park well below the peaks. But meander I do. As an early female adventurer said, "Every valley ends in mystery" (Bird, 1960, p. 106). Being involved with pleasant mysteries and ambiguities helps me to deal with the traumatic ones.

How Do You Strengthen Your Own Resilience and Health?

It is from witnessing the human spirit and people's resilience after losing loved ones that we are energized and sustained to continue this work. For our clients, we know that the critical variable for resiliency and health is human connection, but sometimes we forget that for ourselves. It is primarily in interaction with others that people find meaning and new hope, personally and professionally. We should not fill our days so full professionally that we have no time for meaningful social connections. We also need to connect with other professionals in consultation, supervision, and continued education for prevention of professional burnout or fatigue. I have always maintained what Whitaker called "a cuddle group"—two or three other professional peers with whom I meet regularly in a private place to discuss cases, ethical dilemmas, professional issues, and new research information. Such groups help a therapist to sustain resilience and health by staying professionally connected. Of course, personal connections are also needed.

How Do You Find Meaning?

Whether it is faith in God to heal, faith in science to cure, or faith in oneself to overcome obstacles or illness, professionals need to reflect on the meanings attributed to ambiguous loss. For me, meaning lies in the middle ground between religion and science. I do not see them as mutually exclusive. With Calvinist free will and faith, my expectations are social action, hard work, and individual responsibility. Meaning and actions are linked— that is, the former motivates the latter. In my practice, meanings vary widely from my own. With tolerance and competence for working with diverse beliefs, therapy for an individual's or family's trauma from ambiguous loss can occur regardless of the match (or mismatch) between the beliefs of the client and the beliefs of the therapist. This is also true for training. Therapists do not need to talk about specific denominational faith or dogma. Most of us are not trained to do this. Our focus instead should be on more general meanings about positive human connections that are common across cultural values and religious beliefs.

How Do You Temper Mastery?

Clinicians need to reflect more about our own need for mastery and control. Because of the need for solutions, many of us become impatient with those who linger too long with hope after ambiguous loss. We hunger for closure even when it is impossible. We must instead permit ourselves to live with an irresolvable situation and see this not as pathological or our failure. The people with the greatest need to control may have the most difficulty tolerating the ambiguity inherent in loss and death. In a culture in which mastering problems is so highly prized, even assumed, we as professionals must counteract the predominant belief in order to sustain resiliency, especially when there is ambiguous loss.

How Do You Reconstruct Your Identity
After Personal Ambiguous Loss?

With ambiguous loss, reconstructing identity is difficult because the ambiguity blocks the process of change. We too must revise our identities in order to stay resilient and avoid the symptoms of unresolved loss. Whether at work or at home, we get our identities from the symbolic interactions with others. We receive clues from the verbal, symbolic, and emotional responses we elicit from others, personally and professionally. Based on this interaction with others, we gradually reconstruct who we are and the roles we play at home and at work. We see that the larger community in which we live and work helps shape identity. When there is discrimination or stigmatization, the impact is toxic and deeply challenges resiliency. Intolerance for diversity, it seems, also indicates intolerance for ambiguity. Ideally, the larger community is one that tolerates ambiguity and diversity and allows each of us to reconstruct who we are without prejudice, personally and professionally, after any ambiguous loss.

How Do You Deal With Ambivalence and Guilt?

As professionals, we too are vulnerable to the ambivalent feelings that follow ambiguous loss. Our task is to be aware of them and to minimize them. To deal with ambivalence and guilt, we need consultation, supervision, or therapy. It may be as difficult for professionals to see the dark side of their

ambivalent feelings as it is for clients. But we are human, too. We are expected to be empathic, patient, and caring, but sometimes we feel angry at
clients. What we may need to talk more about is the fact that it is very trying for professionals to work with people who are traumatized and victimized by a situation that has no resolution. Because it goes on and on, we
may begin to find clients who resist closure irritating and unlikable. This is
not unusual, but we need to talk more about it with other professionals.
Each of us needs to be aware of our own ambivalence as we do this therapeutic work with ambiguous loss.

How Do You Revise Attachment?

Even though you are a busy professional, do you take time to tend to your
own close relationships, family boundaries, roles, rules, and ritual celebrations? Even if you have had losses, clear or ambiguous, do you continue to
connect with others in meaningful relationships? We need professional
peers and good friends with whom to laugh and cry. I recall a time, not too
long ago, when a colleague's brother was dying and she had flown across
the country to be at his bedside. She was a licensed family therapist, social
worker, and an Ojibway elder, a great honor for a woman so young. The
entire extended family had gathered to see her brother off "to the spirit
world." At the same time, my husband was dangerously ill. She responded
through the technology of email but with her cultural way of giving comfort
to a colleague. "I am putting him in my prayers," she said, "and will smoke
the pipe for him from here" (M. Gordon, personal communication, October
6, 2002). With deep respect for each other's spiritual ways, we comforted
each other during those anxious days when our loved ones were partly
here and partly gone. Two therapists struggling with the possibility of having to revise attachments, we found strength by connecting with each other
during stressful times.

How Do You Remain Hopeful?

Our hope as professionals lies in our ability to find meaning for the people
we work with professionally, but we also must find meaning in order to
discover hope with our own ambiguous losses at home. Through dialectical processes and the acceptance of paradox, we find resiliency (just as
clients do) by redefining mastery, normalizing ambivalence, reconstructing
identity, revising attachment, and discovering a new hope. In this way, we
can move forward despite unanswered questions. To discover hope in our
own lives and in the despair of the people we work with professionally, we
must make our peace with ambiguity.

CONCLUSION

In the healing professions, many of us feel helpless when there is no clear diagnosis or prescription for making things better. We are trained to cure, not just to witness. But witness we must, especially when we do therapeutic work with ambiguous loss.

As clinicians, we have to trust in something outside of ourselves in order to let go of the (dare I say) hubris that to be a good professional, we must have all the answers all the time. Until we can accept ambiguity more comfortably ourselves, we cannot ease the trauma of ambiguous loss for others. Paradoxically, knowing we can live with not knowing provides us with the resiliency we need to be effective when treating ambiguous loss.

Therapists today are under immense outside pressures. Few have time to explicitly focus on "the self of the therapist." Emphasis instead is on technique and strategies that serve the needs of providers rather than easing the pressure on the professionals. Families, too, are under immense pressure. They have become the defacto case managers for the demented, traumatized, victimized, terminally ill, and war-wounded. Caring for loved ones who are partially present and partially absent is confusing work and a demanding task for family members. Understanding ambiguous loss and the effect that it can have on family and professional relationships is essential. For client and therapist alike, the goal is health and resiliency despite uncertainty. Resiliency grows from a tolerance for doubt and ambiguity rather than from a rigid adherence to absolute certainty.

Ambiguous losses are abundant now due to war and terrorism, but also because of advanced technology that makes it possible to both create and prolong life. Human absence and presence becomes increasingly unclear as the beginning and end of life are disputed. The work of therapists may be constrained by modern technologies that can traumatize as well as help clarify losses. When so many external factors impinge on therapy, when so many constraints are placed on therapists, when families are asked to be case managers for serious physical and mental illnesses, and when families are at such odds with each other's cultures and religions, it is essential that we strengthen ourselves for whatever ambiguities may come. For come they will. Knowing we can be effective without always having the perfect solution is empowering—and the core of professional resiliency.

Across the disciplines, from Elisabeth Kubler-Ross (1969) to James Agee (1969), I have read about death in the family. But I learned about ambiguous loss from decades of research and experience with families who had missing loved ones from war, Alzheimer's disease, head injury, stroke, addiction, mental illness, genocide, kidnappings, earthquakes, hurricanes, the terrorism of 9/11, and the tsunami. These experiences have changed me.

Like enduring a lesson that one is resisting, I learned with each onslaught that "getting over it" was not possible. I now walk with the tension of imperfect solutions and balance them with the joys and passions in my daily life. I intentionally hold the opposing ideas of absence and presence, because I have learned that most human relationships are indeed both. Although some losses are more ambiguous than others, there is no perfect closure.

Acknowledgments

I began this book in St. Paul at the University of Minnesota, and finished it in New York City at Hunter School of Social Work. So my thanks go to the University of Minnesota Experiment Station for their support of my time, and especially to Hunter School of Social Work for my year as the Moses Distinguished Visiting Professor, 2004-2005, which made possible the full concentration I needed to complete this book. I am grateful to Dr. James Blackburn for inviting me to Hunter. I thank the immensely helpful librarians and staff at both institutions. I thank my able assistant, Carol Mulligan, whose technical help was absolutely invaluable throughout the process, no matter where I was located. Above all, I thank my editor, Michael McGandy, who invited me to write a Norton book. For his support, I remain deeply grateful. His editorial skills were immensely helpful in organizing this book, and in making it accessible to professional readers from multiple disciplines, as well as to the general public.

Throughout the process, colleagues from different fields have read drafts of this book. While I may not always have followed their feedback in the ways they had intended, and thus take full responsibility for the final text, I am deeply grateful to: Lorraine Beaulieu and Judy Leventhal who read both early and final drafts in their entirety; to Diane Papalia, Karen Wampler, Froma Walsh, Cherie Collins, Susan Sabor, Bruno Hildenbrand, Dora Schnitman, Tai Mendenhall, Elizabeth Wieling, Lori Kaplan, Carol Riggs, Ann Boss Sheffels, and David Boss, all of whom read parts of the manuscript or later drafts. I am deeply honored that Carlos Sluzki consented to write the foreword to this book.

Whether I am writing, training, doing therapy, or working in the field after a disaster, I could not do this work on ambiguous loss without the support of my family. My children, David Boss, and Ann Boss Sheffels, M.D., have, since their youth, supported my research and writing, and for that I am indeed fortunate. I thank them for their constant love and support and for the wonderful adults and parents they have become with their own families. I also thank Ann for accompanying me to Pristina, Kosovo, on a difficult assignment that remains an unforgettable mother-daughter trip. I thank David for introducing me to the Rocky Mountains where I find respite after such work by taking in the silence and utter beauty. I thank my grandchildren, Erin, Sara, Hayley, and Christopher, for being there with their beautiful faces to cheer me after working with especially horrific ambiguous losses. These wonderful children provide the beauty that is my antidote. Finally, I thank my dear husband, Dudley Riggs, for his constant love and his understanding of the writing process. His presence in my life has never been ambiguous, and for that I am forever grateful.

In the end, I could not do this work on the trauma of ambiguous loss without the individuals, couples, and families who, since 1973, have allowed me into their lives at their most vulnerable times—some for research and others for therapy. I have learned from you all, and hope that this book, in some small way, validates your loss, and honors your resiliency.

Pauline Boss, Moses Professor
Hunter School of Social Work
New York City
June, 2005

Endnotes

INTRODUCTION

1. Portions of this chapter are adapted from the author's Ernest Burgess Award address, "Ambiguous Loss: Three Decades of Research, Theory & Clinical Practice," presented at the National Council on Family Relations Annual Meeting in Houston, Texas, in November 2002.
2. The work on ambiguous loss (and boundary ambiguity) grew out of my original interest in family stress (Boss, 1987, 1992, 2002c; Boss & Mulligan, 2003) and delineated the difference between ambiguous loss and boundary ambiguity.

CHAPTER 2

1. As of January 2004, there are still 1,871 families with members missing from the Vietnam era.

CHAPTER 3

1. George Bonanno (2004), a psychologist at Columbia University, wrote about how we have underestimated the human capacity to thrive after extreme stress and trauma. I agree. Adaptation is not resolution (Walsh, 1998) and recovery is not resilience (Bonanno, 2004).

213

2. The identity of all people in case studies has been protected either by changing names and places with their permission or, in some cases, the use of composite cases.

3. There was a debate about causal and control attributions on emotions, behavior, and self perceptions. Bulman and Wortman (1977) argued that for people to take control of their behaviors and cope, they must first believe that they had something to do with the cause of their problem. In many cases this is indeed helpful. But see Boss (2002c) for concerns about this view which comes dangerously close to blaming the victim. While I understand the relationship between attribution and coping, I remain concerned about self-blame, for example, when a child has been abused, with rape, or when people are traumatized by natural disasters. Instead of blaming themselves, human beings must, at times, face their helplessness, and find some positive meaning in it; e.g., I can go on despite the suffering.

CHAPTER 4

1. After his liberation at the end of World War II, Dr. Frankl began the Third Viennese School of Psychotherapy (after Freud and Adler). He contrasted the motivational force of meaning both with Freud's pleasure principle (or, as Frankl called it, "the will to pleasure") and with Adler's psychology (which stressed "the will to power") (1963, p. 154). Frankl's experience led to his existential analysis and logo (meaning) therapy (1955/1963, 1963).

2. Two theoretical perspectives are recommended for studying marital and family interactions: the symbolic interactionism of George Herbert Mead (Mead & Strauss, 1956) and the phenomenological analysis of the social structuring of reality, especially the work of Schutz (1962, 1967, 1970) and Merleau-Ponty (1945; English translation, 1962). The symbolic interactionism of Sheldon Stryker (1990) represents another compatible theoretical perspective.

3. What is clear is that the phenomenon of phenomenology itself has different meanings to different people. For an in-depth discussion, see Gubrium and Holstein (1993). Phenomenology refers to a broad tradition in the social sciences that is concerned with the actor's frame of reference (see also Psathas, 1973, and Bruyn, 1966). Others use the term more narrowly to refer to the European school of thought in phenomenological philosophy (see, e.g., Schutz, 1962, 1967, 1970). Phenomenology has also been called the microsociology of knowledge (Berger & Kellner, 1964; Kollock & O'Brien, 1994). Today, we might

argue that the original meaning of phenomenology has been socially reconstructed or lost altogether.

4. While Husserl is the father of phenomenology, Martin Heidegger, his student, is regrettably often viewed as the originator. My use of phenomenology here coincides less with Heidegger, who supported the Nazi regime that destroyed Husserl, than with succeeding scholars who left Germany to escape fascism and build on the ideas of Husserl. Safe haven was found in America at Princeton, the University of Chicago, and in New York at the New School for Social Research, where Levi-Strauss, Hannah Arendt, and Alfred Schutz linked Husserl's phenomenology to Weberian sociology. These thinkers were not sullied by the absolute truths of Nazism. In 1945, Heidegger was tried as a collaborator and banned from teaching because his complicity with the Nazis caused many of his colleagues, including his mentor, Husserl, to be put into concentration camps or forced into exile (see Collins, 2000; Philipse, 1998; Ree, 1999). Heidegger continued to deny his complicity with the Nazis; nevertheless, we must ask: Can we separate a man's actions, or inactions, from his philosophy when his very philosophy is "being is doing"? Is his philosophy authentic? For me, the *meaning* of Heidegger's philosophy cannot be separated from his Nazi affiliation and his refusal to defend his mentor.

5. For example, Alaskan natives find that spirituality buffers against problem drinking and addiction (Clay, 2003). Many find sobriety by returning to ancestral ways—eating native foods, spending time in the bush, participating in pow-wows and other ceremonies, and wearing traditional clothes and jewelry. Their return to spiritual roots is the impetus for getting well (Clay, 2003).

CHAPTER 5

1. Presently, Leonard Pearlin directs the Center for the Study of Stress and Health in the department of sociology at the University of Maryland. His research centers on the connection between people's status location in society, the stressors to which they are exposed, and their health and well-being.

CHAPTER 6

1. In 1950, another part of Erikson's identity—his political affiliation—was challenged when Senator Joseph McCarthy insisted professors sign loyalty oaths regarding where they stood politically. Rather than submit,

Erikson left Berkeley and spent 10 years working and teaching at a private clinic in Massachusetts. Following that hiatus from academia, he returned to teaching at Harvard for 10 years. He retired in 1970, another identity shift, and died in 1994.

CHAPTER 7

1. Sociologists Bengtson, Giarrusso, Mabry, and Silverstein (2002) viewed ambivalence theory as complementary to conflict and solidarity theories. Yet assumptions about norms may differ. Researchers Pillemer and Lüscher (2004) viewed ambivalences as normal in intergenerational relations and suggested that behavioral problems and personal disorders may be consequences of the inability to deal constructively with ambivalence (as opposed to deficits in solidarity).
2. Kling, Seltzer, and Ryff (1997) studied whether emotion- or problem-focused coping leads to stronger well-being in caregivers when there is an adult child with mental retardation. Parents who used problem-focused coping reported more positive changes in well-being across time. Gender and personality differences emerged, and the success of this intervention depended on the type of problems. In this light, problem-focused coping was related more to environmental mastery and purpose in life. Emotion-focused coping was more strongly associated with declining well-being with respect to mastery of the environment, declining self-acceptance, and depression. Thoits (1994) proposed that problem-focused "copers" might be psychological activists who want to shape their own destinies. Kling and colleagues. (1997) cautioned strongly, however, that there could be particular life challenges that were not amenable to an activist orientation. I think of victims of genocide, tsunami, and terrorism. Although being mastery- and activist-oriented may not always be enough, it appears that building mastery is important for resilience, whichever clinical model is used. The findings of Kling and colleagues (1997) with caregivers of adult children who are retarded are similar to the findings from research with wives of Alzheimer's disease patients, where feelings of low mastery (along with high boundary ambiguity) predicted depressive symptoms in caregivers (Boss, Caron et al., 1990; Caron et al., 1999). In sum, therapists need both cognitive- and emotion-based skills in their repertoire or on their collaborative team.
3. According to Erdelyi, Freud actually warned against the inference that repression is only a conscious process: "For Freud, defensive repression could be conscious or unconscious" (2001, p. 762). Cramer dis-

agreed: "The features of being unconscious and unintentional are critical for defining the defense mechanism and for differentiating this process from other methods of adaptation" (2001, p. 763). I am, however, not so sure. Working with traumatized people who need stress management more than analysis, this failure to discern the difference about intent has not had an appreciable detrimental effect on the therapeutic work. Rather, the focus in the field is on the degree of immobilization, with less attention to whether its source is repression or conscious intent.

4. One example of this is an elderly couple that came to see me. The wife was complaining that her husband, now with Alzheimer's disease, wanted sex too often. I asked her to bring him with her the next time, and she seemed happy to do this. When the appointment time came, I was a half hour late! Even worse, I forgot their next appointment altogether. There was nothing I could do ethically but to call her and tell her I was not serving them well and recommend that she see another therapist whom I felt was more competent than I in the area of sex and Alzheimer's disease. After talking it over with my peer consultation group, I realized that as I am getting older, there must be some fear in me about such a disability as dementia and I simply did not have the answer as to how this couple should proceed sexually. Because I am rarely late for clinical appointments and don't ordinarily forget them, I knew my ambivalence about working with this couple on this issue was problematic.

CHAPTER 8

1. Detachment was originally illustrated in the literature by the abandoned person (usually an infant) being sociable with others and not needing the attachment figure so much anymore (Ainsworth, 1985; Bowlby, 1973, 1980; Papalia & Olds, 1992). More recently, there have been efforts to apply attachment theory and adult attachment to family dynamics (Mikulincer & Florian, 1999). Today, researchers are expanding attachment theories from infant-mother interactions to adult attachment (Main, 1995; Wampler, Shi, Nelson, & Kimball, 2003).

   In human developmental psychology, attachment is defined as an "active, affectionate, reciprocal relationship specifically between two persons (usually infant and parent), in which interaction reinforces and strengthens the link" (Papalia & Olds, 1992, p. 555).

2. Although it did not address ambiguous loss, the work of John Bowlby (1973, 1980) introduced ideas about the pain of loss in the context of

attachment. Kübler-Ross (1969) also wrote about the persistence of relational connections and the need for some people to tell loved ones
that it is okay for them to go (that is to die). Without this so-called permission, the dying person may suffer longer in order to continue being
there for the person who is attached. There is natural reluctance to separate.

3. Bowen (1978), for example, included in his concept of fusion a heavy
reliance on significant others to confirm one's own beliefs and decisions. From this view, few beliefs are formed or held in isolation from
a relational context. He wrote:

> The solid self does not participate in the fusion phenomenon. The solid
> self says, "This is who I am, what I believe, what I stand for, and what I
> will do or will not do in a given situation. The solid self is made up of
> clearly defined beliefs, opinions, convictions, and life principles . . . in-
> corporated into self from one's own life experiences, by a process of in-
> tellectual reasoning and the careful consideration of the alternatives
> involved in the choice." (p. 365).

What Bowen did not think about was the impossibility of letting go
from attachments that were, through no fault of the patient's, ambiguous and undefined. Clearly defined beliefs, opinions, and convictions
about a loved one's status as dead or alive were not forthcoming. In
such cases, a clear, solid sense of self is impossible even for healthy
persons. A father who was securely attached to his wife and well dif-
ferentiated is likely to regress with more emotional reactivity if she
goes missing. He may become overprotective of his children or detach
altogether. With traumatic and ambiguous losses, early interventions
are needed to interrupt such relational processes that can become maladaptive.

CHAPTER 9

1. On a December Sunday in 1817, the poet John Keats wrote to his
brothers that he had been talking with friends about "what quality went
to form a Man of Achievement, especially in Literature, and which
Shakespeare possessed so enormously—I mean *Negative Capability,*
that is, when a man is capable of being in uncertainties, mysteries,
doubts, without any irritable reaching after fact and reason. Coleridge,
for instance, would let go by a fine isolated verisimilitude caught from
the Penetralium of mystery, from being incapable of remaining content
with half-knowledge" (Forman, 1935, p. 72).

2. Luepnitz wrote that Schopenhauer believed that the human "will" was a permanent source of suffering for people, meaning that there was no life without suffering. However, "Schopenhauer's notion of will was not a matter of personal agency—'what I want'—but, almost the opposite: a blind striving that characterizes all living things" (Luepnitz, 2002a, p. 6). Luepnitz also wrote: Our contentment then according to Schopenhauer is "the eradicating or transcending of the will. . . . When absorbed in art, literature, or music, he said, we free ourselves from the prison of will". . . . Schopenhauer was the first Western philosopher to study the Vedic and Buddhist texts" (2002a, pp. 6–7). See Schopenhauer's *The World as Will and Representation* (1966).

EPILOGUE

1. While working in a hospital in Chicago, Swiss psychiatrist Elizabeth Kübler-Ross noticed the demoralization of physicians, theologians, nurses, and social workers who were working with terminally ill patients. Feelings of professional failure made them deny death (even beyond what Becker, in 1973, called the American culture's general denial of death). From her many interviews with dying patients, she concluded that the professional discomfort with dying interfered with the patient's dying process. Although she was a controversial figure, Kübler-Ross is unequivocally credited with inspiring the present hospice movement.
2. Landau (1997) used personal reflection to enlighten her professional work in the current epidemic of HIV/AIDS. Graziano (1997) also used self-reflection, in her case for teaching social workers about trauma.
3. Although I refer here to my favorite idea from Bowen, overall I see theory differently than he did. My view is that theories—even research-based theories—are social constructions and should not be adhered to blindly. Rather, theory should be considered a guide or map to shape your interventions—which may need adaptations due to diversity in people and cultural context (Boss, 2004b). Theories, after all, reflect the context in which they were developed. They are not gospel. Your professional judgment is always an essential part of applying any theory to shape your particular work.
4. For more on "That Man, Whitaker!" see Boss (1995).

References

Abrahams, F., Stover, E., & Peress, G. (2001). *A village destroyed, May 14, 1999: War crimes in Kosovo*. Berkeley: University of California Press.

Agee, J. (1969). *A death in the family*. New York: Bantam.

Ainsworth, M. D. (1985). Patterns of attachment. *Clinical Psychologist, 38*(2), 27–29.

Albom, M. (1997). *Tuesdays with Morrie: An old man, a young man, and life's greatest lesson*. New York: Doubleday.

Allende, I. (2003). *My invented country: A nostalgic journey through Chile* (1st U.S. ed.). New York: HarperCollins.

American Psychiatric Association. (1980). *Diagnostic and statistical manual of mental disorders (DSM-III)* (Rev. ed.). Washington, DC: Author.

American Psychiatric Association. (2000). *Diagnostic and statistical manual of mental disorders (DSM-IV-TR)* (Rev. ed.). Washington, DC: Author.

Andersen, T. (1991). *The reflecting team: Dialogues and dialogues about the dialogues*. New York: Norton.

Anderson, H., & Goolishian, H. (1992). The client is the expert: A not-knowing approach to therapy. In S. McNamee & K. J. Gergen (Eds.), *Therapy as social construction. Inquiries in social construction* (pp. 25–39). Thousand Oaks, CA: Sage.

Anderson, S. (1921). *Winesburg, Ohio: A group of tales of Ohio small town life*. New York: Huebsch.

Antonovsky, A. (1979). *Health, stress, and coping: New perspectives on mental and physical well-being*. San Francisco: Jossey-Bass.

Antonovsky, A. (1987). *Unraveling the mystery of health: How people manage stress and stay well*. San Francisco: Jossey-Bass.

Armour, M. P. (2002). Journal of family members of homicide victims: A qualitative study of their posthomicide experience. *American Journal of Orthopsychiatry, 72*(3), 372–382.

221

Armstrong, K. R., Lund, P. E., McWright, L. T., & Tichenor, V. (1995). Multiple stressor debriefing and the American Red Cross: The East Bay Hills fire experience. *Social Work, 40*(1), 83–90.

Barry, H. J., Barry, H., III, & Lindemann, E. (1965). Dependency in adult patients following early maternal bereavement. *Journal of Nervous & Mental Disease, 140*(3), 196–206.

Bayley, J. (1999). *Elegy for Iris* (1st ed.). New York: St. Martin's Press.

Beardslee, W. (2003). *When a parent is depressed: How to protect your children from the effects of depression in the family.* Boston: Little, Brown.

Becker, E. (1973). *The denial of death.* New York: Free Press.

Becvar, D. S. (2001). *In the presence of grief: Helping family members resolve death, dying, and bereavement issues.* New York: Guilford.

Bengston, V. L., Giarrusso, R., Mabry, J. B., & Silverstein, M. (2002). Solidarity, conflict, and ambivalence: Complementary or competing perspectives on intergenerational relationships? *Journal of Marriage and the Family, 64,* 568–576.

Berger, P. L., & Kellner, H. (1964). Marriage and the construction of reality. *Diogenes, 64,* 1–25.

Berger, P. L., & Luckmann, T. (1966). *The social construction of reality: A treatise in the sociology of knowledge* (1st ed.). Garden City, NY: Doubleday.

Bird, I. L. (1960). *A lady's life in the Rocky Mountains.* Norman, OK: University of Oklahoma Press.

Bisson, J. I., Jenkins, P. L., Alexander, J., & Bannister, C. (1997). Randomised controlled trial of psychological debriefing for victims of acute burn trauma. *British Journal of Psychiatry, 171 July,* 78–81.

Bixler, M. T. (1992). *Winds of freedom: The story of the Navajo code talkers of World War II.* Darien, CT: Two Bytes.

Blackburn, J. A., Greenberg, J. S., & Boss, P. (1987). Coping with normative stress from loss and change: A longitudinal study of rural widows. *Journal of Gerontological Social Work, 11*(1–2), 59–70.

Bleuler, E. (1911). *Dementia praecox oder gruppe der schizophrenien* [Dementia praecox or the group of schizophrenias]. Leipzig and Wien: Franz Deuticke.

Blumer, H. (1969). *Symbolic interactionism: Perspective and method.* Englewood Cliffs, NJ: Prentice-Hall.

Blumstein, P. (2001). The production of selves in personal relationships. In J. O'Brien & P. Kollock (Eds.), *The production of reality* (3rd ed., pp. 296–308). Thousand Oaks, CA: Pine Forge Press.

Bonanno, G. A. (2004). Loss, trauma, and human resilience: Have we underestimated the human capacity to thrive after extremely aversive events? *American Psychologist, 59*(1), 20–28.

Bonanno, G. A., Field, N. P., Kovacevic, A., & Kaltman, S. (2002). Self-enhancement as a buffer against extreme adversity: Civil war in Bosnia and traumatic loss in the United States. *Personality & Social Psychology Bulletin, 28*(2), 184–196.

Bonanno, G. A., & Keltner, D. (1997). Facial expressions of emotion and the course of conjugal bereavement. *Journal of Abnormal Psychology, 106*(1), 126–137.

Bonanno, G. A., Noll, J. G., Putnam, F. W., O'Neill, M., & Trickett, P. K. (2003). Predicting the willingness to disclose childhood sexual abuse from measures of repressive coping and dissociative tendencies. *Child Maltreatment, 8,* 302–318.

Bonanno, G. A., Papa, A., & O'Neill, K. (2001). Loss and human resilience. *Applied & Preventive Psychology, 10*(3), 193–206.

Bonanno, G. A., Wortman, C. B., & Nesse, R. M. (2004). Prospective patterns of resilience and maladjustment during widowhood. *Psychology & Aging, 19*(2), 260–271.

Boss, P. (1972, November). Father absence in intact families. In *Research and Theory Section.* Presentation at the annual meeting of the National Council on Family Relations, Toronto, Canada.

Boss, P. (1975). Psychological father presence in the missing-in-action (MIA) family: Its effects on family functioning. *Proceedings: Third Annual Joint Medical Meeting Concerning POW/MIA Matters* (pp. 61–65). San Diego, CA: Naval Health Research Center, Center for Prisoner of War Studies.

Boss, P. (1977). A clarification of the concept of psychological father presence in families experiencing ambiguity of boundary. *Journal of Marriage & the Family, 39*(1), 141–151.

Boss, P. (1980a). Boundary ambiguity intervention for families of the Iranian hostages. In C. Figley (Ed.), *Mobilization: Part I. The Iranian crisis. Final report of the task force on families of catastrophe.* West Lafayette, IN: Purdue University, Family Research Institute.

Boss, P. (1980b). Normative family stress: Family boundary changes across the lifespan. *Family Relations, 29,* 445–450.

Boss, P. (1980c). The relationship of psychological father presence, wife's personal qualities and wife/family dysfunction in families of missing fathers. *Journal of Marriage & the Family, 42*(3), 541–549.

Boss, P. (1983a). Family separation and boundary ambiguity. *The International Journal of Mass Emergencies and Disasters, 1,* 63–72.

Boss, P. (1983b). The marital relationship: Boundaries and ambiguities. In C. Figley & H. McCubbin (Eds.), *Stress and the family: Vol. 1. Coping with normative transitions* (pp. 26–40). New York: Brunner/Mazel.

Boss, P. (1986). Psychological absence in the intact family: A systems approach to the study of fathering. *Marriage & Family Review, 10*(1), 11–39.

Boss, P. (1987). Family stress. In M. B. Sussman & S. K. Steinmetz (Eds.), *Handbook of marriage and the family* (pp. 695–723). New York: Plenum.

Boss, P. (1992). Primacy of perception in family stress theory and measurement. *Journal of Family Psychology, 6,* 113–119.

Boss, P. (1993a). Boundary ambiguity: A block to cognitive coping. In A. P. Turnbull & J. M. Patterson (Eds.), *Cognitive coping, families, and disability* (pp. 257–270). Baltimore, MD: Brookes.

Boss, P. (1993b). The construction of chronicity: Coping with ambiguous loss. In R. Welter-Enderline & B. Hiltebrand (Eds.), *System familie* (pp. 161–170). Heidelberg, Germany: Springer-Verlag.

Boss, P. (1993c). The experience of immigration for the mother left behind: The use of qualitative feminist strategies to analyze letters from my Swiss grandmother to my father. *Marriage & Family Review, 19*(3–4), 365–378.

Boss, P. (1993d). The reconstruction of family life with Alzheimer's disease: Generating theory to understand family stress from ambiguous loss. In P. Boss, W. Doherty, R. LaRossa, W. Schumm, & S. Steinmetz (Eds.), *Sourcebook of family theories and methods: A contextual approach* (pp. 163–166). New York: Plenum.

Boss, P. (1995). That man Whitaker! *Family Therapy Networker, July–August,* 58–59.

Boss, P. (1996). They did it quietly: The meaning of immigration for women. In H. Ryhner (Ed.), *Jubilaumsbuch 150 Jahr New Glarus: America's little Switzerland errinert sich* [150 years anniversary of New Glarus, Wisconsin: America's little Switzerland remembers.] (pp. 35–102). Glarus, Switzerland: Tschudi AG.

Boss, P. (1999). *Ambiguous loss: Learning to live with unresolved grief.* Cambridge, MA: Harvard University Press.

Boss, P. (2002a). Ambiguous loss: Working with the families of the missing. *Family Process, 41,* 14–17.

Boss, P. (2002b). Ambiguous loss in families of the missing. *The Lancet, 360,* 39–40.

Boss, P. (2002c). *Family stress management: A contextual approach* (2nd ed.). Thousand Oaks, CA: Sage.

Boss, P. (2004a). Ambiguous loss. In F. Walsh & M. McGoldrick (Eds.), *Living beyond loss: Death in the family* (2nd ed., pp. 237–246). New York: Norton.

Boss, P. (2004b). Ambiguous loss research, theory, and practice: Reflections after 9/11. *Journal of Marriage & Family, 66*(3), 551–566.

Boss, P. Panel Moderator. (2004c). *Integrity and survival in families and communites.* (Video). www.grovesconference.org

Boss, P., Beaulieu, L., Wieling, E., Turner, W., & LaCruz, S. (2003). Healing loss, ambiguity, and trauma: A community-based intervention with families of union workers missing after the 9/11 attack in New York City. *Journal of Marital & Family Therapy, 29*(4), 455–467.

Boss, P., Caron, W., & Horbal, J. (1988). Alzheimer's disease and ambiguous loss. In C. S. Chilman & E. W. Nunnally (Eds.), *Chronic illness and disability: Families in trouble series* (Vol. 2, pp. 123–140). Thousand Oaks, CA: Sage.

Boss, P., Caron, W., Horbal, J., & Mortimer, J. (1990). Predictors of depression in caregivers of dementia patients: Boundary ambiguity and mastery. *Family Process, 29*(3), 245–254.

Boss, P., & Couden, B. (2002). Ambiguous loss from chronic physical illness: Clinical interventions with individuals, couples and families. *Journal of Clinical Psychology, 58*(11), 1351–1360.

Boss, P., & Greenberg, J. (1984). Family boundary ambiguity: A new variable in family stress theory. *Family Process, 23*(4), 535–546.

Boss, P., Greenberg, J., & Pearce-McCall, D. (1990). *Measurement of boundary ambiguity in families.* (Minnesota Agricultural Experiment Station Bulletin No. 593-1990: Item No. Ad-SB-3763). St. Paul, MN: University of Minnesota.

Boss, P., & Kaplan, L. (2004). Ambiguous loss and ambivalence when a parent has dementia. In K. Pillemer & K. Lüscher (Eds.), *Intergenerational ambivalences:*

New perspectives on parent-child relations in later life (pp. 207–224). Oxford, UK: Elsevier.

Boss, P., & Mulligan, C. (Eds.). (2003). *Family stress: Classic and contemporary readings.* Thousand Oaks, CA: Sage.

Boss, P., Pearce-McCall, D., & Greenberg, J. (1987). Normative loss in mid-life families: Rural, urban, and gender differences. *Family Relations, 36*(4), 437–443.

Boss, P., & Weiner, J. P. (1988). Rethinking assumptions about women's development and family therapy. In C. J. Falicov (Ed.), *Family transitions: Continuity and change over the life cycle. Guilford family therapy series* (pp. 235–251). New York: Guilford.

Bowen, M. (1978). *Family therapy in clinical practice.* New York: Aronson.

Bowlby, J. (1973). *Separation: Anxiety and anger.* New York: Basic.

Bowlby, J. (1980). *Loss: Sadness and depression: Vol. 3. Attachment and loss series.* New York: Basic.

Bruyn, S. T. H. (1966). *The human perspective in sociology: The methodology of participant observation.* Englewood Cliffs, NJ: Prentice-Hall.

Bulman, R. J., & Wortman, C. B. (1977). Attributions of blame and coping in the "real world": Severe accident victims react to their lot. *Journal of Personality & Social Psychology, 35*(5), 351–363.

Burgess, A. W., & Holmstrom, L. L. (1979). *Rape, crisis and recovery.* Bowie, MD: Brady.

Burgess, E. W., & American Sociological Association. (1968). *The urban community; selected papers from the proceedings of the American Sociological Society, 1925.* New York: Greenwood.

Burke, P. J. (1991). Identity processes and social stress. *American Sociological Review, 56*(6), 836–849.

Burke, P. J., & Reitzes, D. C. (1991). An identity theory approach to commitment. *Social Psychology Quarterly, 54*(3), 239–251.

Burton, L. M. (2001). One step forward and two steps back: Neighborhood and adolescent development. In A. Booth & A. C. Crouter (Eds.), *Does it take a village? Community effects on children, adolescents, and families* (pp. 149–159). Mahwah, NJ: Erlbaum.

Burton, L. M., & Jarrett, R. L. (2000). In the mix, yet on the margins: The place of families in urban neighborhood and child development research. *Journal of Marriage & the Family, 62*(4), 1114–1135.

Burton, L. M., Winn, D., Stevenson, H., & Clark, S. L. (2004). Working with African American clients: Considering the "homeplace" in marriage and family therapy practices. *Journal of Marital & Family Therapy, 30*(4), 397–410.

Calaprice, A. (Ed.). (2000). *The expanded quotable Einstein.* Princeton, NJ: Princeton University Press.

Campbell, C. L., & Demi, A. S. (2000). Adult children of fathers missing in action (MIA): An examination of emotional distress, grief, and family hardiness. *Family Relations, 49*(3), 267–276.

Caron, W., Boss, P., & Mortimer, J. (1999). Family boundary ambiguity predicts Alzheimer's outcomes. *Psychiatry: Interpersonal & Biological Processes, 62*(4), 347–356.

Carroll, J. S., Boss, P., & Buckmiller, N. (2003, November). *Family boundary ambiguity: A 30-year review of research, measurement, and theory.* Poster session presented at the annual meeting of the National Council on Family Relations (NCFR), Vancouver, BC, Canada.

Carter, B., & McGoldrick, M. (1999). *The expanded family life cycle: Individual. family, and social perspectives* (3rd ed.). Boston: Allyn and Bacon.

Clay, R. (2003). The secret of the 12 steps. *Monitor on Psychology, 34*(11), 50–51.

Collins, J. (2000). *Heidegger and the Nazis.* New York: Totem.

Conger, R. D., Rueter, M. A., & Elder, G. H. J. (1999). Couple resilience to economic pressure. *Journal of Personality & Social Psychology, 76*(1), 54–71.

Cooper, S. H. (2000). *Objects of hope: Exploring possibility and limit in psychoanalysis.* Hillsdale, NJ: Analytic.

Corbett, S. (2001, April 1). The long, long, long road to Fargo. *New York Times Magazine, 48–55,* 75, 80, 84–85.

Cousins, N. (1979). *Anatomy of an illness as perceived by the patient: Reflections on healing and regeneration.* New York: Norton.

Cowan, P. A. (1991). Individual and family life transitions: A proposal for a new definition. In P. A. Cowan & E. M. Hetherington (Eds.), *Family transitions: Advances in family research series* (pp. 3–30). Hillsdale, NJ: Erlbaum.

Cramer, P. (2001). The unconscious status of defense mechanisms. *American Psychologist, 56*(9), 762–763.

Crawford, M. (1993). Identity, "passing" and subversion. In S. Wilkinson & C. Kitzinger (Eds.), *Heterosexuality* (pp. 43–45). London: Sage.

Dahl, C., & Boss, P. (2005). The use of phenomenology for family therapy research: The search for meaning. In D. Sprenkel & F. Piercy, (Eds.), *Research methods in family therapy* (2nd ed., pp. 63–84). New York: Guilford.

Danieli, Y. (1985). The treatment and prevention of long-term effects and intergenerational transmission of victimization: A lesson from Holocaust survivors and their children. In C. Figley (Ed.), *Trauma and its wake* (pp. 295–313). New York: Brunner/Mazel.

Davies, J. (Speaker). (2003). *Breaking up is hard to do: A relational reconsideration of the termination process.* (Cassette Recording No. D3903-G47). Washington, DC: American Psychological Association.

Dickerson, V. C. (2004). Young women struggling for an identity. *Family Process, 43*(3), 337–348.

Dingfelder, S. (2003). Tibetan Buddhism and research psychology: A match made in nirvana? *Monitor on Psychology, 34*(11), 46–48.

DiNicola, V. F. (1997). *A stranger in the family: Culture, families, and therapy.* New York: Norton.

Dittmann, M. (2003). Struggling to keep the faith. *Monitor on Psychology, 34*(11), 52–53.

Ebaugh, H. R. F. (2001). Creating the ex-role. In J. O'Brien & P. Kollock (Eds.), *The production of reality: Essays and readings on social interaction* (3rd ed., pp. 330–345). Thousand Oaks, CA: Pine Forge Press.

Ekman, P. (2003). *Emotions revealed: Recognizing faces and feelings to improve communication and emotional life.* New York: Times Books.

Eliot, T. S. (2004). The hollow men. In M. Ferguson, M. J. Salter, & J. Stallworthy (Eds.), *The Norton anthology of poetry* (5th ed.). New York: Norton. (Originally published in 1927.)

Elkind, D. (1998). *All grown up and no place to go: Teenagers in crisis* (Rev. ed.). Reading, MA.: Addison-Wesley.

Erdelyi, M. H. (2001). Defense processes can be conscious or unconscious. *American Psychologist, 56*(9), 761–762.

Erikson, E. H. (1950). *Childhood and society* (1st ed.). New York: Norton.

Erikson, E. H. (1968). *Identity, youth, and crisis* (1st ed.). New York: Norton.

Everly, G. S. (1989). *A clinical guide to the treatment of the human stress response.* New York: Plenum.

Everly, G. S., & Mitchell, J. T. (1992). *The prevention of work-related post-traumatic stress: The critical incident stress debriefing process (CISD).* Second APA/NIOSH Conference on Occupational Stress, Washington, DC.

Everly, G. S., & Mitchell, J. T. (2003). *Critical incident stress management (CISM): Individual crisis intervention and peer support.* Ellicott City, MD: International Critical Incident Stress Foundation, Inc.

Fadiman, A. (1997). *The spirit catches you and you fall down: A Hmong child, her American doctors, and the collision of two cultures* (1st ed.). New York: Farrar, Straus, and Giroux.

Falicov, C. J. (1988). *Family transitions: Continuity and change over the life cycle.* New York: Guilford.

Falicov, C. J. (1998). *Latino families in therapy: A guide to multicultural practice.* New York: Guilford.

Farley, R. (Ed.). (1993). *Women of the native struggle: Portraits and testimony of Native American women.* New York: Orion.

Feigelson, C. (1993). Personality death, object loss, and the uncanny. *International Journal of Psycho-Analysis, 74*(2), 331–345.

Ferreira, A. (1966). Family myths. *Psychiatric Research Reports, 20,* 85–90.

Festinger, L. (1957). *A theory of cognitive dissonance.* Evanston, IL: Row, Peterson.

Figley, C. R. (1978). *Stress disorders among Vietnam veterans: Theory, research, and treatment.* New York: Brunner/Mazel.

Figley, C. R. (Ed.) (1985). *Trauma and its wake.* New York: Brunner/Mazel.

Figley, C. R. (1989). *Helping traumatized families* (1st ed.). San Francisco: Jossey-Bass.

Figley, C. R. (1995). *Compassion fatigue: Coping with secondary traumatic stress disorder in those who treat the traumatized.* New York: Brunner/Mazel.

Firestone, R. W., Firestone, L. A., & Catlett, J. (2003). Psychotherapy: Past, present, and future? In R. W. Firestone & L. A. Firestone (Eds.), *Creating a life of meaning and compassion: The wisdom of psychotherapy* (pp. 347–365). Washington, DC. American Psychological Association.

Fishbane, M. D. (2001). Relational narratives of the self. *Family Process, 40*(3), 273–291.

Ford, F. R., & Herrick, J. (1974). Family rules: Family lifestyles. *American Journal of Orthopsychiatry, 44*(1), 61–69.

Forman, M. H. (Ed.). 1935. *The letters of John Keats.* (2nd ed.). New York: Oxford University Press.

Fossum, M. A., & Mason, M. J. (1986). *Facing shame.* New York: Norton.

Fraenkel, P. (2002). The helpers and the helped: Viewing the mental health profession through the lens of September 11. *Family Process, 41,* 20–23.

Framo, J. L. (Ed.), Eastern Pennsylvania Psychiatric Institute, Philadelphia. (1972). *Family interaction: A dialogue between family researchers and family therapists.* New York: Springer.

Frankl, V. E. (1955/1963). *The doctor and the soul. An introduction to logotherapy.* New York: Knopf.

Frankl, V. (1963). *Man's search for meaning: An introduction to logotherapy.* New York: Washington Square.

Fravel, D. L., & Boss, P. (1992). An in-depth interview with the parents of missing children. In J. F. Gilgun & K. Daly (Eds.), *Qualitative methods in family research* (pp. 126–145). Thousand Oaks, CA: Sage.

Fravel, D. L., McRoy, R. G., & Grotevant, H. D. (2000). Birthmother perceptions of the psychologically present adopted child: Adoption openness and boundary ambiguity. *Family Relations, 49*(4), 425–433.

Freud, S. (1957). Mourning and melancholia. In J. Strackey (Ed.), *The standard edition of the complete psychological works of Sigmund Freud* (pp. 237–258). New York: Norton. (Original work published 1917.)

Friedman, S., & Fanger, M. T. (1991). *Expanding therapeutic possibilities: Getting results in brief psychotherapy.* New York: Lexington Books/Macmillan.

Garmezy, N. (1985). Stress-resistant children: The search for protective factors. In J. E. Stevenson (Ed.), *Recent research in developmental psychopathology* (pp. 213–233). Oxford, UK: Pergamon.

Garmezy, N. (1987). Stress, competence, and development: Continuities in the study of schizophrenic adults, children vulnerable to psychopathology, and the search for stress-resistant children. *American Journal of Orthopsychiatry, 57*(2), 159–174.

Garmezy, N., & Masten, A. S. (1986). Stress, competence, and resilience: Common frontiers for therapist and psychopathologist. *Behavior Therapy, 17,* 500–521.

Garmezy, N., Masten, A. S., & Tellegen, A. (1984). The study of stress and competence in children: A building block for developmental psychopathology. *Child Development, 55,* 97–111.

Garmezy, N., & Rutter, M. (1985). Acute reactions to stress. In M. Rutter & L. Hersov (Eds.), *Child psychiatry: Modern approaches* (2nd ed.). Oxford: Blackwell Scientific Press.

Garwick, A. W., Detzner, D., & Boss, P. (1994). Family perceptions of living with Alzheimer's disease. *Family Process, 33*(3), 327–340.

Gates, R. D., Arce de Esnaola, S., Kroupin, G., Stewart, C. C., van Dulmen, M., Xiong, B., & Boss, P. (2000). Diversity of new American families: Guidelines for therapists. In W. C. Nichols, M. A. Pace-Nichols, D. S. Becvar, & A. Y. Napier (Eds.), *Handbook of family development and intervention. Wiley series in couples and family dynamics and treatment* (pp. 299–322). New York: Wiley.

Gaugler, J. E., Zarit, S. H., & Pearlin, L. I. (2003). The onset of dementia caregiving and its longitudinal implications. *Psychology & Aging, 18*(2), 171–180.

Gergen, K. J. (1994). *Realities and relationships: Soundings in social construction.* Cambridge, MA: Harvard University Press.

Gergen, K. J. (2001). *Social construction in context.* London: Sage.

Gilgun, J. F. (1994). Hand into glove: The grounded theory approach and social work practice research. In. E. A. Sherman & W. J. Reid (Eds.), *Qualitative research in social work* (pp. 115–125). New York: Columbia University Press.

Gilgun, J. F., Daly, K., & Handel, G. (1992). *Qualitative methods in family research.* Newbury Park: Sage.

Gilligan, C. (1982). *In a different voice: Psychological theory and women's development.* Cambridge, MA: Harvard University Press.

Goffman, E. (1959). *The presentation of self in everyday life.* Garden City, NY: Doubleday.

Goffman, E. (1974). *Frame analysis: An essay on the organization of experience.* New York: Harper & Row.

Goldberger, L., & Breznitz, S. (1993). *Handbook of stress: Theoretical and clinical aspects* (2nd ed.). New York: Free Press.

Goldner, V. (1985). Feminism and family therapy. *Family Process, 24*(1), 31–47.

Goldner, V., Penn, P., Sheinberg, M., & Walker, G. (1990). Love and violence: Gender paradoxes in volatile attachments. *Family Process, 29*(4), 343–364.

Gouldner, A. W. (1970). *The coming crisis of Western sociology.* New York: Basic.

Graziano, R. (1997). The challenge of clinical work with survivors of trauma. In J. R. Brandell (Ed.), *Theory and practice in clinical social work* (pp. 380–403). New York: Free Press.

Groopman, J. (2004, January 26). The grief industry. *The New Yorker,* 31–32.

Gubrium, J. F., & Holstein, J. A. (1993). Phenomenology, ethnomethodology, and family discourse. In P. Boss & W. J. Doherty (Eds.), *Sourcebook of family theories and methods: A contextual approach* (pp. 651–675). New York: Plenum.

Haber, R. (1990). From handicap to handy capable: Training systemic therapists in use of self. *Family Process, 29*(4), 375–384.

Handel, G. (1967). *The psychosocial interior of the family: A sourcebook for the study of whole families.* Chicago: Aldine.

Hardy, K. V., & Laszloffy, T. A. (1995). The cultural genogram: Key to training culturally competent family therapists. *Journal of Marital & Family Therapy, 21*(3), 227–237.

Hare-Mustin, R. T. (1978). A feminist approach to family therapy. *Family Process, 17*(2), 181–194.

Hauser, S. T. (1999). Understanding resilient outcomes: Adolescent lives across time and generations. *Journal of Research on Adolescence, 9*(1), 1–24.

Hauser, S. T., DiPlacido, J., Jacobson, A. M., Willett, J., & Cole, C. (1993). Family coping with an adolescent's chronic illness: An approach and three studies. *Journal of Adolescence, 16*(3), 305–329.

Havel, V. (1990). *Disturbing the peace: A conversation with Karel Hvížďala/Vaclav Havel.* New York: Knopf.

Hawley, D. R., & DeHaan, L. (1996). Toward a definition of family resilience: Integrating life-span and family perspectives. *Family Process, 35*(3), 283–298.

Henry, J. (1971). *Pathways to madness* (1st ed.). New York: Random House.

Herman, J. L. (1992). *Trauma and recovery.* New York: Basic.

Hess, R. D., & Handel, G. (1959). *Family worlds: A psychosocial approach to family life*. Chicago: University of Chicago Press.

Hetherington, E. M., & Blechman, E. A. (1996). *Stress, coping, and resiliency in children and families*. Mahwah, NJ: Erlbaum.

Hill, P. C., & Pargament, K. I. (2003). Advances in the conceptualization and measurement of religion and spirituality: Implications for physical and mental health research. *American Psychologist, 58*(1), 64–74.

Hill, R. (1949). *Families under stress: Adjustment to the crises of war separation and return*. Oxford, England: Harper.

Hobfoll, S. E., & Spielberger, C. D. (1992). Family stress: Integrating theory and measurement. *Journal of Family Psychology, 6*(2), 99–112.

Imber-Black, E. (1993). Secrets in families and family therapy: An overview. In E. Imber-Black (Ed.), *Secrets in families and family therapy* (pp. 3–28). New York: Norton.

Imber-Black, E., & Roberts, J. (1992). *Rituals for our time: Celebrating, healing, and changing our lives and our relationships* (1st ed.). New York: HarperCollins.

Imber-Black, E., Roberts, J., & Whiting, R. A. (1988). *Rituals in families and family therapy* (1st ed.). New York: Norton.

Jackson, D. (1965). Family rules: The marital quid pro quo. *Archives of General Psychiatry, 8,* 343–348.

Johnson, S. M. (1996). *The practice of emotionally focused marital therapy: Creating connection*. New York: Brunner/Mazel.

Johnson, S. M. (2002). *Emotionally focused couple therapy with trauma survivors: Strengthening attachment*. New York: Guilford.

Jordan, K. (2003). Supervision bulletin: Trauma supervision. *Family Therapy Magazine, 2*(5), 41–44.

Kagitcibasi, C. (1983). How does the traditional family in Turkey cope with disasters? *International Journal of Mass Emergencies and Disasters, 1*(1), 145–152.

Kaplan, L., & Boss, P. (1999). Depressive symptoms among spousal caregivers of institutionalized mates with Alzheimer's: Boundary ambiguity and mastery as predictors. *Family Process, 38*(1), 85–103.

Keiley, M. K., Dolbin, M., Hill, J., Karuppaswamy, N., Liu, T., Natrajan, R., Poulsen, S., Robbins, N., & Robinson, P. (2002). The cultural genogram: Experiences from within a marriage and family therapy training program. *Journal of Marital & Family Therapy, 28*(2), 165–178.

Kersting, K. (2003). Religion and spirituality in the treatment room. *Monitor on Psychology, 34*(11), 40–42.

Kiecolt-Glaser, J. K., Dura, J. R., Speicher, C. E., Trask, O. J., & Glaser, R. (1991). Spousal caregivers of dementia victims: Longitudinal changes in immunity and health. *Psychosomatic Medicine, 53*(4), 345–362.

Kiecolt-Glaser, J. K., Glaser, R., Williger, D., Stout, J., Messick, G., Sheppard, S., Bonnell, G., Bruner, W., Ricker, D., & Romisher, S. C. (1985). Psychosocial enhancement of immunocompetence in a geriatric population. *Health Psychology, 4,* 25–41.

Kirmayer, L. J., Boothroyd, L. J., Tanner, A., Adelson, N., & Robinson, E. (2000). Psychological distress among the Cree of James Bay. *Transcultural Psychiatry, 37*(2), 35–56.

Klein, M. (1984). *Love, guilt, and reparation and other works 1921–1945 (the writings of Melanie Klein, volume 1)*. New York: Free Press.

Kleinman, A., & Good, B. (1985). *Culture and depression: Studies in the anthropology and cross-cultural psychiatry of affect and disorder*. Berkeley: University of California Press.

Kling, K. C., Seltzer, M. M., & Ryff, C. D. (1997). Distinctive late-life challenges: Implications for coping and well-being. *Psychology & Aging, 12*(2), 288–295.

Kluckhohn, F. R., & Strodtbeck, F. L. (1961). *Variations in value orientation*. Westport, CT: Greenwood.

Kobasa, S. C., Maddi, S. R., & Kahn, S. (1982). Hardiness and health: A prospective study. *Journal of Personality & Social Psychology, 42*(1), 168–177.

Kohut, H. (1972). Thoughts on narcissism and narcissistic rage. *Psychoanalytic Study of the Child, 27 Feb*, 360–400.

Kollock, P., & O'Brien, J. (1994). *The production of reality*. Thousand Oaks, CA: Pine Forge Press.

Kroeger, B. (2003). *Passing: When people can't be who they are*. Cambridge, MA: Persus Books Group.

Kübler-Ross, E. (1969). *On death and dying*. New York: Macmillan.

Kurtz, D. C., & Boardman, J. (1971). *Greek burial customs*. Ithaca, NY: Cornell University Press.

Kushner, H. S. (1981). *When bad things happen to good people*. New York: Schocken.

Landau, J. (1981). Link therapy as a family therapy technique for transitional extended families. *Psychotherapeia, 7*(4), 382–390.

Landau, J. (1997). Whispers of illness: Secrecy versus trust. In S. H. McDaniel, J. Hepworth, & W. J. Doherty (Eds.), *The shared experience of illness* (pp. 13–22). New York: Basic.

Landau, J., & Saul, J. (2004). Facilitating family and community resilience in response to major disaster. In F. Walsh & M. McGoldrick (Eds.), *Living beyond loss: Death in the family* (2nd ed., pp. 285–309). New York: Norton.

Lasch, C. (1978). *The culture of narcissism: American life in an age of diminishing expectations* (1st ed.). New York: Norton.

Lazarus, R. S. (1966). *Psychological stress and the coping process*. New York: McGraw-Hill.

Lerner, M. J. (1971). Observers evaluation of a victim: Justice, guilt, and veridical perception. *Journal of Personality & Social Psychology, 20*(2), 127–135.

Lerner, M. J., & Simmons, C. H. (1966). Observer's reaction to the "innocent victim": Compassion or rejection? *Journal of Personality & Social Psychology, 4*(2), 203–210.

Leys, R. (2000). *Trauma: A genealogy*. Chicago: University of Chicago Press.

Liebow, E. (1967). *Tally's corner: A study of Negro streetcorner men*. Boston: Little, Brown.

Lindemann, E. (1944). Symptomatology and management of acute grief. *American Journal of Psychiatry, (101)*, 141–148.

Lipchik, E. (1993). "Both/and" solutions. In S. Friedman (Ed.), *The new language of change: Constructive collaboration in psychotherapy* (pp. 25–49). New York: Guilford.

Lipchik, E. (2002). *Beyond technique in solution-focused therapy: Working with emotions and the therapeutic relationship*. New York: Guilford.

London, L. (1995). Dealing with the pain of apartheid's past: South Africa's truth and reconciliation commission. In H. Marcussen & F. Rasmussen (Eds.), *Rehabilitation and Research Centre for Torture Victims (RCT) and International Rehabilitation Council for Torture Victims (IRCT) 1995 annual report* (pp. 7–8). Copenhagen, Denmark: Author.

Luepnitz, D. A. (2002a). *Schopenhauer's porcupines: Intimacy and its dilemmas: Five stories of psychotherapy*. New York: Basic.

Luepnitz, D. A. (2002b). *The family interpreted: Feminist theory in clinical practice*. New York: Basic.

Lüscher, K. (2004). Conceptualizing and uncovering intergenerational ambivalence. In K. Pillemer & K. Lüscher (Eds.), *Intergenerational ambivalences: New perspectives on parent-child relations in later life* (pp. 23–62). Kidlington, Oxford, UK: Elsevier.

Main, M. (1995). Recent studies in attachment: Overview, with selected implications for clinical work. In S. Goldberg, R. Muir, & J. Kerr (Eds.), *Attachment theory: Social, developmental, and clinical perspectives* (pp. 407–474). Hillsdale, NJ: Analytic.

Mandela, N. (2002). *Nelson Mandela's favorite African folk-tales*. New York: Norton.

Mandler, G. (1993). Thought, memory, and learning: Effects of emotional stress. In L. Goldberger & S. Breznitz (Eds.), *Handbook of stress: Theoretical and clinical aspects* (2nd ed., pp. 40–55). New York: Free Press.

Maslow, A. (1961). Peak experiences as acute identity experiences. *American Journal of Psychoanalysis, (21),* 254–262.

Masten, A. S. (2001). Ordinary magic: Resilience processes in development. *American Psychologist, 56*(3), 227–238.

Matsakis, A. (1996). *Vietnam wives: Facing the challenges of life with veterans suffering post-traumatic stress* (2nd ed.). Lutherville, MD: Sidran.

Mayou, R. A., Ehlers, A., & Hobbs, M. (2000). Psychological debriefing for road traffic accident victims: Three-year follow-up of a randomised controlled trial. *British Journal of Psychiatry, 176 Jun,* 589–593.

McAdoo, H. P. (1995). Stress levels, family help patterns, and religiosity in middle- and working-class African American single mothers. *Journal of Black Psychology, 21*(4), 424–449.

McCubbin, H. (1979). Integrating coping behavior in family stress theory. *Journal of Marriage and the Family, 41,* 237–244.

McCubbin, M. A., & McCubbin, H. I. (1993). Families coping with illness: The resiliency model of family stress, adjustment, and adaptation. In C. Danielson, B. Hamel Bissell, & P. Winstead-Fry (Eds.), *Families, health, and illness* (pp. 21–64). St. Louis, MO: Mosby.

McGoldrick, M., Gerson, R., & Shellenberger, S. (1999). *Genograms: Assessment and intervention* (2nd ed.). New York: Norton.

Mead, G. H., & Strauss, A. L. (1956). *The social psychology of George Herbert Mead*. Chicago: University of Chicago Press.

Meadows, W. C. (2002). *The Comanche code talkers of World War II* (1st ed.). Austin: University of Texas Press.

Mendelsohn, H., & Ferber, A. (1972). Is everybody watching? In A. Ferber, M. Mendelsohn, & A. Napier (Eds.), *The book of family therapy* (pp. 431–444). New York: Science House.

Merleau-Ponty, M. (1962). *Phenomenology of perception*. London: Routledge & K. Paul; New York: Humanities Press. (Translated from French 1945.)

Merleau-Ponty, M. (1964). *The primacy of perception, and other essays on phenomenological psychology, the philosophy of art, history, and politics*. Evanston, IL: Northwestern University Press.

Merriam-Webster's collegiate dictionary (11th ed.). (2003). Springfield, MA: Merriam-Webster.

Middleton, W., Moylan, A., Raphael, B., Burnett, P., & Martinek, N. (1993). An international perspective on bereavement related concepts. *Australian & New Zealand Journal of Psychiatry, 27*(3), 457–463.

Mikulincer, M., & Florian, V. (1999). The association between parental reports of attachment style and family dynamics, and offspring's reports of adult attachment style. *Family Process, 38*(2), 243–257.

Miller, J. (2002). Affirming flames: Debriefing survivors of the World Trade Center attack. *Brief Treatment & Crisis Intervention, 2*(1), 85–94.

Miller, W. R., & Thoresen, C. E. (2003). Spirituality, religion, and health: An emerging research field. *American Psychologist, 58*(1), 24–35.

Mitchell, J. T. (1983). When disaster strikes. . . : The critical incident stress debriefing process. *Journal of Emergency Medical Services 8*, 36–39.

Mitchell, J., & Everly, G. S. (1993). *Critical incident stress debriefing (CISD): An operations manual for the prevention of traumatic stress among emergency services and disaster workers*. Ellicott City, MD: Chevron Publishing.

Mitchell, J. T., & Everly, G. S. (2000). Critical incident stress management and critical incident stress debriefings: Evolutions, effects and outcomes. In B. Raphael & J. P. Wilson (Eds.), *Psychological debriefing: Theory, practice and evidence* (pp. 71–90). New York: Cambridge University Press.

Mitchell, J. T., & Everly, G. S. (2003). *Critical incident stress management (CISM): Group crisis intervention*. Ellicott City, MD: International Critical Incident Stress Foundation, Inc.

Mortimer, J., Boss, P., Caron, W., & Horbal, J. (1992). Measurement issues in caregiver research. In B. D. Lebowitz, E. Light, & G. Niederehe (Eds.), *Alzheimer's disease and family stress* (pp. 370–384). New York: Springer.

Murry, V. M., Brown, P. A., Brody, G. H., Cutrona, C. E., & Simons, R. L. (2001). Racial discrimination as a moderator of the links among stress, maternal psychological functioning, and family relationships. *Journal of Marriage & the Family, 63*(4), 915–926.

Newman, L. S. (2001). Coping and defense: No clear distinction. *American Psychologist, 56*(9), 760–761.

Nichols, M. P., & Schwartz, R. C. (2004). *Family therapy: Concepts and methods* (6th ed.). Boston: Allyn and Bacon.

Norris, F. H., Friedman, M. J., Watson, P. J., Byrne, C. M., Diaz, E., & Kaniasty, K. (2002). 60,000 disaster victims speak: Part I. An empirical review of the empirical literature, 1981–2001. *Psychiatry: Interpersonal & Biological Processes, 65*(3), 207–239.

O'Brien, J., & Kollock, P. (Eds.). (2001). *The production of reality* (3rd ed.). Thousand Oaks, CA: Pine Forge Press.

Olds, S. (1992). *The father* (1st ed.). New York: Knopf.

Olson, D. H., & DeFrain, J. (2003). *Marriages and families: Intimacy, diversity, and strengths* (4th ed.). New York: McGraw-Hill.

Orwell, G. (1949). *1984.* New York: Harcourt Brace. (Signet Classic 1955.)

Osterweis, M., Solomon, F., Green, M., & Institute of Medicine. Committee for the Study of Health Consequences of the Stress of Bereavement. (1984). *Bereavement: Reactions, consequences, and care.* Washington, DC: National Academy Press.

Papalia, D. E., & Olds, S. W. (1992). *Human development* (5th ed.). New York: McGraw-Hill.

Papalia, D. E., Olds, S. W., & Feldman, R. D. (2004). *Human development* (9th ed.). New York: McGraw Hill.

Pargament, K. I. (1997). *The psychology of religion and coping: Theory, research, and practice.* New York: Guilford.

Parker, R. (1995). *Mother love, mother hate: The power of maternal ambivalence.* New York: Basic.

Patterson, J. M., & Garwick, A. W. (1994). Levels of meaning in family stress theory. *Family Process, 33*(3), 287–304.

Pearlin, L. (1995). Some conceptual perspectives on the origins and prevention of social stress. In *Socioeconomic conditions, stress and mental disorders: Toward a new synthesis of research and public policy* collection (pp. 1–35). [on-line] Bethesda, MD: National Institute of Mental Health. Retrieved from http://www .mhsip.org/nimhdoc/socioeconmh_home2.htm.

Pearlin, L. I., Menaghan, E. G., Lieberman, M. A., & Mullan, J. T. (1981). The stress process. *Journal of Health & Social Behavior, 22*(4), 337–356.

Pearlin, L. I., & Pioli, M. F. (2003). Personal control: Some conceptual turf and future directions. In S. H. Zarit & L. I. Pearlin (Eds.), *Personal control in social and life course contexts. Societal impact on aging* (pp. 1–21). New York: Springer.

Pearlin, L. I., Pioli, M. F., & McLaughlin, A. E. (2001). Caregiving by adult children: Involvement, role disruption, and health. In R. H. Binstock (Ed.), *Handbook of aging and the social sciences* (5th ed., pp. 238–254). San Diego, CA: Academic.

Pearlin, L. I., & Schooler, C. (1978). The structure of coping. *Journal of Health & Social Behavior, 19*(1), 2–21.

Philipse, H. (1998). *Heidegger's philosophy of being: A critical interpretation.* Princeton, NJ: Princeton University Press.

Piers, M. W., & Landau, G. M. (1979). In D. Sils (Ed.), *International encyclopedia of social sciences* (Vol. 18, pp. 172–176). New York: Free Press.

Pillemer, K. A., & Lüscher, K. (2004). *Intergenerational ambivalences: New perspectives on parent-child relations in later life.* Oxford, UK: Elsevier.

Pillemer, K., & Suitor, J. J. (2002). Explaining mothers' ambivalence toward their adult children. *Journal of Marriage & the Family, 64*(3), 602–613.

Polanski, R. (Director/Producer), Benmussa, R. (Producer), & Sarde, A. (Producer) (2002). *The Pianist* [Motion picture]. Universal City, CA: Focus Features.

Pollner, M., & McDonald-Wikler, L. (1985). The social construction of unreality: A case study of a family's attribution of competence to a severely retarded child. *Family Process, 24*(2), 241–254.

Posttraumatic Stress Disorder (PTSD) Alliance. (2005). *Myths and facts about PTSD.* Retrieved August 25, 2005, from *http://www.sidran.org/ptsdmyths.html.*

Powell, L. H., Shahabi, L., & Thoresen, C. E. (2003). Religion and spirituality: Linkages to physical health. *American Psychologist, 58*(1), 36–52.

Psathas, G. (1973). *Phenomenological sociology: Issues and applications.* New York: Wiley.

Rando, T. A. (1993). The increasing prevalence of complicated mourning: The onslaught is just beginning. *Omega: Journal of Death & Dying, 26*(1), 43–59.

Ree, J. (1999). *Heidegger.* New York: Routledge.

Reiss, D. (1981). *The family's construction of reality.* Cambridge, MA: Harvard University Press.

Reiss, D., Neiderhiser, J. M., Hetherington, E. M., & Plomin, R. (2000). *The relationship code: Deciphering genetic and social influences on adolescent development.* Cambridge, MA: Harvard University Press.

Reiss, D., & Oliveri, M. E. (1991). The family's conception of accountability and competence: A new approach to the conceptualization and assessment of family stress. *Family Process, 30*(2), 193–214.

Resick, P. A. (2001). *Stress and trauma.* Philadelphia, PA: Psychology Press.

Rettig, K. D., & Dahl, C. M. (1993). Impact of procedural factors on perceived justice in divorce settlements. *Social Justice Research, 6*(3), 301–324.

Riskin, J. (1963). Methodology for studying family interaction. *Archives of General Psychiatry, 8*(4), 343–348.

Rober, P. (1999). The therapist's inner conversation in family therapy practice: Some ideas about the self of the therapist, therapeutic impasse, and the process of reflection. *Family Process, 38*(2), 209–228.

Rolland, R. (1994). *Families, illness, and disability: An integrative treatment model.* New York: Basic.

Rolland, J. (2004). Family legacies of the Holocaust: My journey to recover the past. In F. Walsh & M. McGoldrick (Eds.), *Living beyond loss: Death in the family* (2nd ed., pp. 423–428). New York: Norton.

Rose, S., Brewin, C. R., Andrews, B., & Kirk, M. (1999). A randomized controlled trial of individual psychological debriefing for victims of violent crime. *Psychological Medicine, 29*(4), 793–799.

Rosenwald, G. C., & Ochberg, R. L. (Eds.). (1992). *Storied lives: The cultural politics of self-understanding.* New Haven, CT: Yale University Press.

Saul, J. (2003). Promoting community recovery in lower Manhattan after September 11, 2001. *Bulletin of the Royal Institute for Inter-Faith Studies, 5*(2), 69–84.

Schopenhauer, A. (1966). *The world as will and representation.* New York: Dover Publications.

Schulz, R., & Beach, S. (1999). Caregiving as a risk factor for mortality: The caregiver health effects study. *Journal of the American Medical Association, 282*(23), 2215–2219.

Schutz, A. (1962). *Collected papers: Volume 1. The problem of social reality.* The Hague: Nijhoff.

Schutz, A. (1967). *The phenomenology of the social world.* Evanston, IL: Northwestern University Press.

Shutz, A. (1970). *On phenomenology and social relations.* Chicago: University of Chicago Press.

Seeman, T. E., Dubin, L. F., & Seeman, M. (2003). Religiosity/spirituality and health: A critical review of the evidence for biological pathways. *American Psychologist, 58*(1), 53–63.

Seligman, M. E. P. (1991). *Learned optimism.* New York: Knopf.

Seligman, M. E. P. (1992). *Helplessness: On depression, development, and death.* New York: W. H. Freeman.

Seligman, M. E. P., & Csikszentmihalyi, M. (2001). "Positive psychology: An introduction": Reply. *American Psychologist, 56*(1), 89–90.

Sexton, L. G. (1994). *Searching for Mercy Street: My journey back to my mother, Anne Sexton* (1st ed.). Boston: Little, Brown.

Shapiro, E. R. (1994). *Grief as a family process: A developmental approach to clinical practice.* New York: Guilford.

Sheinberg, M., & Fraenkel, P. (2000). *The relational trauma of incest: A family-based approach to treatment.* New York: Guilford.

Sifton, E. (2003). *The serenity prayer: Faith and politics in times of peace and war.* New York: Norton.

Sluzki, C. E. (1990). Disappeared: Semantic and somatic effects of political repression in a family seeking therapy. *Family Process, 29*(2), 131–143.

Sluzki, C. (2004). Hin und züruck: Back to where we came from. In F. Walsh & M. McGoldrick (Eds.), *Living beyond loss: Death in the family* (2nd ed., pp. 428–432). New York: Norton.

Sluzki, C. E., & Agani, F. N. (2003). Small steps and big leaps in an era of cultural transition: A crisis in a traditional Kosovar Albanian family. *Family Process, 42*(4), 479–484.

Speck, R. V., & Attneave, C. L. (1973). *Family networks* (1st ed.). New York: Pantheon.

Sprang, G. (1999). Post-disaster stress following the Oklahoma City bombing: An examination of three community groups. *Journal of Interpersonal Violence, 14*(2), 169–183.

Sroufe, A. (2002). Attachment in developmental perspective. *Journal of Infant, Child, and Adolescent Psychotherapy, 2*(4), 19–25.

Stacey, J. (1998). *Brave new families: Stories of domestic upheaval in late-twentieth-century America.* Berkeley: University of California Press.

Stanton, A. (Director & Cowriter), & Unkrich, L. (Codirector). (2003). *Finding Nemo* [Motion picture]. Emeryville, CA: Pixar Animation Studios/Walt Disney Pictures.

Steinglass, P., Bennett, L. A., Wolin, S. J., & Reiss, D. (1987). *The alcoholic family.* New York: Basic.

Strang, S., & Strang, P. (2001). Spiritual thoughts, coping and "sense of coherence" in brain tumor patients and their spouses. *Palliative Medicine, 15*(2), 127–134.

Stroebe, M., & Stroebe, W. (1991). Does "grief work" work? *Journal of Consulting & Clinical Psychology, 59*(3), 479–482.

Stryker, S. (1990). Symbolic interactionism: Themes and variations. In M. Rosenberg & R. H. Turner (Eds.), *Social psychology: Sociological perspectives* (pp. 3–29). New Brunswick, NJ: Transaction Publishers.

Styron, W. (1990). *Darkness visible: A memoir of madness.* New York: Random House.

Taylor, J. M., Gilligan, C., & Sullivan, A. M. (1995). *Between voice and silence: Women and girls, race and relationship.* Cambridge, MA: Harvard University Press.

Terr, L. C. (1985). Remembered images and trauma: A psychology of the supernatural. *Psychoanalytic Study of the Child, 40,* 493–533.

Thoits, P. A. (1994). Stressors and problem-solving: The individual as psychological activist. *Journal of Health & Social Behavior, 35*(2), 143–160.

Till, E. (Director & Cowriter), & Jones, G. (Cowriter) (2000). *Bonhoeffer: Agent of Grace.* [Film]. Berlin, Germany: NFP Berlin; Potsdam-Babelsberg, Germany: Ostdeustscher Rundfunk Brandenburg (ORB); Toronto, Canada: Norflicks Productions Ltd.

True, F., & Kaplan, L. (1993). Depression within the family: A systems perspective. In H. S. Koplewicz & E. Klass (Eds.), *Depression in children and adolescents. Monographs in clinical pediatrics* (Vol. 6, pp. 45-54). Langhorne, PA: Harwood Academic Publishers/Gordon.

Turnbull, A. P., Patterson, J. M., Behr, S. K., Murphy, D. L., Marquis, J. G., & Blue-Banning, M. J. (Eds.). (1993). *Cognitive coping, families, and disability.* Baltimore, MD: Brookes.

van der Kolk, B. A. (2002). The assessment and treatment of complex PTSD. In R. Yehuda (Ed.), *Treating trauma survivors with PTSD* (pp. 127–156). Washington, DC: American Psychiatric Press.

van der Kolk, B. A., McFarlane, A. C., & Weisaeth, L. (Eds.) (1996). *Traumatic stress: The effects of overwhelming experience on mind, body, and society.* New York: Guilford Press.

Waller, W. (1938). *The family, a dynamic interpretation.* New York: Cordon.

Wallis, C. (2005, January 17). The new science of happiness. *Time,* A2–A9.

Wallis, V. (1993). *Two old women.* Seattle, WA: Epicenter.

Walsh, F. (1996). The concept of family resilience: Crisis and challenge. *Family Process, 35,* 261–281.

Walsh, F. (1998). *Strengthening family resilience.* New York: Guilford.

Walsh, F. (1999). *Spiritual resources in family therapy.* New York: Guilford.

Walsh, F. (2004). Spirituality, death, and loss. In F. Walsh & M. McGoldrick (Eds.), *Living beyond loss: Death in the family* (2nd ed., pp. 182–210). New York: Norton.

Walters, M., Carter, B., Papp, P., & Silverstein, O. (1988). *The invisible web: Gender patterns in family relationships.* New York: Guilford.

Wampler, K. S., Shi, L., Nelson, B. S., & Kimball, T. G. (2003). The adult attachment interview and observed couple interaction: Implications for an intergenerational perspective on couple therapy. *Family Process, 42*(4), 497–515.

Waters, M. (1994). *Modern sociological theory.* Thousand Oaks, CA: Sage.

Waters, R. (2005). After the deluge: Is disaster mental health serving tsunami survivors? *Psychotherapy Networker, 29*(3), 17–18.

Weber, M., Parsons, T., & Tawney, R. H. (1930). *The Protestant ethic and the spirit of capitalism.* New York: C. Scribners Sons.

Weigert, A. J. (1991). *Mixed emotions: Certain steps toward understanding ambivalence.* Albany: State University of New York Press.

Weingarten, K. (1994). *The mother's voice: Strengthening intimacy in families* (1st ed.). New York: Harcourt, Brace.

Welter-Enderlin, R. (1996). A view from Europe: Gender in training and continuing education of family therapists. In K. Weingarten & M. L. Bograd (Eds.), *Reflections on feminist family therapy training* (pp. 53–74). New York: Haworth.

Whitaker, C. A. (1989). *Midnight musings.* New York: Norton.

Whitaker, C. A., & Malone, T. P. (1981). *The roots of psychotherapy.* New York: Brunner/Mazel.

White, M. (Speaker). (1989). *Escape from bickering* (Video #AAMFT197119/V008). Alexandria, VA: American Association for Marriage and Family Therapy.

White, M. (1995). *Reauthoring lives: Interviews and essays.* Adelaide, Australia: Dulwich Centre Publications.

White, M., & Epston, D. (1990). *Narrative means to therapeutic ends* (1st ed.). New York: Norton.

Wiens, T. W., & Boss, P. (2006). Maintaining family resilience before, during and after military separations. In C. Castro, A. Adler, & T. Britt (Eds.), *Minds in the military: Volume 3. The family.* Westport, CT: Praeger.

Wilson, J. P. (1989). *Trauma, transformation, and healing: An integrative approach to theory, research, and post-traumatic therapy.* New York: Brunner/Mazel.

Wolin, S., & Wolin, S. (1993). *The resilient self: How survivors of troubled families rise above adversity.* New York: Villard.

Wood, B. L., Klebba, K. B., & Miller, B. D. (2000). Evolving the biobehavioral family model: The fit of attachment. *Family Process, 39*(3), 319–344.

Wortman, C. B., & Silver, R. C. (1989). The myths of coping with loss. *Journal of Consulting and Clinical Psychology, 57,* 349–357.

Wright, L. M. (1997). Suffering and spirituality: The soul of clinical work with families. *Journal of Family Nursing, 3,* 3–14.

Wright, L. M., Watson, W. L., & Bell, J. M. (1996). *Beliefs: The heart of healing in families and illness.* New York: Basic.

Wright, M. O., & Masten, A. S. (2005). Resilience processes in development: Fostering positive adaptation in the context of adversity. In S. Goldstein & R. Brooks (Eds.), *Handbook of resilience in children* (pp. 17–37). New York: Kluwer Academic/Plenum.

Zarit, S. H., Pearlin, L. I., & Schaie, K. W. (2003). *Personal control in social and life course contexts.* New York: Springer.

Index

Abrahams, F., 77
absence, *see* physical absence; psychological
    absence
abuse, 58, 87
acceptance, 29, 96, 111–12, 127–28
adaptability, 54, 58, 87
adaptation(s), 2, 130, 211
addiction, 9f
    ethics, 172
    family, 120–21, 133–34, 140
    mastery, 112
    systems thinking, 64–65
    workshop, 14
Adelson, N., 3
adolescents, 116, 120, 175
adoption, 8, 9f, 79, 86
African-Americans, 13, 58, 125, 135; *see
    also* women
Agani, F. N., 191
Agee, J., 209
agency, 28–30, 52, 66, 155; *see also* women
Ainsworth, M. D., 215
Al-Anon, 68
Album, M., 1
alcoholism
    and family, 120–21, 133–34, 140
    in spouse, 67–69, 100, 200–2
    systems thinking, 64
Alexander, J., 56
Allende, I., 126, 141
Alzheimer's disease, 9f
    and ambivalence, 147, 151–53

and dialectical approach, 89
and families, 54–55, 57, 192
and Holocaust, 14
as punishment, 16
and sex, 215
spouses, 94–95, 153–56, 214–15
see also psychological absence
ambiguity
    versus ambivalence, 144–45, 146, 150
    and attachment, 163–65
    of boundaries, 12–13, 75
    living with, 48, 91
    and mastery, 102
    opposing ideas, 16, 31, 84, 141
    painfulness, 6–7
    and therapists, 190–91, 198, 203, 205
    and therapy, 32, 34, 58–59, 195
    tolerance, 10, 16, 28–30, 73, 140
    and trauma, 36
ambiguous loss
    and coping, xv (*see also* coping)
    definition, xv, 144
    interventions, xvi (*see also* community-
        based intervention; family-based
        interventions; therapy)
    multiple occurrences, 8
    pervasiveness, xvii, 6
    physical absence with psychological
        presence, 8, 9f, 21, 31
    physical presence with psychological
        absence, 8, 9f, 21, 31
    and PTSD, 6, 41–42

239